THE PARLIAMENTS OF AUTONOMOUS NATIONS

DEMOCRACY, DIVERSITY, AND CITIZEN ENGAGEMENT SERIES

Series editor: Alain-G. Gagnon

With the twenty-first-century world struggling to address various forms of conflict and new types of political and cultural claims, the Democracy, Diversity, and Citizen Engagement Series revitalizes research in the fields of nationalism, federalism, and cosmopolitanism, and examines the interactions between ethnicity, identity, and politics. Works published in this series are concerned with the theme of representation – of citizens and of interests – and how these ideas are defended at local and global levels that are increasingly converging. Further, the series advances and advocates new public policies and social projects with a view to creating change and accommodating diversity in its many expressions. In doing so, the series instills democratic practices in meaningful new ways by studying key subjects such as the mobilization of citizens, groups, communities, and nations, and the advancement of social justice and political stability.

Under the leadership of the Interdisciplinary Research Centre on Diversity and Democracy, this series creates a forum where current research on democracy, diversity, and citizen engagement can be examined within the context of the study of nations as well as of nations divided by state frontiers.

1 *The Parliaments of Autonomous Nations*
Edited by Guy Laforest and André Lecours

The Parliaments of Autonomous Nations

edited by

GUY LAFOREST AND ANDRÉ LECOURS

McGill-Queen's University Press

Montreal & Kingston · London · Chicago

ISBN 978-0-7735-4739-1 (cloth)
ISBN 978-0-7735-4740-7 (paper)
ISBN 978-0-7735-9938-3 (ePDF)
ISBN 978-0-7735-9939-0 (ePUB)

Legal deposit second quarter 2016
Bibliothèque nationale du Québec

Printed in Canada on acid-free paper that is 100% ancient forest free (100% post-consumer recycled), processed chlorine free

McGill-Queen's University Press acknowledges the financial support of CRIDAQ toward the publication of this book.

McGill-Queen's University Press acknowledges the support of the Canada Council for the Arts for our publishing program. We also acknowledge the financial support of the Government of Canada through the Canada Book Fund for our publishing activities.

Library and Archives Canada Cataloguing in Publication

The parliaments of autonomous nations / edited by Guy Laforest and André Lecours.

(Democracy, diversity, and citizen engagement series ; 1)
Includes bibliographical references and index.
Issued in print and electronic formats.
ISBN 978-0-7735-4739-1 (hardback). – ISBN 978-0-7735-4740-7 (paperback). – ISBN 978-0-7735-9938-3 (ePDF). – ISBN 978-0-7735-9939-0 (ePUB)

1. Legislative bodies. 2. Nationalities, Principle of. 3. Self-determination, National. 4. Legislative power. 5. Autonomy. 6. Ethnicity – Political aspects. I. Laforest, Guy, 1955–, editor II. Lecours, André, 1972–, editor III. Series: Democracy, diversity, and citizen engagement series ; 1

JF511.P37 2016   328   C2016-901904-7
                                                         C2016-901905-5

This book was set by True to Type in 10.5/13 Sabon

Contents

Figures and Tables

FIGURES

TABLES

Abbreviations for Names
of Political Parties

In the case of Spain, where a party is represented in both an autonomous community and the Cortes Generales, it is listed in both places.

THE BASQUE COUNTRY

AP	Alianza Popular
CDS	Centro Democrático y Social
EA	Eusko Alkartasuna
EB	Ezker Batua
EE	Euskadiko Ezkerra
EH	Euskal Herria
EHAK	Euskal Herriko Alderdi Komunistak
EPK	Euskadiko Partidu Komunista
ETA	Euskadi Ta Askatasuna
HB	Herri Batasuna
IU	Izquierda Unida
PNV	Partido Nacionalista Vasco
PP	Partido Popular
PSE	Partido Socialista de Euskadi
UCD	Unión de Centro Democrático
UPYD	Unión Progreso y Democracia

CANADA

BQ	Bloc Québécois
CPC	Conservative Party of Canada
LPC	Liberal Party of Canada
NDP	New Democratic Party

CATALONIA

C's	Ciutadans
CDC	Convergència Democràtica de Catalunya
CiU	Convergència i Unió
CUP	Candidatura d'Unitat Popular
ERC	Esquerra Republicana de Catalunya
ICV	Iniciativa per Catalunya Verds-Esquerra Unida i Alternativa
PP	Partit Popular
PSC	Partit dels Socialistes de Catalunya
SI	Solidaritat Catalana per la Independència
UDC	Unió Democràtica de Catalunya

FLANDERS

CD&V	Christen-Democratisch en Vlaams
N-VA	Nieuw-Vlaamse Alliantie
Open VLD	Open Vlaamse Liberalen en Democraten
SPA	Socialistische Partij Anders
UF	Union des Francophones

GALICIA

AGE	Alternativa Galega de Esquerda
BNG	Bloque Nacionalista Galego
PP	Partido Popular de Galicia
PSdeG	Partido dos Socialistas de Galicia
PSOE	Partido Socialista Obrero Español

NORTHERN IRELAND

AP	Alliance Party
DUP	Democratic Unionist Party
SDLP	Social Democratic Labour Party
SF	Sinn Fein
UUP	Ulster Unionist Party

QUEBEC

ADQ	Action démocratique du Québec
CAQ	Coalition Avenir Québec
PLQ	Parti libéral du Québec
PQ	Parti Québécois
QS	Québec solidaire

SCOTLAND

SNP   Scottish National Party

SPAIN

BNG	Bloque Nacionalista Galego
CHA	Chunta Aragonesista
CiU	Convergència i Unió
ERC	Esquerra Republicana de Catalunya
ICV	Iniciativa per Catalunya Verds-Esquerra Unida i Alternativa
IU	Izquierda Unida
PNV	Partido Nacionalista Vasco
PP	People's Party
PSOE	Partido Socialista Obrero Español
UPN	Unión del Pueblo Navarro
UPyD	Unión Progreso y Democracia

UNITED KINGDOM

BNP	British National Party
UKIP	United Kingdom Independence Party

Parliament Websites

We provide the readers here with a list of the websites of all parliaments of the autonomous nations in the countries studied in this book. The list goes beyond the various chapters in our table of contents to include the parliaments of Wales, those of the French-speaking and German-speaking communities of Belgium, Wallonia, and the bilingual and bicommunal Parliament of Brussels-Capital.

Assemblée nationale du Québec
   http://www.assnat.qc.ca/en/index.html
Scottish Parliament http://www.scottish.parliament.uk/
Assembly of Northern Ireland http://www.niassembly.gov.uk/
Assembly of Wales http://www.assembly.wales/en/Pages/Home.aspx
Parliament of Catalonia http://www.parlament.cat/web
Parliament of Galicia
   http://www.parlamentodegalicia.es/sitios/web/default.aspx
Parliament of the Basque Country http://www.legebiltzarra.eus/es
Flemish Parliament http://www.vlaamsparlement.be/vp/engels.html
Parliament of Wallonia http://parlement.wallonie.be/
Parliament of Brussels http://www.parlbruparl.irisnet.be/
Parliament of the French Community of Belgium
   http://www.pfwb.be/
Parliament of the German Community of Belgium
   http://www.dgparlament.be/desktopdefault.aspx

THE PARLIAMENTS OF AUTONOMOUS NATIONS

The Parliaments of Autonomous Nations: An Introduction

GUY LAFOREST AND ANDRÉ LECOURS

Research on nationalism in Western societies has convincingly argued that movements seeking to promote the collective identity of a historical territorial community and achieve some measure of self-government are far from anachronistic.[1] Rather, nationalist movements in countries such as Belgium, Canada, Spain, and the United Kingdom fully embrace modernity and seek to achieve their political goals within liberal and democratic frameworks. For example, the 2014 Scottish referendum on independence, whose parameters were negotiated by the United Kingdom government and the Scottish executive, and the Catalan government's attempt to find ways that fall within the Spanish constitutional framework to consult its population on Catalonia's political future demonstrate a commitment to liberalism and the democratic process. The result of the Scottish referendum (55 percent for the "no" and 45 percent for the "yes") was accepted by all Scots.

Substate nationalism[2] in Western societies has generated a literature too dense to cite here but, despite the many angles taken in studying nationalist movements in such countries as Belgium, Canada, Spain, and the United Kingdom (political parties, political economy, political ideas, among others), parliaments have been largely ignored. Yet, both the commitment to liberalism and democracy on the part of the minority national communities and the defence of their identity and pursuit of further autonomy are anchored, in one way or another, in their parliaments. For these communities, parliaments represent not only the democratic expression of a society but also its distinctiveness within the larger state. As such, parliaments have a particular symbolic relevance. A focus on parliaments also allows us to appreciate the possibilities for consensus within minority autonomous nations and, at the same time, the more usual fragmentation linked to ideology and the specific nature of self-determination claims and expectations. Therefore, this book's relevance stems from the almost total absence of parliaments in the literature on nationalism studies despite their importance as agents for the expression of the identity and self-determination claims of their communities. Moreover, beyond the realms of identity and autonomy, substate parliaments contribute significantly to the praxis of political freedom, within their borders and across the larger independent state.

There are, of course, limits to what parliaments can tell us about minority national communities. Formal political institutions, even when they provide the expression of a democratic will, rarely capture all the complexities of societies that are united by a sense of distinctiveness but often divided on the political implications of this difference. Moreover, as actors in contexts of multinationalism, parliaments cannot be analysed in isolation from political parties, which provide parliaments' varying political and partisan perspectives, and executives, which determine much of the parliaments' agendas. Parliaments' actions are also shaped by a constitutional framework and by societal dynamics that inform identity questions and positions on self-government. This book focuses on parliaments, but its contributors are sensitive to the various forces that shape their functioning. Indeed, the parliaments analysed here are situated within their wider political and social contexts.

The parliaments of minority nations in Belgium, Canada, the United Kingdom, and Spain have two important features. The first is that a formal division of powers limits their sovereignty. Parliaments in Flanders, Quebec, Catalonia, the Basque Country, Galicia, Scotland, and Northern Ireland operate in federal or decentralized states where the scope of their legislative power is specified in constitutional or quasi-constitutional documents. At the same time, in most federal and decentralized states, the formal division of powers (sometimes broad and vague, especially in older federations such as Canada) is permeable to political dynamics: (state) national parliaments, driven by their executives, may look to extend their power in policy fields where the parliaments of the minority national communities operate, and vice-versa.

The second feature is linked to the fact that minority national communities operate in the broader context of multinationalism.[3] In such contexts, central governments typically seek to deploy the nationalism associated with the state-wide community, that is, to promote the (state-wide) national identity and the cultural markers underpinning it. Minority national communities, through their political institutions, most often look to respond to these actions by asserting, developing, and promoting their own identity and cultural distinctiveness. The parliaments of minority national communities typically pay special attention to the protection and promotion of the distinctive culture of their society and its identity. This is helped by the fact that these parliaments most often assume substantial powers over cultural and linguistic policies as well as other policy fields (for example, education) that are conducive to the construction of powerful national symbols.

The dynamic relationship between minority and majority (or statewide) nationalism underscores the importance of thinking about the action of the parliaments of minority national communities in relation to central parliaments. Indeed, efforts by the former to express and promote a distinctive national identity can only be understood in relation to the latter's own mission to strengthen (state) national unity. Not only are central parliaments typically viewed as representing the nation as projected by the state but most of their members defend this nation against self-determination claims coming from minority national communities. In turn, the nature of this defence feeds into the position adopted by the parliaments of minority national communities and the broader nationalist movement.

Differently put, in multinational states, parliaments of minority national communities are not the only legislative bodies concerned with issues of identity and self-government; central parliaments are as well. This book also looks at how central parliaments in Canada, Spain, and the United Kingdom have sought to promote the (state) national identity, represent the country's diversity, and respond to nationalist claims. We believe that such concerns about the institutions and identities of majority nations and central states should play a larger role in all future research on substate nations and nationalism. Unsurprisingly, there are important differences in how these central parliaments have managed the multinational society they represent; most importantly, perhaps, in the extent to which central parliaments even recognize multinationalism (for example, quite extensively in the case of the British Parliament and mostly not for the Spanish Parliament).

The study of parliaments and institutions has paid little attention to parliamentary systems in minority national communities despite the special context in which they operate. Indeed, this literature has tended to focus on parliamentary structure, process, and voting; representation and democracy; and the relationship between executive and legislative powers.[4] This book takes a different focus as it seeks to contribute to the better understanding of parliaments in minority national communities as well as the central parliaments addressing questions of identity and self-government in multinational states. Its point of departure is the qualitative difference between multinational countries and mononational countries where parliaments are not exposed to, and do not have to debate, existential questions about the linkage between state and nation.

Three questions are particularly relevant when it comes to the parliaments of minority national communities. The first relates to the cultural distinctiveness of the community. What initiative does its parliament take to protect and further the community's culture? The second is about identity. What role do parliaments of minority national communities play in the development and promotion of this identity? The third has to do with self-government. What do these parliaments do to alter a political and constitutional status quo they often deem unsatisfactory?

The contributors to this book examine these and other questions linked to the structure, workings, and political dynamics of these parliaments. There are some commonalities among the parliaments, stemming from their position within a multinational state, but also, as could be expected considering the diversity of historical and contemporary experiences, there are important differences. A few remarks can be derived from the chapters on the parliaments of minority national communities.[5]

First, traditions of parliamentarianism in the various cases differ wildly in their trajectories. Quebec has enjoyed uninterrupted parliamentary government for more than a century while other "old" parliaments (for example, in Scotland and Catalonia) have seen their life interrupted either by choice or by force. Some minority national communities' parliaments (for example, Flanders' Parliament) are quite recent.

Second, these parliaments operate in federal and decentralized systems that afford them varying degrees of autonomy. In other words, their legislative scope is conditioned, indeed constrained, by a combination of constitutional provisions and political pressures. This being said, all of these parliaments have almost complete autonomy to organize their own affairs.

Third, parliaments in minority national communities where the language is different from elsewhere in the country have taken a leadership role in ensuring the diffusion and public use of that tongue. Quebec's National Assembly and Catalonia's Parliament, for example, have seen it as their special role to further and promote the use of French and Catalan respectively. In the case of the Basque Country, the task undertaken by Parliament is even more demanding since it has involved building up a tongue that has not been widely used.

Fourth, parliaments of minority national communities have played a very important role in articulating and promoting the collective identity of their society. They have been key actors in the identity politics of the state. In some cases (Quebec, Catalonia), parliaments have explicitly sought to express the idea that they represent a nation and to communicate this idea to the rest of the country.

Fifth, all these parliaments have put forward their views on the level of self-rule their community should enjoy. In most instances, the parliaments of minority national communities have not been satisfied with the constitutional status quo and have claimed greater territorial autonomy. The exact nature of the claims has varied greatly and been conditioned by the particular natures and histories of the states, but these parliaments have often expressed dissatisfaction with the status quo.

Finally, in articulating their preferred self-rule arrangements, the parliaments of minority national communities speak with varying levels of consensus. In this sense, they reflect their societies, some of which (for example, the Basque Country) are deeply divided on the political and constitutional future of the community. Despites divisions on ultimate objectives, some parliaments (for example, Quebec's) can speak with one voice as they criticize the state.

These observations lead us to highlight some of the contributions this book makes to the study of nationalism and of multinational societies. At the broadest level, we can safely say that the study of parliaments and the field of nationalism have really never been connected. Yet parliaments, as institutions representative of the body politic, bear issues of identity and self-determination. From this perspective, this book is a first step in examining the role of these most fundamental institutions in the politics of multinational states.

More specifically, this book contributes to at least three aspects of our understanding of politics in multinational states. The first is democracy. Democratic life in multinational states is qualitatively different from democratic life in mononational states. In the former context, state and nation are not held as congruent by all citizens, which means that the actual *demos* of the political community is contested as are the political, institutional, and constitutional mechanisms for the coexistence of multiple communities within the state. These issues are an important part of the democratic politics of multinational states. The complexity of these politics is reflected, at least partly, in the various parliaments of multinational states. Indeed, both the parliament of a minority nation and the central state's parliament embody in some way the preferences of their polities when it comes to constitutional arrangements, reflecting different degrees of consensus and division. Focusing solely on executives, although democratically formed, does not reveal the whole range of constitutional positions that are an intrinsic component of democracy in multinational states.

Second, this book also makes a contribution to our understanding of multinational states through the insight it brings to federalism. It is often said that federalism features the existence of at least two levels of government, each having some constitutionally protected powers. However, federalism is more than simply a multiplicity of governments; it also involves a multiplicity of duly elected parliaments, which give the constituent units their own political class. These constituent units are also, to varying degrees, political communities (sometimes national communities) whose democratic centres lie in their parliaments. This book suggests that specialists of federalism, and particularly scholars of multinational federations, should not limit their focus to intergovernmental relations (narrowly understood) but rather include that other crucial component of the central and constituent unit political systems, parliaments.

Finally, this book's focus is coherent with a large body of scholarship in political science that has emphasized over the last two decades or so that political institutions matter a great deal. For new institutionalism,[6] political institutions do not simply reflect social, cultural, and political forces; they also shape political outcomes. From this perspective, the politics of multinational states cannot be reduced to its societal components. Political institutions, such as parliaments, acquire a "life of their own" and can develop agency. Indeed, the parliaments of autonomous nations often become crucial agents in the relationships between their community and the state, and in the larger politics of multinational states. Reducing nationalism to societal forces is, as this book and new institutionalist theories both suggest, a major analytical oversight.

NOTES

1 Michael Keating, *Plurinational Democracy: Stateless Nations in a Post-Sovereign Era* (Oxford: Oxford University Press, 2001).

2 Different terms are used to refer to nationalism within states. "Minority nations" is often used, but the case of Flanders renders the term awkward, Flemings being a numerical majority within Belgium.

3 Alain-G. Gagnon and James Tully, eds, *Multinational Democracies* (Cambridge: Cambridge University Press, 2001); Alain-G. Gagnon, Montserrat Guibernau, and François Rocher, eds, *The Conditions of Diversity in Multinational Democracies* (Montreal: Institute for Research on Public Policy, 2003).

4 Jean-François Godbout and Bjørn Høyland, "Legislative Voting in the Canadian Parliament," *Canadian Journal of Political Science* 44, no. 2 (2011): 367–88; David E. Smith, *The Canadian Senate in Bicameral Perspective* (Toronto: University of Toronto Press, 2003, reprinted in 2006); David E. Smith, *The People's House of Commons: Theories of Democracy in Contention* (Toronto: University of Toronto Press, 2007); Peter H. Russell and Lorne Sossin, eds, *Parliamentary Democracy in Crisis* (Toronto: University of Toronto Press, 2009).

5 Minority national communities are, of course, not monolithic entities. The territorial identity landscape in multinational states is typically characterized by shared identities. For example, some Scots feel as or more British than Scottish. The same is true for Catalans, Flemings, and Quebecers.

6 See André Lecours, ed., *New Institutionalism: Theory and Analysis* (Toronto: University of Toronto Press, 2005).

The Catalan Parliament's Contribution to the Consolidation and Development of Self-Government and the Defence of Catalonia's National Identity

CARLES VIVER PI-SUNYER
AND MIREIA GRAU CREUS

In this chapter, we first present an overview of the characteristics of the Catalan Parliament and offer a brief analysis of the contributions it has made to consolidating and developing self-government and defending Catalan national identity. Then we focus on three topics: the fight to obtain recognition for Catalonia as a differentiated national reality; the defence of the right to be consulted and the right to self-determination; and the defence of Catalan as the language of Catalonia. We also analyse all the resolutions, motions, declarations, committee reports, studies, and laws emanating from Parliament, and all the recourses before the Tribunal Constitucional (Constitutional Court), from Parliament's re-establishment in 1980 to the present day.[1]

Our analysis leads us to the general conclusion that although the Catalan Parliament has the general functions and institutional status of a modern parliament in a "rationalized parliamentary system," it has also, in relation to the topics analysed here, played an outstanding and pre-eminent role with respect to government, even though in practice the effectiveness of the role has been extremely limited. This pre-eminent role was even more remarkable throughout the process to reform the Statute of Autonomy (2005–06), as we explain below, and stands out as one of the distinctive aspects of this Parliament. The other two remarkable features of the Parliament of Catalonia are, first, its age – it is one of the oldest parliaments in Europe – and second its multi-party composition, when most of the parliaments (with the exception of those of Navarra and the Basque Country) have kept a bipartisan profile, at least until 2015.

STRUCTURAL AND FUNCTIONAL CHARACTERISTICS
OF THE PARLIAMENT OF CATALONIA

The Parliament of Catalonia can be justly proud of its status as one of the oldest of modern-day parliaments.[2] Its origin can be traced back to the thirteenth century and the General Court (Cort General), although its roots go back even earlier, to the twelfth-century Sanctuary and Truce Assemblies[3] and the Court of the Counts of Barcelona.[4]

The Cort General brought together the king and the three orders of the kingdom (the clergy, nobility, and city representatives). In 1283 the annual convening of the Cort General became compulsory, limiting the king's discretionary power, and the institution's key characteristic was established: the consensual nature of all the legislation enacted by the Cort General.

The institution's evolution led, in the fourteenth century, to the establishment of an executive entity attached to the Cort General: the Diputació del General (giving rise to the term "Generalitat") which performed functions assigned by the Cort, including taxation. The Diputació del General gradually took over the leading institutional role played by the Cort and became, de facto, the main governmental institution in the region, in particular when, after the dynastic union of the Castilian and Catalan-Aragonese kingdoms, the sovereigns stopped convening the Cort General on a regular basis in the mid-fifteenth century.

In the eighteenth century, the institutions of the Catalan government were abolished following the War of the Spanish Succession (1702–14), fought between the Bourbons and the Habsburgs to establish the succession to the Spanish throne. It involved several European powers, competing for the ultimate prize of domination over the European and American continents. In 1706, the Cort General of the Principality of Catalonia sided with the Habsburgs and, in 1713, ratified its decision by declaring war on the Bourbons in the Edict of War to the Uttermost, which relied on support from the kingdoms of Aragon and Valencia. The Bourbon victory led to the abolition in 1714, under the Nueva Planta decrees, of the institutions of government, the rights of the Catalan-Aragonese monarchy, and the Cort General.

Self-government and parliament were not re-established until the Second Spanish Republic (1931–39). However, this Parliament had a short life and faced many obstacles, despite its intense political and legislative activity.[5] The first elections, held in 1932 by universal suffrage, were also the last, since in 1934 the Spanish government suspended self-government in Catalonia following its president's unilateral proclamation of the Estat Català (Catalan State) as part of the Spanish federal republic during a period of heightened social and political tension. In early 1936 the Catalan government and parliament were re-established – and then, in July of the same year, the military rebelled against the republican government, leading to the Spanish Civil War. The Parliament of Catalonia had no further opportunities to meet in normal circumstances. The government of the Generalitat, with Parliament's authorization, took over all its functions. In late 1938 the government of General Franco repealed the Statute of Catalonia. In 1954, the deputies of the Parliament of Catalonia in exile in Mexico elected Josep Tarradellas as president of the Generalitat of Catalonia.

The Contemporary Parliament, 1980–2015

The 1979 Statute of Autonomy of Catalonia led to the re-establishment of Catalonia's institutions of self-government and introduced a parliamentary, unicameral system. The president of the Generalitat (with dual status as president of the autonomous community and head of government) is elected by Parliament from among its members following an election. The relationship between Parliament and the executive has the fundamental characteristics of a parliamentary system dominated by the executive – or, in the case of Catalonia, dominated by the head of the executive, the president of the Generalitat. For example, the president dissolves Parliament and calls elections; and although the parliamentary term is four years, the president of the Generalitat may dissolve the assembly before the end of the term and call an early election (which presidents have done on three separate occasions). Similarly, the president may table a vote of confidence, while Parliament can divest the president of his or her office by passing a no-confidence motion. In thirty years, no vote of confidence has been tabled, while none of the three no-confidence motions presented has had any concrete result.

The Parliament of Catalonia comprises 135 seats (which can be considered adequate in comparative terms for a population of 7.5 million people). It is elected by direct universal suffrage in four electoral divisions: Barcelona (eighty-five seats), Girona (seventeen), Lleida (fifteen), and Tarragona (eighteen). The electoral system is established, in accordance with the Spanish Constitution, as a proportional system based on the Hondt method, with a 3 percent threshold in each electoral division, and closed, blocked party lists. In Lleida, Girona, and Tarragona, the relatively small dimensions of the electoral division and the application of the Hondt method generally lead to over-representation of the most successful party list. However, during each legislature, between five and seven parties or coalitions have obtained representation in Parliament, and in only three legislatures did the party forming the government obtain an absolute majority.

Functions and Relations with Institutions of the Central State and the European Union

The Catalan Parliament possesses the classic functions of a parliamentary system: a legislative function; a supervisory and "encouragement" – as stated in the Statute of Autonomy – function with respect to the government's political action; an elective function (for the members of the other institutions of the Generalitat); and a "publicity" function for the programs and options of Catalonia's main parties.

Concerning the relations between Parliament and the institutions of the state, the legal framework provides for various participatory mechanisms although, in practice, their effectiveness is somewhat limited. For instance, the Parliament of Catalonia can table legislative proposals in the Parliament of the central state, and has done so on forty-nine occasions. However, none of these proposals has been acted on, except in connection with the reform of the Statute of Autonomy in 2006, when the Catalan Parliament's proposal was partially accepted. This type of proposal is completely different from other legislative proposals.

The Parliament of Catalonia also has the power to elect some of the members of central state institutions. For example, it appoints eight of the twenty-four senators from Catalonia, and may suggest candidates when the Senate appoints its two designated members of the Constitutional Court. These powers, common to all the parliaments of the autonomous communities, do not prevent the Senate from selecting as magistrates candidates whose names do not appear on the lists submitted by the parliaments. (The Constitutional Court ruling 31/2010, on the 2006 Statute of Autonomy, made the numerous "elective" functions in the statute inoperative.)

The third means of participation gives the Catalan Parliament the possibility of contesting Spanish legislation before the Constitutional Court. In this area the Parliament of Catalonia has been quite active, although not as active as the Catalan government, which has contested forty statutes over the years.

With respect to relations with other parliamentary institutions, the Parliament of Catalonia maintains few ties with the parliaments of the other autonomous communities. On the other hand, it has an active relationship, within the European Union (EU), with parliaments in other European regions that have been granted legislative functions (via the Conference of European Regions with Legislative Powers, or ReGleg), with the Conference of European Regional Legislative Assemblies (CALRE), and also with the EU's Committee of the Regions and the representatives of the EU Commission in Barcelona. The Catalan Parliament has always responded actively when the EU has requested the opinion of regional parliaments, although the success rate for its proposals remains extremely low.

Parliamentary Entities and Operations

Parliament is organized on the basis of parliamentary groups. A group must have a minimum of five deputies, no one political party can form more than one group, and parties with fewer than five deputies belong to the mixed group.

The deputies' seats are not tied to a party although, in practice, voting discipline is almost always respected. For this reason, deputies who leave or are expelled from their parliamentary group retain their seat automatically and become unassigned deputies. If a deputy resigns his or her seat (and status as deputy), and only in this case, the seat is retained by the parliamentary group concerned and assigned to the next candidate on the list. Each parliamentary group appoints a chair and a spokesperson. The chairs of the parliamentary groups, along with the Speaker of the Parliament and the other members of the Office, belong to the Council of Spokespersons. The operation of Parliament relies on the work of the legislative and special committees.

The Office of the Parliament is a collegial entity with a speaker, two vice-speakers, and four secretaries. The members are elected by separate ballot during the assembly's first sitting. In general, the composition of the Office reflects the distribution of the seats held by the political parties and alliances. The speaker is the second-in-charge of the Generalitat of Catalonia, and chairs and adjourns parliamentary debates.

Composition of the 2012 Parliament

The most recent elections, called early, were held on 25 November 2012. The party platforms and pre-election debates focused mainly on two topics: the economic crisis and, in particular, the continuation of the "budget cuts," and the "accommodation" of Catalonia by the central state. This second topic has two aspects: the right of Catalans to be consulted on their own future (it is important to remember that Catalonia cannot organize a referendum unilaterally), and the "accommodation" or "non-accommodation" model that should be adopted. With respect to the latter question, the members of today's Parliament represent an array of options, ranging from independence to maintenance of the status quo, through the intermediate stages of confederation, federalism, and partial reforms of the current system.

The parties that obtained parliamentary representation defend the following positions:

- Convergència i Unió, CiU (a federation of two parties, Convergència Democràtica de Catalunya – CDC – and Unió Democràtica de Catalunya – UDC): continuation of austerity measures and right to be consulted. UDC defends a confederal system, whereas CDC prefers, majoritarily and implicitly, independence.
- Esquerra Republicana de Catalunya (ERC): changes to economic policies, right to be consulted, and independence.
- Partit dels Socialistes de Catalunya (PSC): changes to economic policies and federalism. During the campaign the party was in favour of the right to be consulted, but only if the consultation was conducted in a legal way; after the elections it supported abstention if a legal referendum was held.
- Partit Popular (PP): continuation of economic policy, against the right to be consulted and for the maintenance of the status quo, with the possibility of supporting changes to the financing system.
- Iniciativa per Catalunya Verds-Esquerra Unida i Alternativa (ICV): reform of economic policies, right to be consulted, and, with respect to the model for the future, the coalition would like to see consultation on three options: independence, confederation, and federation.
- Ciutadans (C's): no clear position on economic policy, against the right to be consulted, supports the status quo.
- Candidatura d'Unitat Popular (CUP): defines itself as "anti-system" and supports the right of Catalans to be consulted, as well as independence.

After the elections, the composition of Parliament was as shown in Figure 1.1 and Table 1.1.

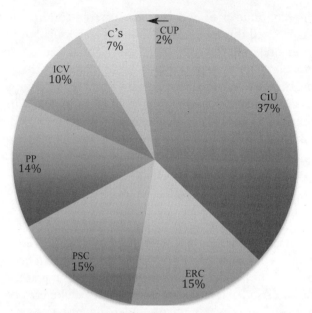

Figure 1.1   Political composition of Parliament (% of seats, 2012 election)

Table 1.1
Political parties (2012–)

Political Parties		Seats
CiU	Federation of 2 Catalan nationalist parties: majoritarily liberal (CDC) and Christian-Democrat (UDC), the governing party in Catalonia	50
ERC	Left-wing Catalan party	21
PSC	Socialist Catalan party (federated with the Spanish socialist party)	20
PP	Regional branch of the Spanish conservative party	19
ICV	Left-wing eco-socialist coalition	13
C's	"Spanish-leaning" Catalan party	9
CUP	Anti-system independent candidates	3

Parliament voted on 24 January 2013 on the right to be consulted. The results are shown in Figure 1.2 and Table 1.2: eighty-five votes for the right to be consulted and for the organization of a consultation of the people, forty-one against such a right, nine abstentions and absences.

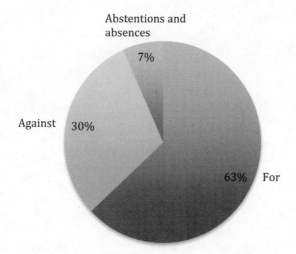

Figure 1.2   Vote on the right to be consulted, 24 January 2013

Table 1.2
Distribution of votes on 24 January 2013

	Seats	Parties/Deputies
For	85	CiU, ERC, CUP (1)
Against	41	PP, PSC,[1] C's
Abstentions and absences	9	CUP (2), 5 PSC deputies, 2 "real" absences

[1] The PSC supported the right to be consulted on two conditions: that there were negotiations with the central state, and that the legal rules in force were followed. When the PSC learned that the resolution had failed to meet these two conditions, it voted against.

Figure 1.3 and Table 1.3 summarize the parliamentary parties' support for the models for the future relationship between Catalonia and Spain (independence, confederation, federation, and status quo). The official position of one of the parties (ICV) has not yet been decided, but will be one of the first three options. For independence, sixty deputies (CDC, ERC, and CUP); for confederation, thirteen (UDC); for federalism, twenty (PSC); for the status quo, twenty-two (PP and C's).

If a referendum were held, based on the latest official surveys (October 2012), 57 percent of citizens would vote for independence (see Figure 1.4).[6] This figure continues to move incrementally upward, even though there is a gap between the result and the preferences indicated

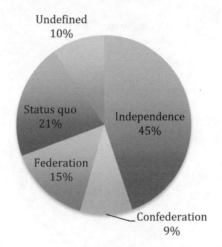

Figure 1.3   Parliamentary parties' support for models of future Catalonia-Spain relationships

Table 1.3
Parliamentary parties and votes for models of the future Catalonia-Spain relationship

	Votes	*Parties*
a) Independence	60	CDC, ERC, CUP
b) Confederation	13	UDC
c) Federation	20	PSC
d) Status quo	28	PP, C's
e) Undefined (one of a, b or c)	13	ICV

for the institutional model for the relationship between Spain and Catalonia, where 44 percent support independence.

Last, the socio-professional profile of the members of the 2012 Parliament shows close ties to the public sector with 64 percent having worked in the public sector at least once in their career. Professional experience in the public sector is also apparent in two parties: 66 percent of ICV deputies and 44 percent of CiU deputies have professional experience in the public sector. Similarly, 75 percent of deputies have previously held elected office; 85 percent have post-secondary education qualifications, and 36 percent have studied law. Male/female parity has not been achieved, since 60 percent of the deputies are men.[7]

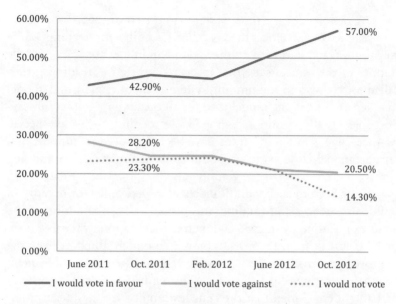

Figure 1.4   If a referendum on the independence of Catalonia were held
tomorrow —

The Catalan Parliament's Contribution to the
Consolidation and Development of Self-Government in Catalonia

An analysis of Parliament's activities since 1980 with respect to the consolidation and development of self-government leads to three fundamental conclusions that confirm the key importance of Parliament's
role, as mentioned above.

The first conclusion is that Parliament has repeatedly denounced the
low degree of self-government in Catalonia in terms of competences
and financing and, in another area, transfers from the central state of
material and human resources for the exercise of its competences. Parliament has also continually denounced the central state's interpretation and application of the Constitution and Statute of Autonomy of
Catalonia since it fails to respect what it calls the "State pact" set out in
the two defining texts and deprives the Generalitat of the political
power, financial means, and national recognition inherent in those texts.

The second conclusion concerns the solutions adopted or proposed
by Parliament to resolve the deficiencies of self-government. There has
been a radical change in the proposals made over the years and it is possible to discern four separate stages in this process, occurring with in-

creasing rapidity. During the first stage, from 1981 to 2002, Parliament's proposals for competences merely called for a different "reading" of the constitution and statute (with the logical requirement of amending the statutes of the central state that imposed "restrictive" readings); they called for changes to the funding system without requesting a model that departed from the model used for all the autonomous communities subject to the "common regime." However, since 1992 and especially since 1999, some resolutions have been approved in support of a separate model, close to the "economic concertation" model (or funding system) used for the Basque Country and Navarra. During the second stage, from 2002 to 2010, significant changes were called for, in terms of both competences and funding; this process led to the reform of the Statute of Autonomy in 2006 and then to the decision by the Constitutional Court in June 2010 that removed absolutely all effect from the improvements made to the statute. The ensuing period, up to September 2012, constituted the third stage, during which a clear majority in Parliament concluded that the constitution and the statute, as interpreted and applied by the central state and Constitutional Court, did not allow the level of self-government a majority of Catalans desired and proposed as a solution the establishment of a "fiscal pact" in order to provide Catalonia with a funding system "based on the model of economic concertation" used in the Basque Country. The rejection of this proposal by the head of the Spanish government, Mariano Rajoy, in September 2012, and the vast demonstration organized one week earlier in Barcelona under the banner "Catalonia, the new European state," marked the beginning of the fourth stage, during which a majority of the members of parliament (MPs) decided to launch a process to allow Catalans to exercise their right to be consulted about the political future of Catalonia and, depending on the response, the right to separate from Spain. This last stage will culminate with the elections that the president of the Generalitat, Artur Mas, has called for 27 September 2015.

Prior to Parliament's decision to launch the reform process, criticism of the way in which the central state gradually shaped government in the autonomous communities and proposals for corrections – besides proceedings filed at the Constitutional Court[8] – appear in resolutions and motions targeting specific actions, generally draft legislation, but especially in assessments and proposals of a general nature adopted each year following the annual debate on the Generalitat's general political program.

We cannot, in this chapter, analyse these resolutions in depth and exhaustively. As examples of resolutions with a specific goal, it is sufficient to mention Resolution 28/I from September 1981, which denounced the negative effects of the draft legislation to harmonize the autonomy process – known as the LOAPA (Ley Orgánica por la Armonización del proceso Autonómico) statute – on self-government in Catalonia. The statute, passed following the attempted military coup of February 1981, resulted from an agreement between the two majority parties in Spain, the Unión de Centro Democrático (UCD), the governing party, and the socialist party (PSOE), the main opposition party. The draft legislation drastically limited the autonomy of the autonomous communities, and was declared to be partially unconstitutional by the Constitutional Court in 1983. Similarly, Resolution 34/I from December 1981 reiterated the grounds for denunciation in the previous resolution, and then denounced the excessive detail in the process established by the central state for the exercise of shared competences. These resolutions are important not only for their content (denunciation of the fact that the draft legislation constituted an "underlying reform of the Constitution and of the Statute") but also because they demonstrate that disagreement in this area and the defence of self-government had begun only two years after the re-establishment of Parliament.

With respect to the resolutions that included more general assessments and proposals, we should highlight Resolution 106/II from 1987, which followed a general debate known at the time as the "debate on the Statute of Autonomy of Catalonia." Even today this resolution is surprisingly "topical," in the sense that the deficiencies in self-government that it denounces are exactly those currently reported in Catalonia. In fact, the resolution of 1987 is repeated each year with a few small changes, amplifications, and details. This old, recurrent demand is also futile, judging by its practical effect. Nevertheless, it helps explain why a majority of Catalans have decided to call for a new model rather than for continued efforts to reform the existing model. It also points to the third conclusion mentioned above, since it highlights the fact that the causes of the current demands for a radical new model and even for independence can be traced back a long way and are not exclusively economic; they do not result from the economic crisis of 2008, although they may have been amplified by it.

However this may be, given the topicality of the criticism detailed above, it is interesting to review at least part of the 1987 resolution. It begins by stating that "the Parliament of Catalonia notes that, on many occasions, the State pact that led to the 1979 Statute of Autonomy has not been respected by the various levels of government." It calls on the Catalan government to immediately take all possible steps with the central state government to "re-establish an interpretation of the 1979 Statute that is consistent with the reading of the Statute made by the political forces when they asked the Catalan people to ratify it." Certain criteria must be taken into account: limit the scope of framework or basic legislation to leave room for its development; respect the exclusive nature of exclusive competences; limit the spending power of the central state in areas of autonomous jurisdiction by setting generic goals but giving the autonomous communities responsibility for final regulation and execution; approve a "funding system for the Generalitat that is fair"; ensure that the central state's horizontal competency to establish the basis for and coordinate general economic planning is limited to the establishment of a "truly general framework"; complete transfers of material and human resources; guarantee that "EEC [European Economic Community] membership in no way involves changes to the internal distribution of competences"; "ensure, in an effective way, that the Generalitat participates in the formation of the central state's political aims with respect to the EEC in areas under the jurisdiction of the autonomous communities"; "have representatives of the Generalitat as members of the central state delegation during EEC negotiations"; "promote the absolute normalization of Catalan"; "negotiate amendments to organic, framework and regular statutes on autonomy"; and "conduct a study of the development of self-governing capacity using the section of the Constitution that provides for the delegation of central State competences to the autonomous communities." The resolution concludes, "Clearly, all the criteria making our Statute a true statute of self-government [must be applied]. If it becomes apparent that it is impossible to implement the Statute of 1979 in accordance with the State pact that defined it and if the criteria mentioned above are not respected, the Parliament of Catalonia should begin a process to reform the Statute."

As previously mentioned, until 2000, when it was decided to begin the statutory reform process, the content of the resolution was repeated year after year with some small additions.[9]

Similarly, with respect to funding, until 2000, recurrent resolutions were passed to point out deficiencies in the system and demand improvements, without questioning Catalonia's adhesion to the common regime.[10] Nevertheless, in 1992, in a motion dated 27 November, Parliament for the first time suggested claiming a funding model for Catalonia based on the economic concertation model used in the Basque Country and Navarra, if it was not possible to obtain an improvement to the existing system.[11] In fact, in 1996 (Resolution 5/V), during a plenary session of Parliament, a study committee was set up under the name "Study Committee on Economic Concertation" as a way of providing for the adequate funding of the Generalitat of Catalonia. The committee tabled its report in May 1999, defining the criteria that should govern the new funding system it referred to as a "fiscal pact." The criteria predetermined a unique funding model very similar to the economic concertation used in the Basque Country and Navarra, the only difference being that the Generalitat would not collect the total yield of all taxes but a share of the taxes collected by the central state based on criteria established jointly with the central state. The report's conclusions were adopted by Parliament's Committee on Economy, Finance, and Budgets in 2000 as Resolution 257/VI and, despite the fact that during 2001 several resolutions were approved expressing Parliament's satisfaction with the improvements made to the "common regime" funding system in effect in Catalonia,[12] the following year the plenary assembly approved a major resolution (1489/VI), contemporary with the resolutions calling for reform of the statute, in which after noting the insufficiency of the funding for the autonomous community and discrimination in central-state investment in Catalonia, it stated the need to establish a new funding system based on the criteria of Resolution 257/VI, in other words criteria similar to the Basque economic concertation model.

With respect to competences, we have already mentioned that up to the late 1990s, Parliament regularly denounced the low level of self-government and defended a new reading of the constitution and statute by proposing reforms to improve the quality of self-government. Obviously, these improvements could, objectively, be implemented in other autonomous communities, protecting the Parliament of Catalonia from the accusation that it was explicitly calling for asymmetrical treatment. However, as we will see below in connection with the "national question," in some – quite rare – cases, Parliament protested against a tendency to homogenize the competences of the autonomous communities,[13] not only because homogenization further weakened the level of self-government of all the autonomous communities, including Catalonia, but also because it risked diluting Catalonia's specific identity.

However this may be, in early 2000, after noting that the quality of self-government had not improved despite repeated protests, Parliament, on the basis of an accord between all the parties except the Partit Popular (PP), decided to establish a "study committee to extend self-government," which tabled its report two years later, clearly demonstrating that proposals to re-read the constitution and statute had evolved into proposals for reform.

The committee's long and detailed report, tabled at a plenary session of Parliament in December 2002,[14] diagnosed deficiencies in the extent of the competences of the Generalitat and in national recognition for Catalonia – summarizing what politicians, specialists, and Parliament itself had previously denounced – and made a series of proposals, for re-reading – in the form of long lists of amendments to the statutes of the central state – and for reform of the statute and of the constitution, without indicating a preference for any of the three possibilities. Nevertheless, after a plenary debate, all the parties except the PP chose a renewal of the statute as the only way to extend self-government.

The process of drafting the new statute began in early 2004. Significantly, this process was exclusively parliamentary, that is, Parliament was the sole institutional player involved. In comparison with other parliaments considered in this book, among them the legislative assemblies of Quebec and Scotland, the role of the Catalan Parliament on this issue is quite exceptional. The Catalan government remained, at least formally, outside the process. The objective of the reform of the statute was, in particular, to resolve the problems denounced by Parliament since 1987 in connection with the competences and funding of the Generalitat, in addition to the question of national recognition for Catalonia. The proposal, approved by a plenary session of Parliament on 25 September 2005 and sent to the Congress of Deputies in Madrid for debate and approval, made substantial improvements to the list of competences (by seeking to ensure respect for the exclusive nature of exclusive competences, to limit the scope of the central state's basic and "horizontal" competences, to restrict the central state's spending power, etc.) and, with respect to the funding system, introduced radical changes without going so far as to propose an economic concertation model. The proposal from the Catalan Parliament was heavily amended by the central Parliament; next, following a recourse launched by the PP, each and every improvement still present in the text of the statute approved by the Spanish Parliament was "deactivated" in a ruling by the Constitutional Court, which found that most of the provisions in the statute concerning competences and funding were not legally binding on the ordinary legislator of the central state.

After the statute came into force in 2006 and until the release of the July 2010 ruling, Parliament gradually enacted laws in its fields of jurisdiction, but encountered numerous difficulties in obtaining the transfer of material and human resources from the central state. Even more remarkably, the central legislature – except in the field of funding and, even then, incompletely – refused to enact legislation to allow the development of the new statute.

Once the ruling had been issued, the Parliament of Catalonia took up the defence of self-government and tried to make the Spanish state keep its word and limit the devastating effects of the ruling by enacting legislation to match the relatively numerous cases where the Constitutional Court had found the statute unconstitutional not because its contents were unconstitutional but because the matter needed to be dealt with by the ordinary legislator of the central state and not by the statutory legislator. Once again, Parliament's efforts to develop the 2006 statute had come to nothing. Even the laws of the central state concerning funding, enacted in 2009, and its undertaking to invest in Catalonia, set out in the statute, were implemented in a partial or restrictive manner or simply ignored.

At this point, the parliamentary majority concentrated on its objective of improving self-government by establishing, as part of a fiscal pact with the central state, a system of funding "based on the model of economic concertation" in the Basque Country. To attain its goal, in June 2011 Parliament set up a new "committee to study a new funding model based on economic concertation." The committee presented its conclusions in October 2011. Unlike the 1999 report, the new report contained all the criteria that defined the Basque and Navarra model, including the collection of all yields from all taxes raised in Catalonia. In Resolution 275/IX from October 2011, which followed a debate on general political aims, a plenary session of Parliament endorsed the conclusions of the committee; on the other hand, with respect to competences, it limited itself to calling on the central government to support and recover the original content of the statute. Last, as mentioned above, Parliament concentrated all its efforts on obtaining a new funding system outside the common regime. Finally, in July 2012, the government of the Generalitat presented a proposal for a solution to the plenary session of Parliament, which was debated on 25 July 2012 – 737/IX from July 2012 – and which called on the government of the Generalitat to begin a process of negotiation with the central government on the basis of the approved conclusions of the committee and the criteria established in the resolution itself. The resolution was approved by an absolute majority with support from the CiU, ICV, ERC, one independent deputy, and one from the PSC; the PP and C's parties voted against, while the PSC voted against the sections "inspired" by economic concertation and abstained for the rest of the resolution; Solidaritat

Catalana per la Independència (si) also voted against, but for other reasons: it believed that the central state would not accept the proposal and that, as a result, supporting the process would simply delay independence.

The president of the Generalitat, Artur Mas, presented the proposal for a fiscal pact to the head of the Spanish government, Mariano Rajoy, and the latter rejected it out of hand in a meeting that lasted less than two hours, alleging that a text that had not yet been written was unconstitutional. This fact, and the huge demonstration on 11 September, led to Parliament's Resolution 742/IX of 27 September 2012, which we analyse in more detail below. In it, Parliament stated its opinion that autonomy was a dead-end option and set the objective of obtaining recognition for the right of Catalans to be consulted and, if supported by the vote of a majority of Catalans, transforming Catalonia into a new European state.

Thus, there can be no doubt that Parliament has acted as a protagonist in the promotion of self-government in Catalonia, that the low level of self-government has been repeatedly denounced over many years, and that the proposals made by Parliament in this area have evolved over time.

THE CATALAN PARLIAMENT'S CONTRIBUTIONS TO THE DEFENCE OF CATALONIA'S NATIONAL IDENTITY

The Parliament of Catalonia has contributed to the defence of Catalan national identity through three fundamental actions.[15] First, it has repeatedly affirmed the fact that Catalonia is a differentiated national reality, and that the central state needs to recognize its plurinational (plurilingual and pluricultural) character. Second, it has supported the right to self-determination which, for Parliament, is one of the consequences of its national character. Last, it has provided ongoing support for Catalan as the language of Catalonia. Besides a common history and the awareness of belonging to a differentiated community (the desire "to be" sometimes mentioned by Parliament), language is the fundamental element of the Catalan nation. Rocher and Gilbert make a similar argument with regard to the role of Quebec's National Assembly in the promotion of the French language in their chapter on Quebec further on in this book.

In the next section, we analyse each question, although Parliament considers the three questions an undifferentiated whole, in the same way that it considers self-government overall to be the guarantee and inevitable consequence of the fact that Catalonia is a differentiated national entity.

Catalonia as a Nation and Spain as a Plurinational (Pluricultural and Plurilingual) State

Despite the fact that the Spanish Constitution uses the word "nation" to refer to Spain itself, and only admits to the possible existence of "nationalities," the Parliament of Catalonia has proclaimed openly and frequently that Catalonia is a nation, and has used the adjective "national" in numerous statutes concerning a wide range of realities.[16] It is clearly significant that the first statute enacted by the re-established Catalan Parliament concerned the "national holiday of Catalonia," and that in one of its first resolutions (76/I from September 1982), approved on the date marking the fiftieth anniversary of Parliament's establishment, a unanimous vote by the plenary assembly stated that "Catalonia is a nation." However, it must be admitted that only a few resolutions have been passed on this question, that they are laconic – as though referring to an existing situation – and that they do not constitute a general theory of nationhood.

Until the late 1990s a reference to the national character of Catalonia was used only three times as the basis for the right to self-determination. It occurred in Resolution 98/III from 1989,[17] and at a later date, in a more generic international context, in Resolution 229/III from 1991. In 1999, in Resolution 944/V (discussed in the next section), the concept of "historic nationality" and its inherent "historic rights" was invoked in a demand for the creation of instruments to allow Catalonia to effectively exercise its right to self-determination (through a pact with the central state or the organization of referendums, although they were not expressly provided for by law).

Starting in 2000, Parliament approved four resolutions that marked progress in two different directions. First, these resolutions demanded that the central state recognize, if only indirectly, the national character of Catalonia, by recognizing the plurinational, plurilingual, and pluricultural nature of the Spanish state; second, they demanded that the central state implement a series of measures to make this plurinational nature more visible.

For example, Resolution 241/VI, which resulted from a debate on the general political program in 2001, begins by stating that Parliament "demonstrates that symbolic aspects are important in Catalonia's national identification process, particularly in a context where those who

claim that national affirmations have been overtaken in an era of glob-
alization and European construction seek unremittingly to support the
unitarist symbols of Spanish national identity," and "notes ... the need
to strengthen recognition for Spain's plurinational reality and reiterates, once again, the urgent need to promote and develop the self-government of Catalonia as a historic nationality."

The reference to Spain's plurinational, pluricultural, and plurilingual
character, along with the need to strengthen self-government in order
to support the national identity, appears once again in Resolution
1489/VI, which resulted from the debate on the general political program in 2002. It defends the reform of the statute "as a definitive solution to safeguard the rights of Catalonia as a nation and escape from the
currently stagnant situation of self-government."

These resolutions culminate in a report by the committee formed to
study the extension of self-government, tabled, as mentioned above, in
December 2002. The report, under the heading "deficits in institutional accommodation for the plurinational character of the State," states
that this characteristic of the central state is recognized in sections 2
and 3 of the constitution, and that the Statute of Autonomy of 1978
confirms that Catalonia is a nationality that forms part of the central
state "with its own differentiated personality, manifested in its language,
culture, civil law and institutional tradition, and also in a firm and permanent political intention to achieve – and develop – self-government."
It also denounces the fact that "the Catalan difference, in terms of both
language and culture and also purely political aspects, is not reflected
in terms of symbols and competences in the organization of the State"
and, as a result, proposes a series of specific measures that the central
state should adopt. More specifically, in the area it describes as "symbolic," it mentions involvement (apparently of Catalonia and other nationalities) in designating the members of the Constitutional Court
and other state institutions; the use of Catalan or the symbols of Catalonia on currency, stamps, identity documents, and vehicle plates; the
use of Catalan in the Senate, courts, and civil and military administration; the presence of Catalonia in cultural policy abroad and at UNESCO;
the promotion of sports teams in international competitions; and so
on. In the area of competences, the report focuses in particular on a
more "flexible" distribution of competences, through the delegation of
state competences under section 150.2 of the constitution in order to
"take into account the Catalan difference and the political desire to obtain broader self-government," and emphasizes the need for full recognition of the plurinational character of the central state.

The proposal to reform the Statute of Autonomy, approved by Parliament in September 2005, was intended to take a definitive step to ensure that the central state recognized Catalonia's national character. It is therefore not by chance that the first paragraph of section 1 proclaims that "Catalonia is a nation." Approval for this proposal by the central Parliament would, for the first time, have constituted recognition of this fact. Section 3 attests to the plurinational character of the state, section 8 refers to the "national" symbols of Catalonia, and section 5 states that the "self-government of Catalonia as a nation" is based on "the historic rights of the Catalan people," in addition to the constitution and statute.

The Spanish Parliament largely limited the aspirations of the Parliament of Catalonia since, in the text as finally approved, the reference to the nation was moved to the preamble and there is no recognition from the central state, other than the observation that the text is simply a unilateral affirmation by the Parliament of Catalonia.[18] The reference to the plurinationality of the state in section 3 of the Catalan proposal was removed.

In a resolution from 2007 (Resolution 70/VIII, resulting from the debate on the general political program for that year), Parliament enjoined the Catalan government to "strengthen national recognition for Catalonia." Nevertheless, the ruling by the Constitutional Court concerning the statute found that in Spain, from a legal point of view, there was only one nation – the Spanish nation. Even though an indirect mention of the Catalan nation appeared only in the preamble of the statute, the court specified in the ruling that the reference to the national character of Catalonia had no interpretive legal effect on the rest of the text of the statute. In this way, the court wanted to avoid the possibility of a broader interpretation of several provisions such as those concerning historic rights, competences, and relations between the state and the Generalitat; above all, though, as revealed in its second legal argument, it wanted to avoid the possibility that a mention of the national character of Catalonia would "introduce ambiguity concerning the indissoluble unity of the Spanish nation, proclaimed in section 2 of the Constitution."

Right to Self-Determination

Since the re-establishment of the Parliament of Catalonia in 1980, it has proclaimed Catalonia's right to self-determination nine times (including two in an implicit, but clear, manner[19]), almost always founding the right on Catalonia's national character.[20]

Except in the last two resolutions (from September 2012 and January 2013), which have specific features, the resolutions and motions proclaiming Catalonia's right to self-determination are of exclusively parliamentary origin, resulting from proposals made by the various parties supporting the Catalan government. In addition, in all cases, the proposals were presented by independence-supporting parties (ERC and/or SI), but always with support from Convergència i Unió which, in fact, often helped to draft the definitive content of the resolutions. This continued, especially in recent years, with the proposals made by ICV. Ordinarily, the PSC abstained,[21] and the PP and C's voted against. In many cases, the resolutions were approved first by a parliamentary committee, and then endorsed by the plenary assembly.

From the first (1989) to the last (2013) resolution, the content has changed considerably. The early resolutions reflect a desire to announce that Catalonia, as a nation, has a right to self-determination, although the right is not one that will be exercised in the immediate future. They correspond to the imperatives of the international context at a time when various nations were engaged in a process of self-determination, but do not indicate a desire to exercise the right in order to change Catalonia's political status.

In the first resolution, Resolution 98/III from 12 December 1989, which was approved by a committee, the scope of the right is extremely limited in terms of both the objectives pursued and the means chosen to implement them. The main objective is to proclaim the possibility of "increasing the level of self-government and, in general, adapting the regulation of national rights to the circumstances of each historic time." This objective is to be achieved "by means of actions provided for in the constitutional order itself." However, the constitution does not give the autonomous communities the ability to call referendums and, with respect to statutory and constitutional reform, gives them only the power to make proposals, for a decision by the central state. The international background to the first resolution was the fall of the Berlin Wall and German reunification. The resolution mentions the principles governing "international organizations" and, as part of the debate that preceded its approval, Point VIII of the Helsinki Final Act which, as is well known, concerned the right of peoples to freely determine their political status. The resolution was approved with only the PSC voting against.

The second resolution, Resolution 229/III from September 1991, was passed by a plenary assembly of Parliament. Self-determination is one on the five points in the resolution that ended the annual debate on the general political program of the Catalan government. The proclamation of Catalonia's right to self-determination remained relatively vague and indirect. It is in three parts: the first proclaims that Catalonia represents a differentiated national identity; the second rejoices that "in eastern and central Europe, formerly oppressed nations are in the process of recovering their freedoms (during the debate, Estonia and Latvia were mentioned)"; and the third notes that "the recovery of national freedoms in the deployment of the right to self-determination must shape ... the new reality of a Europe of Peoples, in which Catalonia wishes to participate with its differentiated national personality."

The third resolution, Resolution 679/V from October 1998, was passed by a plenary assembly following the debate on the general political program. Briefly, but more openly than in the 1991 resolution, it proclaims Catalonia's right to self-determination. In particular, the single point of the resolution dealing with self-determination states that "As part of the celebration marking the fiftieth anniversary of the Universal Declaration of Human Rights, the Parliament of Catalonia ratifies, once again, the right of the Catalan people to freely determine its future as a people, in peace, democracy and solidarity."

In contrast, Resolution 944/V from June 1999 already belongs to the transition between the three resolutions discussed above and the new model, which appeared for the first time in 2010. The resolution does not mention the right to self-determination specifically. It refers to the "rights of Catalonia as a historic nationality." Its key feature, though, is that for the first time it introduces an explicit reference to the procedures through which the right to self-determination or, as phrased in the resolution, "the majority will of Catalans concerning the current status of historic nationality," should be made manifest. The procedures are bilateral agreements with the central state and other "mechanisms and ... specific procedures" to give effect to the "majority will of Catalans," such as "the calling of consultations of the people or referendums on the political status of Catalonia."

The five parliamentary agreements passed since 2010 (two resolutions and two motions) point to a new possibility. First, they demand a right to self-determination and the ability to exercise it effectively and, depending on the circumstances, immediately and in order to solve specific problems; second, the debates surrounding the approval procedure for the motions focus on the instruments that would allow the right to be exercised.

The first of the agreements, Resolution 631/VIII from March 2010, was tabled by ERC and debated and passed by an absolute majority of the members of a parliamentary committee.[22] It resulted from "non-official" consultations organized by private institutions with indirect support from the mayoralties of over 250 municipalities in Catalonia;[23] respondents were asked if they agreed that the "Catalan nation should become an independent, democratic and social State founded on law, integrated into the European Union." The participation rate was 25 percent of potential electors, and over 90 percent of votes were affirmative. Parliament's resolution comprised four clear, precise declarations: it ratified the 1989 and 1998 resolutions "on the right to self-determination of the Catalan nation"; it recognized the previous consultations "as an expression of society's willingness to participate in shaping the future of Catalonia"; it encouraged organized civil society to plan more consultations; and it ratified "the will to use all legal instruments in force and all necessary policies to ensure that the Catalan people can exercise its right to decide."

Although the resolution recognized that the "non-official" consultations were a valid instrument, it did not ignore the other "legal instruments in force" to make exercise of the right to self-determination possible. At the time, and still today, they were not available by a unilateral decision of the Generalitat, although there was – and is – a law passed by Parliament on consultations that are not referendums, drafted on the basis of the Statute of Autonomy. The resolution even states that recourse may be had to other "necessary political instruments" that are not specified, although the party promoting the resolution, and other independence-leaning parties represented in Parliament, have always defended the possibility of a unilateral declaration of independence by Parliament and a demand for the recognition of Catalonia as an independent state by the international community.

The second agreement, Motion 6/IX from March 2011, was passed by a plenary assembly. It was tabled by SI and has similar content to the resolution approved by the committee: it demands the right to self-determination as a right that the Catalan people cannot renounce; it defines the Parliament of Catalonia as the seat of the "sovereignty of the Catalan people"; it supports the right of civil society to express itself freely through consultations of the people; last, it expresses Parliament's support for consultations of the people organized throughout Catalonia. The resolution was approved by eighty-five deputies (CiU, ERC, SI, and ICV – except for the last point), while forty-seven deputies voted against (PSC, PP, Ciutadans).

The third agreement, Motion 11/IX from March 2011, records Parliament's rejection of the recourse tabled by the central government

(PSOE) against the Catalan statute concerning consultations of the people by way of referendums which regulated the consultation procedure; however, it gave the power to authorize consultations to the central state government, as required by the constitution. Parliament took advantage of the motion to highlight its "active support for the right to self-determination of the Catalan people."

Last, Resolution 742/IX from September 2012, approved just after the large demonstration of 11 September in support of Catalonia becoming a new European state, constitutes the culmination of the process started in 1989. This is a long, strongly worded and, clearly, politically significant declaration. It begins by expressing satisfaction with the success of the demonstration and undertaking to fight to make Catalonia a new European state; it notes the failure of attempts to obtain accommodation for Catalonia in the central state over a period of thirty years; it states that the current approach – and, in fact, the autonomous communities – is a dead-end (I.2); it accuses the central state of failing to understand the serious situation created by the 2010 ruling of the Constitutional Court on the Statute of Catalonia and of doing nothing to improve the situation and, in fact, of launching a "recentralization offensive" (II.1).

As a result, the resolution proclaims the objective of "beginning a new stage based on the right to decide" (I.2) and emphasizes that the Catalan government could call a poll "as a priority during the next legislature" (I.5). Despite the priority given to the right to decide – synonymous with the right of the population to be consulted – the resolution also states that the ultimate objective of the process is for Catalonia to become a new European state. Federal or confederal options are not totally excluded. However this may be, "it is essential for Catalonia to equip itself with an instrument that allows the population to be consulted"; in this connection, a reference is made to a referendum – requiring authorization from the central state – and the draft Catalan legislation on non-referendum consultations of the people being prepared by Parliament; in addition, the resolution states that these participatory instruments must be based "on the legality and legitimacy of the Parliament of Catalonia" (III.1). Parliament solemnly proclaims Catalonia's "imprescriptible and inalienable right of self-determination, as a democratic expression of its sovereignty as a nation" (II.4); it emphasizes that the process must take place in a pacific and democratic way (I.4 and 5); it refuses threats of the use of force (IV.3 and 4); it pays particular attention to the need to internationalize "the process of building an independent State [here, independence is specifically mentioned as an objective] for the Catalan nation" (V.1.1); it notes that "the achievement of sovereignty necessarily includes an administrative reform" (V.1.2); and, for the first time, it raises the possibility of not applying the legislation of the central state and the jurisprudence of the courts of law with respect to the Education Act (V.6.1.2).

As mentioned above, on this occasion CiU, ERC, ICV, and PSC tabled their proposals for a resolution on Catalonia's right to self-determination. In addition, CiU and ERC tabled a joint proposal. During this period, the president of the Generalitat, in the opening speech for a debate on the general policy of the Catalan government, announced the dissolution of Parliament and the calling of an election, and expressed clear support for the right to decide. For this reason, on this occasion, unlike in previous cases, we can consider that Parliament's role as a protagonist was shared, in practice, with the Catalan government, acting through the intermediary of deputies from the parties forming the government coalition. Several elements from the five proposals mentioned above were included in the final resolution. The result of the vote was as follows: eighty-four votes for (CiU, ICV, Esquerra, and SI),[24] twenty-one against (PP and C's), and twenty-six abstentions (PSC).

The last resolution on self-determination is dated 25 January 2013, and is referred to as the "sovereignist" resolution. It bears a strong resemblance to the resolution of September 2012, although the former declared that Catalonia is a "sovereign political and legal subject" and, most importantly, that the process to consult the Catalan people is open. As mentioned above, this resolution was supported by the vote of eighty-five deputies.

Catalan as the Language of Catalonia

Protection for the Catalan language has been one of Parliament's key objectives over the thirty-two years since it was re-established. Parliament considers Catalan to be one of the fundamental elements of the Catalan identity and thus protection for the Catalan language is crucial for Catalonia's construction as a nation. In fact, in all the resolutions and motions on the Catalan language approved during the period, the inseparable link between Catalan and the existence of the Catalan people or nation is highlighted.

The importance of the recovery, defence, and promotion of Catalan in parliamentary activity is clearly reflected in two pieces of data. First, the normalization and defence of the Catalan language is the issue that has produced by far the greatest number of parliamentary resolutions and motions; in all, 336 between 1980 and 2012 (for more details, see Table 1.3); second, this question, although normally supported by the "Catalanist" parties – ERC, CiU, SI – also received unanimous support until the late 1990s, and still attracts vast majorities.[25]

The content of the resolutions on language has hardly changed from one legislature to the next. Safeguarding the Catalan language is founded on two main considerations: first, compared to Spanish, Catalan is still in a socially and institutionally disadvantaged situation and, second and more specifically, Catalan is the language of Catalonia and plays a fundamental role in the process of reconstructing the national identity. Next, depending on the sector concerned, there can be further reasons, such as the decision not to separate students by language in the education sector. On the other hand, the PP, strengthened since 2006 by the presence in Parliament of a new type of "centralist" party, Ciutadans (C's), focused on defending the (individual) language rights of Spanish speakers and ensuring consideration for the fact that Spanish is also a language found in Catalonia and one that deserves to be treated on an equal footing with Catalan.

The resolutions and motions on language approved by Parliament can be divided into three groups based on their content and objectives. The largest group contains resolutions that seek to promote and support the effective normalization of the Catalan language in all areas (educational, social, institutional, media); the next group contains resolutions on outreach for Catalan language and culture, especially within the European Union; the last group contains resolutions on the promotion of plurilingualism in the operations of the state, including draft legislation addressed to the Spanish Parliament.

In the first group, it is possible to define at least four sub-groups: the regulation of Catalan in everyday life, in other words, promotion of the re-establishment and normalization of the use of Catalan in social life (road signage, traffic signals, signs in airports and museums, place names, etc.); promotion of Catalan in public and private media; normalization of the use of Catalan in the public administration of the autonomous community and central government, with a special focus on the administration of justice; and, last, the use of the Catalan language in the education sector as a mechanism for social integration. The four subgroups account for 65.5 percent of all the resolutions and motions on Catalan approved between 1984 and 2012.

In terms of the evolution and content of the resolutions and motions and, more generally, support for Catalan as the language of Catalonia, three main stages can be identified.

Table 1.4
Approved resolutions and motions on language, 1984–2012

Legislature	Daily life	Media	Administration	Education	Outreach	Plurilingualism in Spain	Unity of the language	Other	Total (by line)
I	4	5	3	1	1	2		2	17
II	2	7		1	5			1	16
III	4	11		1	4	4	1	3	28
IV	7	3	4	4	1	2			21
V	17	17	11	4	6	6	10	4	75
VI	9	19	4	12	5	7		15	71
VII	3	21		3	5	4	1	1	38
VIII	9	10	3	6	3			6	37
IX	1	9	2	3	6	5	1	6	33
Total (by column)	56	102	27	35	35	30	13	38	336

Source: Authors' compilation of data from Diari de Sessions del Parlament de Catalunya and Butlletí Oficial del Parlament de Catalunya

In the first stage, covering the first four legislatures (1980–95), most of the motions and resolutions called on the Catalan government to immediately implement the practical aspects of language normalization and set the conditions needed to meet the objectives (for example, they detail the necessary transfer of competences and material resources by the central government, along with the need to give effect to the undertakings made concerning cooperation). In fact, this first stage corresponds to the process of drafting, approving – unanimously – and applying the act respecting the linguistic normalization of Catalonia (Statute 7/1983).

In the second stage (starting with the fifth legislature, and therefore in 1995), the content of the resolutions and motions highlights the dissatisfaction of the parliamentary forces with the central government's "non-respect" for established agreements, and the impossibility of achieving the objectives set during the preceding stage. It became clear that full normalization of the Catalan language in Catalonia depended not only on the action of the government of the Generalitat but also on the central government, whose inaction, particularly with regard to the administration of justice, constituted a major obstacle to the achievement of the Generalitat's objectives and linguistic policy. The start of the second stage corresponds to the period during which the second statute on language was drafted and approved: the Act Respecting Language Policy (Statute 1/1998).

The third stage began with the PP contesting the 2006 Statute of Autonomy and, more specifically, with the June 2010 ruling of the Constitutional Court. In the area of language, the 2006 Statute regulated in depth the status of Catalan as the official language of Catalonia (section 6), as well as linguistic rights and duties (sections 32 to 36). In particular, section 6 established that "the language of Catalonia is Catalan" and added that "for this reason ... it is the language used habitually and by preference by the public administration and public media in Catalonia; in addition, Catalan is the common language of instruction in the field of education." The second paragraph of the same section specifies that Catalan and Spanish are the official languages of Catalonia, every person has the right to use both official languages, and Catalans have the right and duty to know both official languages.

The ruling of the Constitutional Court was based on the premise that, strictly speaking, Catalan could not be the language of Catalonia since Spanish had the same status. From this premise, and from the official status of Spanish, came the conclusion that the two languages had to have exactly the same status, despite the fact that, paradoxically, the ruling did not apply the same principle with respect to the obligation to know Catalan, recognizing only an obligation to know Spanish. In addition, equality had to be applied to the language rights of individuals who spoke both Catalan and Spanish. As a result, it declared unconstitutional the preferential use of Catalan by the Catalan administration – in other words, by the Generalitat and the local administration – along with the duty to know Catalan, and established that it was not possible to allow individuals to demand that communications from the Catalan administration be addressed to them in Catalan, since this would place an undue burden on the administration. In some areas, such as education, the ruling allowed Catalan to be the preferred language of use, but only in cases where Catalan still needed special support, given its subservient position to Spanish, and not because Catalan was the language of Catalonia.

The application of the Constitutional Court's ruling generated new disputes at the administrative level and in the courts, even in the Supreme Court, which applied the new constitutional doctrine in an even stricter way, on the basis of the absolute equality of the two languages for the immediate future. In addition, the central government, in particular in the area of education, appeared to be pursuing a harder line with Catalan. For example, the Department of Education approved draft legislation making it possible to separate classes and schools by language.

In the final analysis, the fundamental thesis of Parliament, that the Catalan language is a founding element of the Catalan nation and an element that characterizes it as a differentiated society, is under extreme threat. As a result of the ideas pursued by the central state and the courts of justice, Spanish should have exactly the same status as Catalan in Catalonia. The Parliament of Catalonia's most recent resolutions express energetic support for the linguistic model in effect in Catalonia's schools and implement the decision not to apply any central state law that contradicts this model. This reveals, in yet another area, the grave state of disagreement between the Generalitat de Catalunya and the central state.

CONCLUSIONS AND FUTURE PROSPECTS

The leading role played by the Parliament of Catalonia with respect to the four essential issues examined in this chapter has given us a privileged, although partial, viewpoint from which to analyse the evolution of self-government in Catalonia over the thirty-two years that have elapsed since it was re-established.

First, it would be unfair, and in fact it would be denaturing the facts, not to recognize the extraordinary progress that recognition for its political autonomy in the 1978 Constitution and the 1979 Statute has represented for Catalonia. However, as we observed above, since the establishment of the autonomous communities, it has become apparent that the central state and Catalonia interpret the "State pact," which is how the Parliament of Catalonia views both texts, in very different ways. The gap between the two sides is both long-standing and continuous, leading to the current situation of extreme disagreement. In fact, from a political point of view, the bridges between the two parties have been cut; worse still, what has been cut is the minimum level of mutual trust needed by any decentralized state to "function."

This broadening divide can be explained by the fact that all demands by a majority of Catalans to increase their political power, improve the funding system, and obtain national recognition for Catalonia have been persistently and radically rejected. The frustration caused by the crushing of Catalonia's aspirations – possibly illusory, possibly impossible for the central state to grant (a fact that lends weight to arguments for an independent state) – has increased over the years and is now generalized among the population. All attempts to "re-read" the constitution and statute have failed; the proposal to reform the statute and the proposal for a new fiscal pact have been rejected in a spectacular way.

Today, the political future of Catalonia within the central state seems to have only two possible theoretical outcomes: a radical reform of the constitution to respond to Catalonia's political, economic, and national aspirations, and separation. In Catalonia, many people have, like us, concluded that the second option involves enormous difficulties, but that the first option, currently, *rebus sic stantibus*, is simply untenable. In fact, the central government and the party that supports it have rejected the possibility of any reform, while the Spanish socialist party appears to accept the reform as long as it does not cross certain lines – such as equality of all the rights of Spanish people, and not just their fundamental rights – thereby excluding a large proportion of the simplest demands based on what seem to be the aspirations of most Catalans. In addition, over the last two years, the central government has taken no steps to reconsider Catalan aspirations; on the contrary, it has pursued an aggressive recentralization policy that runs against those aspirations.[26]

In these circumstances, it is impossible to predict the future direction of this dispute. That will depend on numerous domestic and international factors, and especially on the percentage of Catalans who choose to support the construction of an independent state. For now, the government and the Parliament of Catalonia have already decided to call a consultation – within the next two years – to gauge the opinion of the Catalan population. They will ask the Spanish government for authorization to hold a referendum and, if necessary, they will organize the consultation, but not as a referendum. If this approach is barred by the central state, the government and Parliament will seek other alternatives that, today, have not yet been determined, although they seem to be leaning toward a non-"official" consultation promoted by private organizations, with the indirect support of public authorities, or, if necessary, a "plebiscitary" election or unilateral declaration of independence by Parliament.

The Spanish government and the two majority parties in Spain have made a firm decision to prevent any sort of consultation, using the argument of unconstitutionality. To date, it is not known whether the people of Catalonia will be able to express their opinion, and what their definitive opinion will be.

All options remain open: an agonizing continuation of the status quo resulting from the extreme polarization between two opposing positions; acceptance by a majority of Catalans of a reduced pact if the central state becomes more flexible; or an increase in the number of citizens who, when surveyed, say that they would vote for independence if a referendum were to be held, since at some point their aspirations must be met.

NOTES

1 The authors wish to thank Ms Rosa Mª López and Ms Rosa Felicitat Escrihuela, at the studies and documentation division of the Catalan Parliament, for their assistance.

2 J.L.Van Zanden, E. Buringh, and M. Bosker, *The Rise and Decline of European Parliaments, 1188–1789*, Discussion Paper No. 7809, Centre for Economic Policy Research, 2010.

3 In the late eleventh century, in the Catalan territories, the Sanctuary and Truce Assembly was created by the church as a purely ecclesiastical institution which, working with the civil authorities, deliberated on and entered into agreements concerning truces during periods of war and regulated the enforcement of truces. In a similar context, in the early twelfth century (1192), the section of the population known as the "braç

popular" was invited for the first time to attend a Sanctuary and Truce Assembly.

4 Starting in the twelfth century, the Cort of the Count of Barcelona brought together feudal nobles, representatives of the church, *pro homes* from the cities, and the count's advisers. The Cort helped the king legislate and administer justice. During the first half of the thirteenth century, under King James I, the kingdom grew larger, the number of Cort members increased, and the presence of representatives of the bourgeoisie was consolidated. Eventually, all the feudal courts in the kingdom were brought together in the Cort General.

5 I. Pitarch, *L'obra legislativa 1932–1936* (Barcelona: Publicacions del Parlament de Catalunya, 1981).

6 *Baròmetre d'Opinió Pública*, 3rd survey, October 2012, Centre d'Estudis d'Opinió, http://www.ceo.gencat.cat/ceop/AppJava/pages, accessed 2 December 2015.

7 This data is from the article "CiU i ICV tenen més diputats del sector public," published in *ARA* on 17 December 2012, p. 10, under the by-line Mireia Miquel, http://www.ara.cat, accessed 2 December 2015.

8 There have been thirty-seven filed between 1981 and 2002.

9 For example, Resolution 115/IV, which followed the debate in 1993, adds the need to ensure that the administration of the Generalitat becomes the ordinary administration of Catalonia. Examples of recurrent demands include Resolutions 15/V from May 1996 (transfers, bases, participation in the EU, ordinary administration, etc.) and Resolution 184/V, which followed the debate on the general political program for that year.

10 For example, in Resolution 115/IV, Parliament expressed its satisfaction with the improvements made to the financing system under the common regime. Similarly, in Resolution 16/V from May 1996, Parliament decided to promote the establishment of a new financing system, but one based on the common model and "applicable to the other autonomous communities."

11 The fundamental characteristic of the "economic concertation" model is that the autonomous community concerned collects all the taxes levied in its territory and manages them through its tax agency, paying the central state an agreed amount on the basis of the competencies and services provided by the central state to all autonomous communities.

12 For example, Resolutions 859/VI and 915/VI.

13 For example, in Resolution 1547/VI from 2002, "Parliament states its opposition to ... the gradual homogenization of the autonomous communities"; Resolution 115/IV from 1993 mentions that "a standardizing

deployment of the competencies of the autonomous communities must be avoided" and that "the Statute of Autonomy of Catalonia must be developed in more depth under the Constitution of 1978, taking the principle of heterogeneity and the Catalan differential into account."

14 See *Butlletí Oficial del Parlament de Catalunya,* dated 5 December 2002.

15 The Catalan Parliament has also helped "build the nation," like all parliaments, by enacting legislation on social affairs, health care, and education. However, an analysis of this important question requires more space than is available here.

16 Over fifteen laws have explicitly mentioned Catalonia's national character, whether in the title or the body of the act. These include the act respecting the national holiday of Catalonia (Statute 1/1980), Statute 1/1993 on the Catalan national anthem, Statute 4/1985, which establishes the national youth council of Catalonia, and the library acts (Statute 3/1981 and Statute 4/1994), which provide for the establishment of the Biblioteca Nacional de Catalunya (National Library of Catalonia).

17 This is the first resolution in which Parliament proclaims Catalonia's right to self-determination. The title of the resolution is "Dret a l'autodeterminació de la Nació catalane" (right to self-determination of the Catalan nation), although the text of the resolution uses the term "differentiated national reality" rather than "nation." ERC, the party that promoted the resolution, agreed to an amendment by CiU, stating that this was a way to recognize Catalonia's place in the broader Catalan environment (which includes the Valencian Community, the Balearic Islands, and Northern Catalonia, in addition to the Principality of Catalonia).

18 The preamble states that the "Parliament of Catalonia, taking upon itself to express the will and sentiment of the Catalan people, defines Catalonia as a nation on the basis of a broad majority. In section 2, the Spanish Constitution recognizes the national reality of Catalonia as a nationality."

19 As discussed below, in Resolutions 229/III from 1991 and 944/V from 1999.

20 In addition to these resolutions, we must point out that Parliament has been especially active in expressing its support for the various self-determination processes underway around the world, taking a stand exactly opposite that of the Spanish state. Examples of parliamentary resolutions include the non-legislative proposal to salute and encourage the peoples and governments of Slovenia and Croatia of 3 December (it has been said that, because it does not have the competency, Parliament cannot recognize the independence and political sovereignty of these countries).

The PS abstained. The other MPs voted for Resolution 742/IX from September 2012, requiring the state to recognize the state of Kosovo.

21 Even so, during the last election campaign, in November 2012, the PSC defended the idea of calling a consultation of the people to allow Catalans to express their opinion on the future of Catalonia, provided the consultation was "legal" and after warning that it would support Catalonia's remaining in the Spanish state and a reform of the constitution on a federal basis.

22 ERC, CiU, and SI voted for, along with one deputy from the mixed group. The PSC and ICV abstained, while the PP and C's voted against.

23 Following the resolution, consultations were organized in 259 municipalities (out of 900 in Catalonia), including all the major cities.

24 Except for the first point, which obtained eighty-five votes because one PSC deputy failed to follow the party line.

25 For example, between the first legislature (1984–88) and the fourth legislature (1992–95), fifty-nine out of seventy-five resolutions were approved unanimously, whether by committees or plenary assemblies.

26 We have analysed this aspect in "El procés de recentralització de l'Estat de les autonomies," C. Viver and G. Martín, to be published in *Informe sobre Federalismo Fiscal '12* by the Institut d'Economia de Barcelona.

2

The Parliament of the Basque Country and the National Issue: The Weaknesses of a Strong Identity

ALBERTO LÓPEZ BASAGUREN

Citizens of the Basque Country possess a very strong, differentiated national awareness. A large proportion of citizens feel "only Basque"; Basque nationalism enjoys considerable political strength, as shown by successive elections; and the basic elements of Basque identity are accepted by most of society, although often they are not totally compatible with the actual characteristics of a large part of the population. Significant, in this sense, is the case of the Basque language (*euskara*). Socially speaking it is a minority language: between 25 and 30 percent may be considered Basque-speaking. Moreover, the language has traditionally been absent from a very large area of the territory; nonetheless, it enjoys considerable legal and social support as a distinctive element of Basque identity.[1] The characterization of the Basque national identity is a nationalist construction, but despite these beginnings, a majority of citizens and political parties have assumed it. Taken together, these elements appear to indicate the great strength of the Basque national awareness.

The existence of the terrorist organization ETA (Euskadi Ta Askatasuna), with the extreme radicalism of its activity, its enormous impact, and the image it has transmitted, has further reinforced the perception of the great strength of the Basque national awareness. But this perception needs to be qualified. Behind this apparent strength lie hidden weaknesses.

The generalized acceptance by citizens of the nationalist construction of the idea of the Basque nation is recent and, to a large extent, superficial.[2] A significant part of Basque society does not share this

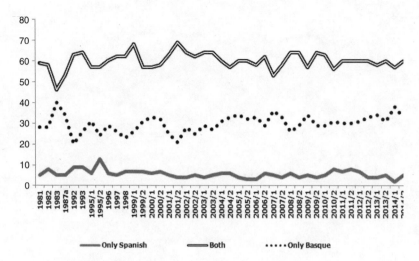

Figure 2.1   The feeling of national identity, 1981–2014
Source: Euskobarometro – UPV/EHU

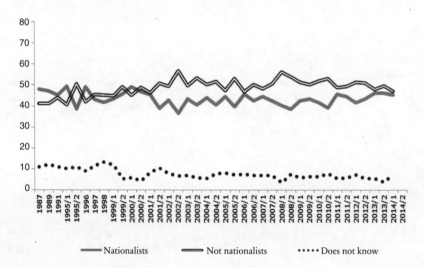

Figure 2.2   Basque nationalist feelings, 1987–2014
Source: Euskobarometro – UPV/EHU

identity, and an even larger part does not accept the meaning and consequences attributed to this identity by the more doctrinaire and radical sectors of nationalism. It is significant that, from the point of view of identity, a large majority do not feel "only Basque" (Figure 2.1), do not consider themselves "(Basque) nationalist" (Figure 2.2), and express

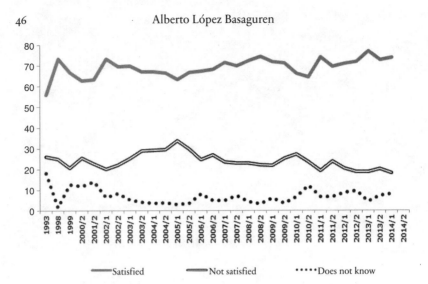

Figure 2.3 Satisfaction with the Statute of Autonomy in the Basque Country, 1993–2014
Source: Euskobarometro – UPV/EHU

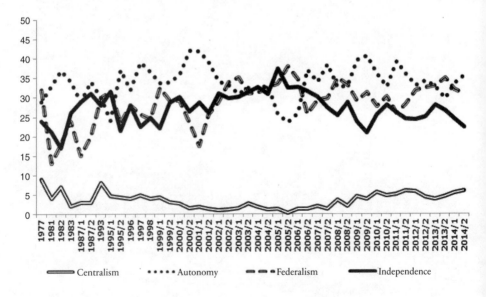

Figure 2.4 Preferences for the form of the Spanish State, 1977–2012
Source: Euskobarometro – UPV/EHU

a high degree of satisfaction with the Statute of Autonomy (SA) (Figure 2.3), and that only a minority regard independence as the best option for the Basque Country (Figure 2.4). This explains the electoral limits of nationalism, despite its strength, and the variations in election results, depending on their nature – general elections or regional elections – and the political scenario.

Among the weaknesses of the nationalist construction of the Basque Country is the hugely important territorial question. The territory of the political nation defended by nationalism[3] is divided between France and Spain; and the presence of nationalism in the French Basque Country is purely cultural. In the Spanish part, there are two separate political-institutional entities: the Basque Provinces and Navarra. Nationalism in Navarra has traditionally been almost insignificant and, although it has grown considerably in recent times – especially radical nationalism – it is still a minority force which is, for now, unable to put an end to Navarra's institutional separation from the Basque Country. Nationalism is impregnated, then, by irredentism; and the attitude to the territorial question constitutes, at the same time, a vital source of recruitment for radical nationalism – which is the strongest nationalist option in Navarra and in the French Basque Country – and an element of irreconcilable confrontation with possibilist sectors of nationalism.

The territoriality issue exists even within the Basque Country, although with different characteristics. The strength of nationalism varies from one province to another. Traditional nationalism (PNV – Partido Nacionalista Vasco) has enjoyed an unchallenged position of strength and majority in Bizkaia since the restoration of democracy. It is largely a possibilist, moderate nationalism, dominated by sectors that favour autonomy. Radical nationalism is strongest in Gipuzkoa where it now contests the hegemony of the PNV, which is led in this province by its more radical sector. Finally, in Araba nationalism has traditionally been very weak. Although it has attained a relative electoral majority in various elections following the death of Franco and the restoration of democracy, its electorate is voluble and largely moderate, and tends to retract when nationalism radicalizes its strategy, relegating it to a secondary position. Non-nationalist political forces have a very strong presence in the province and have won in several elections, general elections in particular, but also in regional and provincial elections.

In conclusion, the sentiment of Basque national identity is very strong. But it is limited and has important political and institutional weaknesses which hinder the construction of a national project in keeping with the nationalists' wishes and with the potential for strong political support in the Basque Country as a whole. These weaknesses are magnified by the deep split between radical and moderate nationalists, which renders barely feasible a common national project shared – and promoted – by all nationalist parties. On the other hand, nationalist and non-nationalist parties have collaborated in government over a long period, necessitating a balance between their visions of how to address the development of Basque autonomy.

THE PARLIAMENT OF THE BASQUE COUNTRY: GENERAL OVERVIEW: THE PRINCIPLE OF "CONFEDERACY"

The Basque Country has not experienced political-institutional unity, at least in the modern and contemporary age. Only the passing of the Statute of Autonomy (SA) in 1979 institutionalized the political unity of the provinces of Araba, Bizkaia, and Gipuzkoa, which form the Autonomous Community (AC) of the Basque Country.[4]

Traditionally, the institutionalization of the Basque Country has been provincial, linking up with the medieval institutionalization in which each territory had its own "particular laws" (*Fueros*). In one way or another, this situation persisted in the Basque Country until recently.[5] Although the paths taken by Navarra and by the Basque Provinces were very different,[6] the end result was, paradoxically, very similar: the creation of a special new administrative system the most notable element of which is the taxation system, known as the Economic Convention (Navarra) or Economic Agreement (Basque Country).[7] This new system maintained the differentiated provincial institutions.

The statute projects drafted during the Second Republic followed this tradition, in which the "principle of confederacy" was particularly influential.[8] Although this element disappears in the text finally approved by the Spanish Parliament (October 1936), that change was insignificant, given the special circumstances in which the text was drafted and passed: in the middle of a civil war, with most of the territory of the Basque Country – except most of the province of Bizkaia – in the hands of the rebels. In these circumstances, the text was drafted as an emergency text, in Parliament itself, unconnected to the project that had been proposed by the Basque political parties and approved in a citizens' referendum.

The effects of this provincial tradition have also been apparent in the current SA (1979). There are two points that are particularly relevant. First, each province – now known as a "Historical Territory" (HT) – is a constituency with an identical number of representatives in the Basque Parliament (sec. 26.1 SA),[9] despite considerable differences in population.[10] The equal representation of the territories in the Basque Parliament ties in with the provincial institutional tradition. But, second, it is also a way of addressing the problem of the scant political integration of the different territories that, for nationalism, integrate the Basque nation. It strove not to complicate a hypothetical integration of Navarra, where there was fear of being diluted within the much more populous Basque provinces,[11] and to do the same with the representatives of Araba, where there was a similar fear. The SA could go ahead without the participation of Navarra (traditional now); but the refusal of Araba, too, would have been very difficult to deal with.

The establishment of the equal representation of each province in the Basque Parliament would have significant consequences, which would reinforce the "principle of confederacy." The considerable demographic (and economic) weight of Bizkaia would make it necessary to compensate for its reduced representation in Parliament via the reservation of important competences for the HT, which would have a very negative effect on the primacy of the shared political institutions of the AC – parliament and government. The SA directly reserves some competences for the HT and provides for Parliament to transfer them when it sees fit (sec. 37); the Law of Historical Territories (LHT) did this comfortably.[12] But the most important power of the HT lies in the sphere of finance or taxation. The competences attributed to the Basque Country by the Economic Agreement correspond to the HT (sec. 41 SA), and not to the shared institutions, which regulate and administer (collect) practically all the taxes of the Spanish tax system in the Basque Country. The distribution within the AC of the tax revenues collected by the HT – discounting the quantity payable to the state – is determined beyond the Basque Parliament, in the Basque Council of Public Finances (BCPF), a body constituted on an equal basis by representatives of the Basque government and the provincial councils of the three HTs. This procedure was established in the LHT (sec. 20 and subsequent), similar to the system for determining the amount the Basque Country must pay to the state for the "powers (competences) not assumed" by the AC. Once this amount had been deducted, the representatives of the government and of the *Diputaciones* (provincial councils) in the BCPF establish what corresponds to the AC and what each HT should contribute to this. This proposal has to be approved in Parliament as a law "of single article or of totality" (sec. 22.2 and 29 LHT), that is, without the capacity to introduce amendments, having to be approved or rejected as a whole. In the latter case, it would return to the BCPF for a new proposal. Only in the exceptional case of there being no agreement in the BCPF does Parliament have the power to determine the content of the law; but only in those aspects in which there is no agreement in the BCPF (sec. 29.2 LHT).

To sum up, the "principle of confederacy" has a profound influence on the institutional organization of the Basque Country, articulating some significantly weakened shared institutions and some provincial institutions invested with considerable power.

THE PARLIAMENTARY SYSTEM OF GOVERNMENT: THE MEMBERS OF PARLIAMENT

The SA establishes a parliamentary system of government for the Basque Country, similar to that established by the constitution for the state. This means that Parliament assumes institutional centrality. Its members are elected by universal suffrage – "responding to criteria of proportional representation" within each constituency (sec. 26.3 SA) – in the number and territorial distribution indicated above, and in respect of its mandate. The legislature lasts four years (sec. 26 SA).

Parliament exercises legislative power, but is limited by obligatory respect for the competences that, as a consequence of the peculiar institutional system, correspond to the HT. The Basque Parliament, in this regard, is protected by "inviolability" (sec. 25.2 SA), as too are its members "in the votes and opinions they issue in the exercise of their responsibility" (sec. 26.6 SA). In other words, parliamentary activity cannot be conditioned nor may its members be accountable for opinions or votes issued in the exercise of their responsibility. Furthermore, members of Parliament (MPs) enjoy special *status* during their mandate: in the case of crimes committed within the territory of the AC of the Basque Country, they cannot be "arrested or held" except when caught in the act of committing a crime; and the competence to decide upon their "indictment, imprisonment, trial and sentencing" corresponds to the High Court of Justice of the Basque Country.[13] In the case of crimes committed outside the AC's territory, the Spanish Supreme Court will ascertain criminal responsibility (sec. 26.6 SA).

In this sphere, it is worth noting the *restrictive status* of the members of Parliament of the AC in comparison with those of the state Parliament's MPs. The latter enjoy *inviolability* in the votes and opinions issued in the exercise of their responsibility and also *immunity* during their mandate, as well as special *status* of trial before the Supreme Court (sec. 71 SC). This means that their being charged or tried will require prior authorization by the respective house. Although the SA does not include this *immunity* among the elements comprising the *status* of the members of Basque Parliament, this body attributed this privilege to them via law, establishing requirement of prior authorization by the house as a condition to charge or try them. The Constitutional Court (Constitutional Court Ruling – CCR–36/1981 of November 12) declared – in the light of the drafting of the SA – that this went far beyond the text.

In addition to legislative power, the Basque Parliament has compe- tence in different fields in relation to some state bodies. Thus, it is the body competent to elect the senators whose election, in accordance with sec. 69.5 of the Spanish Constitution (SC),[14] corresponds to the AC of the Basque Country (known as "regional" senators).

Moreover, the Basque Parliament, like the Basque government, is en- titled to appeal before the Constitutional Court – via the "claim of un- constitutionality" – against state and other AC laws (sec. 162.1, SC). This capacity has been employed with a certain degree of frequency by Par- liament – especially in cases of structural impact or in defence of a par- ticular aspect of constitutionality (anti-terrorist legislation, for example) which had considerable political significance; but, usually, it is the gov- ernment that lodges appeals in defence of the competences of the AC. Legitimacy for the lodging of a claim of unconstitutionality by the in- stitutions of the AC – parliaments and governments – was the object, initially, of a restrictive interpretation by the Constitutional Court (CC), which demanded a direct link with the competences of the AC (CCR 25/1981, 14 July, on anti-terrorist legislation). But that interpretation was relaxed almost immediately and is no longer a practical problem; the CC regards as sufficient the existence of an "interest" in the issue subject to appeal and acknowledges that the ACs have an objective in- terest in the confirmation of the constitutionality of laws.[15]

Finally, the Basque government has the capacity to exercise legisla- tive initiative before the State Parliament (Cortes Generales). This is a function which, during the ten mandates to date, has been exercised only on very specific and very few occasions and usually in questions of no great political significance. The Basque Parliament has exercised legislative initiative, successfully, on two politically insignificant occa- sions (the tax regime applicable to the Basque Radio and TV Corpora- tion, extending that enjoyed by its Spanish counterpart; extension of the period for handling proceedings in the Arbitral Insurance Tribu- nal, to enable completion of processing of claims resulting from the floods suffered by Bilbao and the vicinity in 1983). Successfully, too, in a matter of considerable significance, namely the reform of the Organ- ic Law of the CC to assign to the CC control of the provisions of the HT (known as *Normas Forales*) in fiscal matters, excluding them from ordi- nary jurisdiction. The Basque Parliament presented, also, a draft organic law regarding the rights of those under arrest or held in police facilities, which was abandoned at the end of the Basque legislature. Moreover, the Basque Parliament initiated a reform of the SA with the presentation of the Project for a New Political Statute for Euskadi (generally known as the Ibarretxe Plan), which was rejected by the plenary of the Lower House of the Spanish Parliament on 1 February 2005. Finally, the Basque Parliament presented a draft law for the reform of the General Social Security System legislation, which, theoretically, is being processed in the Lower House. This is, then, a course of action rarely employed by the Basque Parliament.

The most important political competences of the Basque Parliament, as is characteristic of parliamentary systems of government, are exercised in the sphere of relations between parliament and government: it elects the president of the government – known as the *lehendakari* – and promotes and controls government action. In this area, the legal system of the Basque Country lacks any particularly significant novelties. The *lehendakari* is elected by the MPs and he or she freely designates and removes members of government. At the same time, the *lehendakari* is the "highest representative of the Basque Country and the ordinary representative of the State in this territory"' (sec. 33 SA).

POLITICAL REPRESENTATION AND GOVERNMENT
IN THE BASQUE COUNTRY (1980–2012)

The Basque Parliament began its 10th Legislature following the elections in October 2012. The evolution of political representation and of governability during the thirty-two years since the first elections to the Basque Parliament (1980), after the passing of the SA (1979), is fundamental to understanding the development of the national question in the political activity of Parliament and, ultimately, in Basque politics.

The first question is the political hegemony exercised during this period by the PNV, the moderate nationalist party. It has won all the elections, except those of 1986 held immediately after the schism resulting from the creation of Eusko Alkartasuna (EA) (Figure 2.5). But the PNV has never enjoyed a solid parliamentary majority; this has obliged it to govern in minority or in coalition with other parties.

Thus, the second element to highlight is the proliferation of weak governments; governments that, in any case, have always been in the hands of the PNV, except in the 9th Parliament's mandate (Figure 2.6). This weakness was partly counteracted by a specific fact: the refusal of radical nationalism (HB – Herri Batasuna[16]) to participate in parlia-

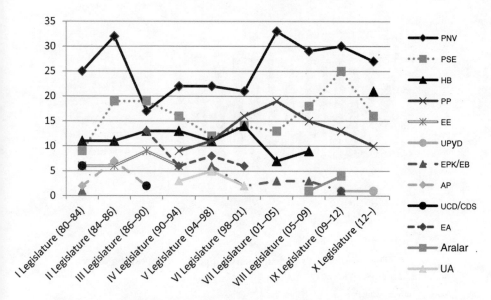

Figure 2.5 The distribution of seats in the Basque Parliament, 1980–2012

Source: Author's calculations

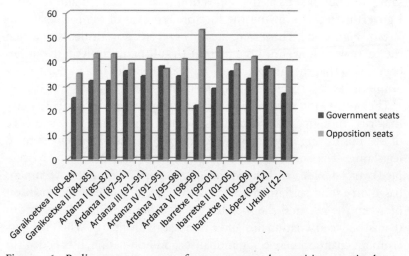

Figure 2.6 Parliamentary support of government and opposition seats in the Basque Parliament, 1980–2012

Source: Author's calculations

mentary activity, except in some exceptional debates. Despite this, the PNV had an absolute parliamentary majority only during the first legislature (Garaikoetxea I Government), while in the second it had the

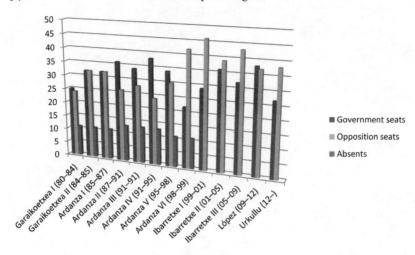

Figure 2.7 The government's parliamentary support and opposition seats, deducted absents, 1980–2012

Source: Author's calculations

same number of seats as the opposition (Garaikoetxea II and Ardanza I governments), following the forcible removal of the former *lehendakari* (Figure 2.7). These were the only two PNV governments in which the party was alone, until the present Urkullu government; the difference being that the latter is much more at the helm of a minority government (27 seats of 75) than the former.

The only period when the government enjoyed a solid parliamentary majority (though due, in almost all parliamentary terms, to the absence of HB) was during the successive Ardanza governments after the third legislature. The 2nd, 4th, and 5th Ardanza governments,[17] which occupied over a decade, constituted the longest period of stable government based on a solid parliamentary majority, made possible by the coalition between the PNV and the socialist PSE (Partido socialista de Euskadi); that is, between a nationalist and a non-nationalist party. When the government coalition between nationalists and non-nationalists ended (in July 1998), the PNV once again fronted weak governments. The Ardanza VI Government was merely a transition to the next elections (between July and October). The 1st, 2nd, and 3rd Ibarretxe governments were coalition governments between the PNV, EA (the party which split from the PNV) and EB-IU (Ezker Batua-Izquierda Unida, the former communists); very much minority governments – especially the 1st and the 3rd – which revolved around the PNV's boldest political strategy.

In the 9th Legislature, the head of the government was, for the first time, a politician who did not belong to the PNV. Patxi López (PSE) was elected *lehendakari* and formed a government of a single hue on the basis of a modest group of twenty-five MPs, but supported by a pact with the PP (conservatives), which afforded it an absolute parliamentary majority. This enabled him to govern with majority support, but subject to significant limitations. He had to withstand the virulent reaction of the PNV, which denied his legitimacy to accede to the position of *lehendakari*, and counter the opposition of the Regional Council of Bizkaia, governed by the PNV.[18] Furthermore, there were significant material limits to the government pact with the PP, as a result of which government action had guaranteed parliamentary support only in limited fields.

Thus, the general rule in the Basque Country has been that of weak governments, or otherwise, of coalition governments between parties with very different visions and aspirations. The effect has been limited legislative activity with the emphasis on administrative action. At the same time, it has meant that in most significant legislative initiatives, consensus was sought between highly divergent political positions, absolutely vital if these were to have sufficient political support.

There is, finally, a question that must be taken into account in order to understand the political development of the Basque Country: the considerable variation in results depending on the nature of the elections: general (to the Spanish Parliament) or regional (to the Basque Parliament). One might refer to a "roller coaster" with regard to the three major political forces: PNV, PSE, and PP (figure 2.8). In general, in elections to the Basque Parliament there is usually significantly lower voter turnout than in general elections of the same period, which penalizes the non-nationalist parties, PSE and PP, although there have been exceptions.[19] On the other hand, these parties tend to benefit in general elections from the electoral climate prevailing in Spain as a whole at the time. This means that the part of the electorate that votes nationalist in elections to the Basque Parliament is probably voting with the government of the AC in mind and not the party's strategic national aims. But even radical nationalism has had its own roller coaster ride.[20]

The elements described reveal a complex political reality, in which nationalism, as a whole, is very strong; in the last elections – both general and to the Basque Parliament – nationalists account for around 50 percent of voters. But there is a significant block of abstainers who participate only in critical situations and significantly alter this equilibrium. On the other hand, cooperation between the two sectors of

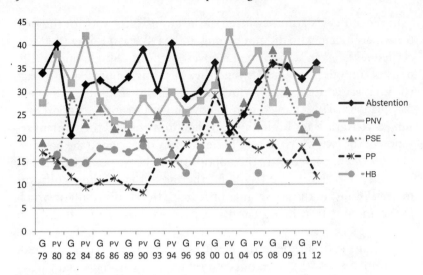

Figure 2.8   Comparison of percentage of abstention and voting for different parties in general elections to Congress of Deputies (G) and in regional elections to the Basque Parliament (PV), reporting data for the four largest parties only

Source: Author's calculations

nationalism, except on very specific issues, does not seem feasible. As the experience of Ibarretxe's plan has shown, the PNV's leadership within the nationalist movement could be at risk. For the PNV to be able to govern, they must be open to non-nationalist political sectors; and the retention of its electorate, particularly in elections to the Basque Parliament, requires that it act with caution, in order not to lose those who, not strongly linked to nationalism, vote for what they regard as the best way to defend regional interests or governability.

THE PARLIAMENT OF THE BASQUE COUNTRY AND THE NATIONAL ISSUE

The Issue of Symbols: From Agreement to Dissent

Initially, the symbolism of Basque nationalism, largely the work of Sabino Arana, was a party symbolism. But, especially during the civil war and in exile, the most important symbols came to be accepted by all parties. Both the term *Euskadi* and the flag were incorporated into the SA with the approval of practically all the political parties.

The SA, however, makes no reference to the anthem of the Basque Country, since this has always been a controversial question. The PNV has always believed that the anthem of Euskadi should be the party anthem. But this anthem was – and is – almost unknown beyond PNV circles. At the end of the 1st legislature the PNV proposed that this become the official anthem. The Anthem Law – Law 3/1983, of 14 April – was passed with twenty-three votes in favour and fourteen against; in other words, with only thirty-seven members present, in a Parliament of seventy-five MPs.

This episode is symptomatic of the political attitude of the PNV and of the deep divisions produced in the Basque Country in different spheres. It is, furthermore, indicative of the way the Basque Parliament functioned for many years during the first two legislatures (1980–86), when the PNV held a narrow majority due to the absence of HB from parliamentary activity and, on many occasions, saw no need to reach a consensus with another political group, pushing through its proposals on its own.

The anthem thus approved lacks any degree of social acceptance and, thirty years later, remains unknown to most citizens. Even bearing in mind its limited significance, the issue of the anthem offers a lesson in Basque politics: moderate nationalism is not strong enough, by itself, to guarantee majority support for its political project; and when, taking advantage of the circumstances, it attempts to impose factional patterns, most of society ignores them.

The Language Question: The Value of Consensus

Compared with the practical insignificance of the anthem, language has been an issue of decisive importance. The Basque language was very much a minority language within Basque society itself, established, traditionally, in a relatively small area of the territory and mainly limited to rural areas and the home. A single literary standard had been adopted little more than a decade before the passing of the SA in 1979, not without considerable resistance from some sectors that were attached to dialectal varieties. The Basque language is, moreover, an isolated language, with no linguistic family, which for a very long time has been in a situation of subordinate coexistence with another language of great social and "linguistic" strength – Spanish or French – languages which are widely spoken by the Basque speakers of each respective territory, and which, therefore, they traditionally employ in different spheres of public life. The result has been that the Basque language is an undeveloped language in important public spheres.

Successfully addressing the issue of language was, therefore, crucial to arresting the deterioration of its social use and permitting its access to spheres from which it had traditionally been excluded. According to the Spanish Constitution (sec. 3), the SA had declared Euskara the official language of the Basque Country, along with Spanish. However, it was necessary to specify both the meaning and consequences of that official status. Achieving a broad consensus, with as much unanimity as possible, was an indispensable condition for any hope of success. But the conflicting positions made this very difficult, particularly when the temptation to politicize the issue had always been so great. However, the integration of Basque society depended on the capacity to effectively resolve this issue, to achieve a regulation that would enjoy widespread social and political support from both nationalist and non-nationalist people and parties. In spite of the absence of radical nationalism – HB – from parliamentary activities, the process was not easy; and there were moments when division seemed inevitable. In the end, however, that absence resulted in a near unanimous parliamentary consensus; this was both fortunate and risky at the same time.

The SA had established the foundations for the linguistic pact (sec. 6). It declared Basque to be an official language of the Basque Country, along with Spanish, in the whole territory of the AC. It excluded territorial limitation of official status, unlike in Navarra. Every citizen of the Basque Country has the right to know and use both languages, which will be guaranteed by the authorities, "taking into account the socio-linguistic diversity of the Basque Country."[21] The principal element of disagreement was the degree to which the use of the Basque language was compulsory, given its decidedly minority character and the traditional concentration of speakers in a relatively small and less populated geographical area.

The process was lengthy. The government presented the project in the Lower House in mid-1981; initially it appeared that the PNV was prepared to push through "its" law alone. However, those who believed it essential to seek a broad consensus prevailed. First, they reached an agreement with Euskadiko Ezkerra (EE); but the fundamental challenge was consensus with the non-nationalist parties. And both parties reached an agreement with the Socialist Party. The law obtained the support of thirty-one votes for, with two against and one abstention.[22] Only the two MPs representing AP – Alianza Popular, predecessor of the PP (conservatives and, one could say, Spanish nationalists) – opted not to support the law. Both sides made a huge effort to tackle the real problems involved in regulating the language and to avoid politicization.

Consensus was possible thanks to a balance between acknowledgment of citizens' linguistic freedom, that is, the right to use the official language of their choice, without any limitation, and the corresponding obligation of the authorities to serve the public in that language, make learning of the official language different from the chosen one compulsory, and promote the knowledge and use of Basque.

The consensus achieved in the law regarding *euskara* has not totally eradicated political differences over language; but it has limited them to a low profile. There has been a broad consensus in its application during these thirty years, except in matters of detail. And this has permitted growth in knowledge and use of the language to an extent that was unimaginable in the late 1970s.[23]

Institutional Organization: The Schism within Nationalism

The PNV has traditionally suffered considerable internal friction between its orthodox and possibilist sectors. In the 1980s, in the wake of the approval of the SA, the traditional confrontation between these sectors assumed peculiar connotations. To the question of nationalist radicalism versus possibilism was added the question of institutional organization and the powers that should correspond to the HT and the political strength that should be assigned to Parliament and the Government of the Basque Country, the shared institutions. These issues became intertwined and flared up during processing of the LHT, which established the powers that would correspond to the provinces.

At the helm of the party in Bizkaia – and in the Regional Council – was a provincialist sector that believed that the province's relatively weak representation in the Basque Parliament should be compensated for by the allocation of significant powers. This turned into a head-on confrontation between the Regional Council of Bizkaia and the Basque government, which had a profound impact upon the PNV. To this were added other kinds of tension between the *lehendakari* Carlos Garaikoetxea and the party leadership.

All this tension came to a head with the passing of the LHT, which the government opposed. The law conferred on the provinces very broad powers, in particular, the power to regulate and collect the taxes, and established a system for allocating public funds between provincial councils and shared institutions according to the "principle of confederacy": a deal has to be agreed upon between representatives of provincial councils and the Basque government on a parity basis body (the Basque Council for Public Finance). The implementation of this regulation sparked the conflict. In January 1985 the situation became unsustainable and led to the dismissal of the *lehendakari*, for refusing to accept the distribution of financial resources between shared institutions of the AC and the provinces.

The removal of Garaikoetxea, who was replaced by José Antonio Ardanza as *lehendakari*, provoked a profound internal divide within the PNV and the creation in 1986 of a new party (EA) led by the former. Collaboration between the two sectors did not resume until the first decade of the twenty-first century, in a process of steady weakening of EA and the radicalization of the PNV's strategy (Ibarretxe Plan).[24]

On the Right to Self-determination: What Meaning with What Nationalist Majority Support?

In February 1990, at the end of the 3rd Legislature, the Basque Parliament passed a declaration regarding the Basque Country's right to self-determination. It had the support of the PNV, EA, and EE, three nationalist parties, and was passed with thirty-eight votes for and twenty-three against. The thirteen HB MPs, for once, took part in the debate, presented an amendment, withdrew it at the end of the debate, and abandoned the session prior to voting.

The debate took place in the context of the still recent schism within the PNV, at the end of the first legislature subsequent to this, in which the battle over the nationalist electorate was at its bitterest. The PNV presented a joint proposal with EE, and EA presented its own proposal. The influence of EE is evident in the drafting of the PNV's initiative. The three parties finally managed to agree on a joint proposal, which by and large preserved the PNV and EE version. The parliamentary agreement required the votes of all three parties.

The adopted text begins by stating that the right to self-determination "resides in the lawful authority of its citizens to take decisions, freely and democratically, on their political, economic, social and cultural status, either by providing themselves with their own political framework or by sharing their sovereignty, totally or in part, with other peoples." But the text returns immediately to the institutions' and to the SA's legitimacy, which was the declaration's essential aim. The text maintains that the SA – "the result of a pact freely endorsed by the Basque citizens" – is "the legitimate expression of the free will of the Basque People." Thus, via the "genuine development of each and every one of [its] contents," the SA is the "legitimate framework for the gradual resolution of the problems of Basque society, as well as in order to progress in the national construction of Euskadi." According to the approved text, the representative institutions – and, in particular, Parliament – as depositaries of sovereignty are "alone in their legitimacy" to promote the exercise of the right to self-determination. Consequently, the addition to the legal system of any appeal should be undertaken via Parliament, which has the legal authority to promote and decide initiatives destined to "make possible the fulfillment of the aspirations of Basque citizens," by means of the reforms it considers necessary "in accordance with the procedures established for this purpose." The content and context of this declaration are indicative of the limits within which nationalism has traditionally moved, always conditioned, moreover, by the weakness of its parliamentary majority and the competition with radical nationalism.

On the "Non-compliance" with the SA:
Between Consensus and Disagreement

Nationalism has shown itself to be, almost permanently, dissatisfied with the development of the system of territorial autonomy. During the 1990s the Basque Parliament undertook an analysis of the "transfers"' yet to be performed by the state. The stance on this issue produced a clear majority consensus.

In 1992 and 1993 a parliamentary commission produced the "Report on Statute's Development," which was approved in the plenary session of 1 July 1993. This report establishes fifty-four competences pending transfer to the AC, urging the Basque government to negotiate these transfers with the government of the state.[25] The report was proposed by the PNV-PSE government coalition and reflects their shared position and an almost unanimous parliamentary consensus. The consensus appeared to be threatened when in 1994 the Basque Parliament passed an agreement on "full and fair development of the Statute" in which, referring to the parliamentary agreement of 1993, it maintains that the central government "must respect the decisions that this House [Basque Parliament] adopts regarding the Statute of Autonomy insofar as they are the democratic and pacific expression of the will of the citizens of the AC and accept them as this institution's reading of our basic rules of self-government"; on this basis, it urges the Spanish government to "assume as in accordance with the Statute" the contents of the report.[26] The PSE (socialists) and other parliamentary groups opposed this declaration, but the PNV supported it. The disagreement lay, fundamentally, in the character attributed to the position of the Basque Parliament with regard to compliance with and development of the SA. Finally, however, the consensus was partially rebuilt and the result was a text in which some points obtained the backing of a strong majority, while others were approved with a narrow majority.[27]

Finally, in 1995 Parliament approved the "Report on Priorities in the Negotiation of Outstanding Transfers."[28] This document clearly states that completing the development of the SA "is starting to become a structural problem" to the extent that Parliament declares that the delay in compliance with the statutory provisions "delays or undermines the model of political cohabitation ... encouraging strategies which delegitimize the way of the Statute of Autonomy and impact upon the process of normalization of the country." However, this was a realist, possibilist document, which achieved unanimity in the house (fifty-six votes for, none against, and no abstentions).

From this moment onward the coalition government between nationalists and socialists began to fall apart, and the PNV began to prepare a new political era in which the nationalists would use parliamentary activity with regard to outstanding transfers for the radical disqualification of the system of territorial autonomy, going so far as to claim that the SA had "died" as a consequence of the disloyalty of the state.

THE PATH TOWARD SOVEREIGNTY: THE *PLAN IBARRETXE* AND "FREE ASSOCIATION"

The new era would begin with a plenary session in the Basque Parliament on self-government (25 October 2001), creating a special commission on this issue. The resolution establishing the commission demanded "full and urgent compliance" with the SA, referring to the 1995 resolution. It acknowledged "the democratic legitimacy of the current legal and political frameworks constructed with the consent of Basque citizens" but also "the democratic legitimacy of options for change and updating it, in the event the necessary majorities are reached within Basque society." On these bases, the commitment was assumed to constitute a commission "of extension of our self-government, which addresses respect for and compliance with the statutory pact and the options for updating the latter, according to its potential."[29]

The report prepared by this commission was approved in the plenary session of Parliament on 12 July 2002,[30] and opened the era of demand by the nationalist political forces for a new political statute for the Basque Country; a project which would go beyond the system of territorial autonomy established in the constitution. The motion was passed with thirty-six votes for and thirty-one against. The consensus between the PNV – and occasionally EA – and the other parties was now completely broken. The Ibarretxe government could tread this path only if the radical nationalists – EH – permitted it to do so; the success of the Ibarretxe government's proposal was in their hands.

This document contains all the elements around which the new nationalist strategy for sovereignty would revolve: the right to self-determination; legitimacy to establish unilaterally a new system of autonomy in the Basque Country; and a bilateral system of political – not judicial – guarantees for it. This strategy began to materialize immediately and continued throughout the three Ibarretxe governments. In the debate of September 2002,[31] the Basque premier presented the document "A New Political Agreement for Cohabitation." With this, the chief executive rooted his proposal in the achievement of "cohabitation." He presented his proposal as a solution to terrorist violence: "the solution to the problem of political normalization lies in accepting that the Basque Country is not a subordinate part of the Spanish State but a People with its own identity, with the capacity to establish their own framework of internal relations and to form part of a truly plurinational state under the terms of free association."

At the heart of the Ibarretxe Plan is the "right to decide." The particular identity of the Basque people is born of a "feeling of national identity." And that "national identity" anchors the "right to be consulted in order to decide their own future," a right based upon both the decision of the Basque Parliament – in its role as representative of the electorate of the Autonomous Community of the Basque Country – and the right of peoples to self-determination acknowledged in article 1 of the International Covenant on Civil and Political Rights and of the International Covenant on Economic, Social and Cultural Rights (1966).

On these bases, on 25 October 2003, the Basque government approved the proposal of a "Political Statute for the Community of Euskadi" for debate in Parliament.[32] On 30 December 2004, it was approved by thirty-nine votes for and thirty-five against. Again, the radical nationalists gave three of their six votes in Parliament in support of the government proposal; without those votes it would not have been approved. In this project, the Basque Country unilaterally established the system of political link with Spain which it considers appropriate, namely, "status of free association": a "singular regime of political relations with the Spanish State" that the Basque Country establishes "on the basis of respect and mutual recognition" (sec. 12). And it includes the "right to decide": "Basque institutions and those of the State are deemed to be committed to guaranteeing a process of negotiation to establish the new political conditions that will enable the implementation, by common agreement, of the democratic will of Basque society," provided that Basque citizens express their clear and unequivocal desire completely or substantially to alter the model and regime of political relations with the Spanish state.

The Project for a New Political Statute was presented before the Spanish Parliament. In a debate in plenary session in which, on behalf of the Basque Parliament, the *lehendakari* Ibarretxe participated, the Lower House rejected it.[33] The rejection led the head of the autonomous Basque government to dissolve Parliament and call new regional elections. The coalition led by Ibarretxe lost a significant number of votes – and four seats – although the leader was able to continue at the head of a very weak minority government.[34] This did not prevent him from persisting with his strategy.

THE CONSULTATION LAW: TOWARD THE "RIGHT TO DECIDE"

In the general policy debate of September 2007 the *lehendakari* laid out his plans for the future. He restated the validity of the proposal for a new political statute, but focused his objectives on the "right to decide," which would culminate in the carrying out of a "consultation." This process would involve the following steps: first, the presentation of an "offer of political agreement to the President of the Spanish Government, until June 2008"; second, a plenary session of the Basque Parliament, in June 2008, to "endorse the political agreement reached with the State and authorize a legally binding consultation for its ratification," or, in the absence of an agreement with the state, to "authorize the holding of an enabling consultation that would initiate a process of solution"; third, the holding of the "consultation," in either of the two forms – with agreement or without – on 25 October 2008. Finally, in the second semester of 2010 the conclusive negotiation process would begin, with the holding of the "definitive referendum," which would constitute the embodiment of the "exercise of the right freely to decide our future."

After the general elections, the *lehendakari* pressed ahead with his political agenda, attempting, once again, to convince the president of the

Spanish government to accept his political proposal. When it was again rejected, the Basque Parliament passed the so-called "Consultation Law."[35] The law consisted of a single section which authorizes Parliament to "consult" the electorate, on a non-binding basis, about two simultaneous questions, on the same ballot paper.[36] It stipulated that the consultation would be held on 25 October 2008.

This law was challenged before the Constitutional Court and was suspended via application of article 161.2 of the constitution.[37] The CC – CCR 103/2008 of 11 September rejected the Basque law's claim that the "consultation"' was not a referendum, denying that the AC of the Basque Country had the power to call a referendum of this nature and to do so without the state's authorization, which is required, in any case, by the constitution (art. 149.1.32).

With the path to consultation blocked and unable to fulfill his commitments, the *lehendakari* dissolved the Basque Parliament and called new elections. In the elections of 2009, in the absence of radical nationalist candidates – outlawed for their links with the terrorist organization ETA – the PNV obtained thirty seats, a number to which must be added one each for its EA and EB-IU allies. This proved insufficient compared with the twenty-five seats of the PSE and the thirteen of the PP, a result that granted them an absolute majority, with the determination to end the nationalist strategy and eliminate ETA from a Basque government which was not in nationalist hands.

NOTES

1 Alberto López Basaguren, "The Legal System of a Bilingual Society," in Pello Salaburu and Xabier Alberdi, eds, *The Challenge of a Bilingual Society in the Basque Country* (Reno: Center for Basque Studies, University of Nevada, 2011), 33–50; Miren Azkarate Villar, "The Current Situation of the Basque Language: Speakers," in Salaburu and Alberdi, *The Challenge of a Bilingual Society in the Basque Country*, 113–35.

2 In Spanish society, in any case, the term "nation" is still a matter of profound disagreement as shown in a recent Constitutional Court ruling, CCR 31/2010, of 28 June (Legal Reasoning –LR–11), regarding the indirect reference to Catalonia as a nation in the reform of the SA (2006) (López Basaguren, "The Legal System of a Bilingual Society").

3 Nationalism conceives of the Basque nation as comprising Araba, Bizkaia, and Gipuzkoa; Navarra; and the French Basque Country. Sabino Arana, the father of Basque nationalism, referred to this whole with a ne-

ologism of his own invention: Euzkadi (subsequently transformed – not
without the resistance of Arana's followers – to *Euskadi*, in an attempt to
adapt it linguistically). He thus attempted to give a political dimension
to what had previously had only a linguistic-cultural dimension: *Euskal
Herria* – or *euskal herria*, to quote Pedro de Aguerre Axular, the most notable classical author in euskara, in the prologue to his work *Guero*
(After), (1643), that is, the people who speak euskara. The leap from linguistic-cultural to political alters reality and, territorially, Euskadi is more
than euskal herria. The circle is completed when radical nationalism demands the construction of *Euskal Herria* as a political reality (in an independentist sense) integrating all those territories, reducing the meaning
of *Euskadi* to that of the AC of the Basque Country, as a disqualification of
the possibilist politics – autonomist, largely limited to the Basque Country – of the PNV (Ludger Mees, "A Nation in Search of a Name: Cultural
Realities, Political Projects, and Terminological Struggles in the Basque
Country," in Salaburu and Alberdi, *The Challenge of a Bilingual Society in
the Basque Country*, 11–32).

4 The political representatives of Navarra did not make use of the possibility afforded them by the constitution to form a part of the AC of the
Basque Country: see Spanish Constitution (SC)'s 4th Interim Provision.

5 Felipe V, at the end of the Succession War (1701–13) – contrary to what
he did with the territories of the former Crown of Aragón (Aragón, Catalonia, Valencia, and the Balearic Isles) – confirmed the Fueros of the
Basque Provinces and Navarra, in recognition of their support for his
cause. Although in a process of continuous erosion, that arrangement
survived until the end of the Carlist Wars – new wars of succession,
which ended with the triumph of the liberals over the traditionalists – in
the nineteenth century.

6 The end of the first Carlist war saw the proclamation of the Law of 25
October 1839, which confirmed the Fueros of the Basque Provinces and
Navarra, "without prejudice to the constitutional unity of the Monarchy"
(sec. 1). The institutions of Navarra accepted this path and the Law of 16
August 1841 was passed, modifying the Fueros of Navarra. At the end of
the second war, the law of 21 July 1876 abolished the Fueros of the
Basque Provinces. This consolidated the divergence of the paths followed
by Navarra and the Basque Country, which has continued to the present
day.

7 The economic Convention for Navarra was established, initially, in the
Law of 16 August 1841. The Economic Agreement for the Basque
Provinces was created via the Royal Decree of 28 February 1878,
developing the Law of 21 July 1876. Alberto López Basaguren, "El

Concierto Económico y la financiación de la Comunidad Autónoma des País Vasco entre mito y realidad," in *El Estado autonómico: integración, solidaridad, diversidad. 25 años de Estatuto de autonomía des País Basco* (Madrid: Colez-INAP, 2005), 619–34. Sec. 41 of the SA of the Basque Country refers to it as the "traditional foral system of economic agreement or convention."

8 Between 1931 and 1933 two projects for a Statute for the Basque Country were presented. The Project for the Statute of Lizarra/Estella (1931), prior to the approval of the Constitution of 1931, was strongly "confederacy." The Legislative Assembly was composed of an equal number of representatives from each province, designated from among their members by each of the provincial legislative assemblies. The executive comprised an equal number of representatives from each province and the presidency was rotational, in accordance with territorial criteria. The second project, elaborated by the commissions that, provisionally, administered the Regional Councils, would be approved in referendum by the electorate in 1933. This draft Statute – now limited to the (three) Basque Provinces (without Navarra) – retained important elements of the "principle of confederacy." With regard to Parliament, this project provided for half the members to be elected by the entire population of the Basque Country; the other half, divided equally among the provinces, was elected by each province. A "principle of confederacy" was maintained in the composition of the executive and in the rotational character of the presidency.

9 The number of representatives for each HT was, provisionally, twenty in the first elections of 1980 (art. 2 of the general Council of the Basque Country Decree of 12 January 1980, which called elections to the Basque Parliament) and twenty-five for each HT following Law 28/1983 of 25 November of elections to the Basque Parliament, currently regulated by Law 5/1990, of 15 June.

10 According to the data of the Basque Institute of Statistics-EUSTAT, in 2011 the AC of the Basque Country had a population of 2,174,033, of which 318,730 corresponded to Araba (just under 15 percent), 1,152,406 to Bizkaia (approximately 53 percent) and 700,897 to Gipuzkoa (just over 32 percent). http://www.eustat.es/elementos/ele0004400/ti_Poblacion _por_ambitos_territoriales_1986-2011/tbl0004435_c.html#axzz2IeBmx DVU, accessed 22 January 2013.

11 In 2012 Navarra had a population of less than 650,000 inhabitants, that is, substantially fewer than Gipuzkoa, although its territory (10.391 km²) is considerably larger than the Basque Provinces (7.234 km²).

12 Law 27/1983 of 25 November, on relations between the Common Institutions of the Autonomous Communities and the Provincial Authorities

of their Historic Territories (Gobierno Vasco, *Boletín Oficial del País Vasco*, no. 182, 10 December 1983, http://www.lehendakaritza.ejgv.euskadi.net /r48-bopv2/es/bopv2/datos/1983/12/8302316a.shtml.

13 The court that, according to the provisions of sec. 152.1, paragraph 2, SC, "will complete the judicial organization in the sphere of the Autonomous Community."

14 As well as the senators directly elected by the citizens – four per province, by universal and direct suffrage (sec. 69.2 CE) – each AC will designate one senator plus one more per million inhabitants, whose designation will correspond to the Legislative Assembly of the AC.

15 There is an interesting change of interpretation in CCR 199/1987, of 16 December, in the same issue of anti-terrorist legislation.

16 The electoral option of radical nationalism has varied during these years owing to changing circumstances. Between 1980 and 1994 it stood for election as HB (Herri Batasuna); in the elections of 1998 and 2001, it assumed the title EH (Euskal Herritarrok). In the elections of 2005 it could not participate under this name, having been outlawed due to its links with the terrorist group ETA; it requested the vote for a party that had been "asleep" until then, the PCTV-EHAK (Communist Party of the Basque Lands). In the elections of 2009 it could not stand because it was still outlawed; it promoted groups of candidates, but these were also declared illegal; finally, it recommended abstention. In the elections of 2012, the now legalized party (Sortu) participated, in coalition with EA and other minor groups, under the name of EH Bildu (Euskal Herria Bildu).

17 The 3rd Ardanza Government lasted only eight months, from February to October 1991. It was a tripartite government (PNV, EA, and EE–Euskadiko Ezkerra); it enjoyed a solid parliamentary majority, but was unstable due to the tension between the PNV and EA, the party born from the split within the former.

18 The PSE's access to government was due to the absence of the radical nationalist option, as a result of its being illegal, and the resulting distribution of seats. But, even in these circumstances, the electoral results would probably not have permitted a government majority alternative to a nationalist one nor, above all, would the socialists have embarked on this adventure, had it not been for the consequences of the *plan Ibarretxe*. An important part of the electorate had grown tired of this strategy that had lasted five years and reached a dead end. The party leadership did not support this strategy, especially in its final phase , but felt incapable of correcting Ibarretxe or replacing him. This led the then-president of the party – Josu Jon Imaz, formerly a member of Ibarretxe's government – to resign from his position.

19 An exception to this rule occurred in the elections of 2001, in which there was an extraordinary mobilization of the electorate provoked by the challenge of the PP and the PSE joining forces to seek to accede to power. The results of the general elections immediately prior (2000) had brought a minimal victory for the PNV, but closely followed by the PP and the PSOE; the combination of these two forces could provide them with a solid majority. A nationalist coalition (PNV-EA) won the elections with thirty-three seats, against the thirty-two resulting from the combination of PP (nineteen) and PSE (thirteen). The three seats of EB-IU were added to the nationalists in a coalition government (Ibarretxe II). HB-EH obtained seven seats.

20 The electoral variations experienced by radical nationalism respond, fundamentally, to the continued activity of ETA. This effect was evident, first, in the 1998 elections, in which it obtained its best results to date as a consequence of the peace declaration which followed the signing of the pact of Lizarra/Estella between the nationalist parties (radical and moderate) and EB-IU; on the other hand, in the elections of 2001, it obtained its worst results following the end of the ceasefire in 1998; in the 2005 elections the nationalists enjoyed a significant electoral recovery, although failing to recover their usual level, after ETA decided to end its campaign of assassinating non-nationalist town councillors and begin negotiations with Zapatero's government. Finally, after being outlawed and therefore absent in the elections of 2009, in those of 2012, when ETA ceased its terrorist activity, nationalism achieved the best results in its history, far superior to those of 1998, obtaining twenty-one seats and becoming the second political force in number of votes with 25 percent.

21 Alberto López Basaguren, "The Legal System of a Bilingual Society," 33–50.

22 The Law 10/1982, 24 of November is the basis of the normalization of the use of *Euskera* (Government of the Basque Country, *Boletín Oficial del País Vasco*, no. 160, 16 December 1982).

23 Miren Azkarate, "The Current Situation of the Basque Language: Speakers," in Salaburu and Alberdi, *The Challenge of a Bilingual Society in the Basque Country*, 113–35; Government of the Basque Country, *Fourth Sociolinguistic Survey. Basque Autonomous Community, Navarra and Iparralde,* 2006, 2008, http://www.euskara.euskadi.net/r59-738/es/contenidos /informacion/argitalpenak/es_6092/adjuntos/IV_incuesta_es.pdf, accessed 29 December 2015; Government of the Basque Country, *Fifth Sociolinguistic Survey. Basque Autonomous Community, Navarra and Iparralde,* 2011, 2012, http://www.euskara.euskadi.net/r59-738/en/contenidos /informacion/sociolinguistic_research2011/en_2011/adjuntos/Euskal

%20Herria%20inkesta%20soziolinguistikoa%202011_ingelesez.pdf, accessed 29 December 2015.

24 Finally, in the 2012 elections to the Basque Parliament – and in the general elections of 2011 – EA joined the coalition EH Bildu, referred to as "Amaiur" in the general elections of 2011, although a significant number of its former members supported the PNV.

·25 Government of the Basque Country, *Boletín Oficial del Parlamento Vasco*, 4th Parliamentary Term, no. 94, 9 July 1993, pp 6072 and following.

26 Government of the Basque Country, *Boletín Oficial del Parlamento Vasco*, 4th Parliamentary Term, no. 122, 4 March 1994, pp 8330 and following.

27 Points 1, 2, 5, and 6 were passed with thirty-three votes for and fifteen abstentions. Points 3 and 4 were passed with twenty-one votes for, twenty against, and seven abstentions. What is significant is not the content of the points that achieved a narrow majority, but the very fact that, without consensus, the nationalist parties could attain only a very precarious majority.

28 Government of the Basque Country, *Boletín Oficial del Parlamento Vasco*, 4th Parliamentary Term, no. 40, 17 October 1995, pp 1860 and following.

29 Government of the Basque Country, *Boletín Oficial del Parlamento Vasco*, 7th Parliamentary Term, no. 18, 9 November 2001.

30 Government of the Basque Country, *Boletín Oficial del Parlamento Vasco*, 7th Parliamentary Term, no. 55, 19 July 2002.

31 Government of the Basque Country. *Diario de Sesiones*. 7th Parliamentary Term, no. 41, session of 27 September 2002. Parliamentary documents may be accessed on the Basque Parliament website, http://parlamento.euskadi.net/.

32 Government of the Basque Country, *Boletín Oficial del Parlamento Vasco*, 7th Parliamentary Term, no. 115, 7 November 2003.

33 The Lower House, in a plenary session held on 1 February 2005, rejected the proposal for a new Political Statute for the Basque Country by 344 to twenty-nine and two abstentions: see the debate in Government of the Basque Country, Congreso de los Diputados, *Diario de Sesiones. Pleno y Diputación Permanente, year 2004*, 8th Parliamentary Term, no. 65, 1 February 2005, pp 3088 and following.

34 The PNV-EA coalition obtained twenty-nine seats and its government ally EB-IU three seats. The PSE obtained eighteen seats, gaining five; the PP fifteen, losing four; and radical nationalism, which supported the *sleeping* party EHAK-PCTV, nine, gaining two. Thus, there were thirty-two seats for the government, thirty-three seats between the PSE and the PP, 1 seat for Aralar – HB splinter group in disagreement with ETA's terrorism – and nine seats for EHAK.

35 Basque Law 9/2008, of 27 June, calling for and regulating a popular consultation with the object of gathering the opinion of the citizenship of the Autonomous Community of the Basque Country regarding the opening of a negotiation process to achieve peace and political normalization: see Government of the Basque Country, *Boletín Oficial del País Vasco*, no. 134, 15 July 2008.

36 The questions are as follows: "a) Do you agree to support a process of dialogue ending the violence if prior to that ETA shows an unequivocal desire to put an end to violence once and for all?; b) Do you agree that the Basque parties, without exclusions, initiate a process of negotiation to reach a Democratic Agreement about exercising the Basque people's right to decide, and that said agreement be submitted to referendum before the year 2010 ends?"

37 Against the Basque Law of Consultation were presented the Appeal of Unconstitutionality no. 5707–2008, filed by the president of the Spanish Government, who invoked article 161.2 of the constitution, as a result of which the law was suspended, and the Appeal of Unconstitutionality 5748–2008, filed by over fifty MPs from the Popular Party in parliament: Government of the Basque Country, *Boletín Oficial del Estado*, no. 173, 18 July 2008. On the problems, both procedural and of content, posed by the law, see Consejo de Estado, Dictamen no. 1.119/2008, of 3 July 2008, with regard to the president of the government's intention to file an appeal of unconstitutionality against the Basque law of consultation, as well as Alberto López Basaguren, "Sobre referéndum y Comunidades Autónomas. La ley vasca de la 'consulta' ante el Tribunal Constitucional (Consideraciones con motivo de la STC 103/2008)," *Revista General de Derecho Constitucional (Iustel)*, no. 13 (2011): 1–25.

3

The Parliament of Galicia

JOSÉ JULIO FERNÁNDEZ RODRÍGUEZ

The elements of the Galician identity were established gradually, over the centuries, and gave rise in particular to a distinct language and distinct socio-cultural traits. During the nineteenth and twentieth centuries, a series of literary, political, and cultural movements forged the Galician identity. Political aspirations led to the creation of Galicianist (*galleguistas*[1]) parties or political associations. Thanks to the influence of Galician emigrants, in particular to America, the effects were felt outside the Galician territory. These movements had even more impact when the integrated Spanish state was established by the Constitution of 1931 following the proclamation of the Second Spanish Republic. In 1936, the Statute of Autonomy was approved by referendum, giving specific autonomy to the Region of Galicia, as it was then known. However, the start of the Spanish Civil War in July of the same year prevented the statute from coming into force.

Galician political aspirations re-emerged after the death of General Franco in 1975 and the start of Spain's transition to democracy, and continued until the establishment of pre-autonomy following the democratic elections of 1977. The Royal Decree of 7/1978 established the pre-autonomous community of Galicia (whose presidents were to be Antonio Roson and José Quiroga Suárez). This brings us to the Spanish Constitution currently in force. I do not claim that there is much institutional originality about the Galician Parliament, although some aspects will be highlighted. But clearly, after the death of Franco, a new era of political freedom was inaugurated and all parliaments played a role in this. Even when the role was more modest, as in Galicia, it remains nevertheless relevant.

Although the Spanish Constitution of 1978 decentralized power, one of the fundamental decisions was to link the principles of unity and

territorial autonomy under section 2,[2] which allows them to be interpreted jointly. The principle of autonomy for specified territories led to
the possibility of establishing autonomous communities, which are territorial entities endowed with political autonomy, in the sense that they
have full legislative power and can, as a result, establish their own legal
system. The possibility offered by the constitution was made generally
available, and the whole of Spain is now made up of seventeen autonomous communities, plus the autonomous cities of Ceuta and
Melilla. As a result of concerns raised during the debate on the Spanish Constitution, the constitutional framework is open-ended, but also
imprecise. The main mechanism is based on a key idea: only territories
that wished to do so were to become autonomous communities, although in practice the autonomy model became generalized, as noted
above. In addition, each community could define its own competences
in its Statute of Autonomy, within the limits prescribed by section 148
and/or 149 of the constitution. The Statute of Autonomy is therefore
the basic institutional standard for each autonomous community.

In this way, Galicia became one of Spain's autonomous communities, just like Catalonia and the Basque Country, as seen in previous
chapters of this book. It was considered one of the historic communities and one of the nationalities mentioned in section 2 of the constitution, although this decision was perhaps more political than legal. As
a result, Galicia was able to use the constitution's second transitional
provision to achieve autonomy more quickly,[3] and Galicia's Statute of
Autonomy was drafted using the special – or fast-track – procedure set
out in section 151 of the constitution. This also allowed Galicia to take
on a greater number of competences. After a number of problems had
been overcome,[4] the statute was passed in the form of Organic Law
1/1981, dated 6 April, following a successful referendum in Galicia on
28 December 1980 and despite an extremely high abstention rate of
71.74 percent.[5]

The statute sets out the powers of the autonomous community, using
the framework established by the constitution, allowing Galicia to take
on a number of competences or, in other words, determining the functions that Galicia could exercise in specific areas. A legal system,
genuinely specific to Galicia, was then established on the basis of
the statute.

Section 152.1 of the Spanish Constitution specifies that, in autonomous communities whose status derives from the procedure in
section 151 – such as Galicia – there will be "a legislative assembly elected by universal suffrage, using a system of proportional representation

that ensures, in particular, representation of the various zones in the territory." In compliance with this provision, Chapter I of Title I of Galicia's Statute of Autonomy created the Parliament of Galicia. A further development of the legislation led to the determination of the rules and procedures of the Parliament of Galicia, first issued in September 1983 and revised in 1993, 1994, and 2012. In addition, a series of interpretative agreements and complementary standards derive from the rules and procedures.

The Parliament of Galicia has the traditional configuration of a liberal legislative assembly, based on the example of the Chamber of Deputies of the Spanish State – the legislative, or lower, assembly which forms, with the Senate, the Spanish Parliament or Cortes Generales. The electoral system of the Autonomous Community of Galicia is also based on the Spanish example.

The Parliament of Galicia began its operations on 19 December 1981, the date on which the first legislature opened. Its first seat was the Gelmírez Palace, followed by the Fonseca Palace, and since 1989, the Pazo do Horreo, all three located in Santiago de Compostela. The ninth legislature is currently under way, and the results are clearly positive: Galician society has attained a high level of well being and quality of life, and its legislative assembly has made a major contribution to this result.

THE GALICIAN PARLIAMENT AND POLITICAL SYSTEM

The Galician political system is centred on the Parliament, a source of primary legitimacy since it is elected by universal suffrage. The unicameral Parliament makes democratic principles a reality and represents all the citizens of the Autonomous Community of Galicia, making political autonomy possible. The two symbols of our political system are the Parliament and the president of the Xunta (the head of the Galician executive), elected by Parliament. Parliament and territorial autonomy have long been, and are still, two interdependent concepts, each reliant on the other. The role of the Statute of Autonomy is to guarantee the inviolability of Parliament in the institutional organization of the Autonomous Community of Galicia (section 10.2 of the Statute of Autonomy).

Parliament has evolved in parallel with the development of an autonomous government in Galicia and the consolidation of the competences assigned to the Autonomous Community. Although the Statute of Autonomy defines the structure of power in Galicia, it is made effective by the work of the assembly. The tangible results of Galicia's autonomous system depend on the work of the assembly; we can even state that the existence of Parliament and its everyday activities have strengthened its representative function, and in fact democracy in Galicia, giving it the symbolic aspect referred to previously.[6] The consolidation of the assembly also signals its key importance in Galician public opinion, since it constitutes a political reference that interacts continuously with society and has, to a large degree, helped forge the modern collective identity of the Galician people.

There is a close relationship between Parliament and the executive, thanks to the parliamentary basis of the political system. Parliament oversees the exercise of power by the autonomous Galician government, and for this reason a series of procedures has been created, such as the investiture of the president of the Xunta, the no-confidence motion, and the vote of confidence. The president and his or her government are politically responsible before Parliament; on the other hand, the president can dissolve Parliament and call an election. Parliament determines and directs the political actions of the Galician executive, in particular through general debates (such as the yearly debate on the state of the autonomous community), inquiries, questions, and examinations of members of the government.

There are few links with the judicial power, since in Spain this remains a jurisdictional function of the central state rather than of the autonomous communities.

Composition

There are currently seventy-five deputies, elected in four electoral divisions (A Coruña, Lugo, Ourense, and Pontevedra) matching the four provinces making up the Autonomous Community of Galicia. The Statute of Autonomy allows for a number of deputies between sixty and eighty (section 11.5 of the Statute of Autonomy), while Statute 8/1985, on elections to the Parliament of Galicia, sets the actual number at seventy-five (section 9.1).

The last elections to the Galician Parliament on 21 October 2012 resulted in four parliamentary groups: the people's group, comprising forty-one deputies from the Partido Popular de Galicia (PP); the socialist group, comprising eighteen deputies from the Partido dos Socialistas de Galicia-Partido Socialista Obrero Español (PSdeG-PSOE); the AGE group, comprising nine deputies from the Alternativa Galega de Esquerda (AGE, made up of Esquerda Unida and Anova-Irmandade Na-

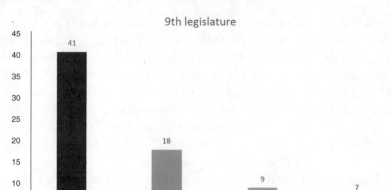

Figure 3.1   Composition of Galician Parliament following 21 October 2012 election

cionalista); and the BNG group, comprising seven deputies from the Bloque Nacionalista Galego (BNG). This composition can be represented graphically as shown in Figure 3.1. With respect to the educational level of the elected representatives, almost all are higher education graduates. Only nine deputies do not have a post-secondary qualification, while of the sixty-six who do, eight hold doctorates.

In terms of the deputies' socio-professional profiles, the most striking feature is their diversity. Law graduates form the largest group (twelve), followed by economists (ten), physicians (six), engineers (six), and historians (five). There are also three political scientists, three philologists, two veterinarians, two education specialists, one biologist, one pharmacist, one architect, one nurse, one computer scientist, one philosopher, one business leader, one kinesitherapist, and employees from various sectors of activity. There are also several teachers (at the elementary, secondary, and university level) and civil servants.

The PP, a centre-right party present throughout Spain, has been the dominant party throughout the history of the Parliament of Galicia, since it has achieved six absolute majorities (in legislatures III, IV, V, VI, VIII, and IX) and three relative majorities (in legislatures I, II, and VII). It has always been the most widely represented party in the Galician Parliament. The second political force is the PSdeG-PSOE, also a party present throughout Spain (and always the second largest party, except for legislatures V and VI, when it obtained the same number of seats as the BNG).

However, this is by no means a two-party system, since other parties have also been represented during the various legislatures, such as the BNG, a left-wing nationalist party that is not present elsewhere in Spain. During five legislatures, all the parliamentary seats were held by the PP, PSdeG-PSOE, and BNG. It would be more appropriate to describe the system as made up of several Galician parties of a pluralist, moderate nature, in which the PP is the dominant party, although its domination does not exclude an alternation of power and a genuine opposition.

This hegemony over the Galician Parliament has allowed the PP (or its predecessor, Alianza Popular) to form the Galician government (Xunta de Galicia) during seven full legislatures (legislatures I, III, IV, V, VI, VIII, and IX). A PSdeG-PSOE/BNG coalition was in power for one legislature (legislature VII), while the government during legislature II was in the hands of the Coalición Popular de Galicia, headed by Alianza Popular, the predecessor of the PP, until a vote of no-confidence proposed by the PSdeG-PSOE and seconded by the Coalición Galega, the Partido Nacionalista Galego (comprising dissident deputies from the Coalición Galega), and a group of dissidents from the Alianza Popular led to the removal from office of the *popular* president Fernández Albor and the appointment of socialist González Laxe. The presidents of the Xunta have been, successively, Gerardo Fernández Albor (PP, 1982–87), Fernando González Laxe (PSdeG-PSOE, 1987–1990), Manuel Fraga Iribarne (PP, 1990–2005), Emilio Pérez Touriño (PSdeG-PSOE, 2005–09), and Alberto Núñez Feijoo (PP, 2009–), who recently began his second successive term of office.

Elections to the autonomous Galician Parliament had, for the first three legislatures, an abstention rate above the rest of Spain (just below 60 percent), but beginning with the fourth legislature (1993), the difference began to disappear. In addition, there is little difference between voting patterns in regional and national elections, in contrast to other Spanish communities.[7]

Deputies are elected on the basis of universal, equal, and direct suffrage by free, secret ballot (section 11.1 of the Statute of Autonomy) to a four-year term. The elections use a system of proportional representation "to ensure, in addition, representation of all zones in the Galician territory" (section 11.2 of the Statute of Autonomy). The Hondt system is used, with each province forming, for the purpose of the elections, an electoral division (section 11.4 of the Statute of Autonomy). The detailed procedure for elections is established in the previously mentioned Statute 8/1985 concerning elections to the Parliament of

Galicia. Each of the four Galician provinces is guaranteed a minimum of ten deputies; the remaining thirty-five are distributed between the provinces in proportion to their population. The election writ specifies the number of deputies to be elected in each electoral division (since 1997, the breakdown has been as follows: A Coruña, twenty-four; Lugo, fifteen; Ourense, fourteen; Pontevedra, twenty-two).[8] The ballot is based on closed, blocked electoral lists. In addition, candidates who fail to obtain at least 5 percent of the votes in their division are excluded from the distribution of seats. Prior to 1993, this limit was 3 percent, until Statute 15/1992, amending Statute 8/1985 concerning elections to the Parliament of Galicia, raised it to 5 percent.

The legal status of the members of the Galician Parliament is based on that of the members of a legislative assembly. They enjoy privileges of inviolability, immunity, and jurisdiction. In addition, parliamentarians are subject to a series of ineligibility and incompatibility clauses, to ensure that they represent their electors properly, without undue interference. They must also comply with a set of rules, while performing multiple duties.

Functions[9]

Parliamentary functions are directly linked to the fact that deputies are the political representatives of Galician citizens. For this reason, their functions mainly involve the following:

- passing laws that develop the competences assumed by or transferred to Galicia (legislation);
- approving, by statute, the budgetary estimates of income and expenditure submitted by the Xunta of Galicia;
- supervising and scrutinizing the activities of the Xunta;
- electing the president of the Xunta of Galicia from among the members of the Parliament;
- requiring political responsibility from the Xunta of Galicia and its president;
- appointing the senators of the Autonomous Community;
- appointing the Valedor do Pobo (Ombudsman of Galicia);
- appointing the members of the Consello de Contas (audit office);
- asking the Spanish government to pass bills, and submitting legislative proposals to the Office of the Chamber of Deputies;
- formally submitting "unconstitutionality proceedings" and appearing before the Constitutional Court in relevant cases.

For the supervisory function mentioned above, a series of tools, such as inquiries, motions, and questions, is available. One key way of ensuring that the executive acts responsibly is the no-confidence motion, related to although the opposite of the vote of confidence, when the president of the Xunta submits his or her administration to the judgment of the assembly.

To pursue its activities in an optimal way, the Parliament of Galicia, like any other legislative assembly, is based on a structure that defines a series of administrative entities. The administration is made up of the Speaker of the Parliament, the Office, and the Council of Party Spokespersons. Parliament elects its Speaker at the opening session of each legislature. The role of the Speaker is to represent Parliament, direct and coordinate the actions of the Office, preside at debates and maintain order, and apply, enforce, and interpret, in cases of doubt, the standing orders.

The Office of the Parliament has five members, and is the main administrative entity. It reviews written documents emanating from Parliament and accepts or rejects them, interprets and supplements the standing orders while the assembly is not sitting (this role is performed by the speaker during debates), and sets the schedule for plenary sessions and committee meetings during each session period, after hearing the Council of Party Spokespersons.

The third entity of governance is the Council of Party Spokespersons which, as its name indicates, is made up of spokespersons from each parliamentary group and the Speaker, along with a vice-chair, secretary or vice-secretary, and an official legal counsel. The Council of Party Spokespersons has an essentially consultative role.

It is also important to note the specific role played by the parliamentary groups formed by the deputies on the basis of their political allegiance. These groups launch initiatives and are a key element in the composition of administrative entities and the organization of debates. To form a group requires a minimum of five deputies; a given deputy can belong to only one group, but is required to belong to a group.

The deliberative entities are the plenary assembly, the committees, and the permanent deputation. The plenary assembly is a formal meeting of all deputies, convened by the Speaker on his or her own initiative or at the request of two parliamentary groups or one-fifth of all members – in other words, fifteen members. A committee is a smaller group of deputies who meet to deal with a limited range of subjects which require specific expertise. There are eight legislative standing committees and six non-legislative standing committees. A committee may also be established for a special purpose, or to inquire into a specific matter.

Last, the permanent deputation comprises a minimum of eleven members representing all the parliamentary groups in proportion to their size. It acts when the parliamentary term has expired, when the legislative assembly has been dissolved, or when it cannot be convened during vacations.

Legislative procedure has three steps: initiation, constitution, and integration. Legislation can be initiated by the Xunta of Galicia, in the form of legislative bills; by Parliament, through a parliamentary group, in the form of a text signed by a spokesperson or a single member, if supported by the signatures of four other deputies; or by the electoral body, in the form of a popular legislative initiative.[10] Initiatives that do not come from the Xunta are legislative proposals, but most are bills tabled by the Xunta. The second step is constitution: publication of the initiative, taking under consideration – but only if it is a bill, and not just a proposal – the presentation of suggested amendments to the committee, the report on the presentation to the committee, the committee debate, the drafting of the committee's opinion, the tabling of the committee's opinion during a plenary session for debate purposes, and the vote. The third step is integration, when the text is promulgated and then published. Promulgation is performed by the president of the Xunta, on behalf of the king of Spain. In parallel with this normal legislative process, several special legislative procedures are also available.

The situation in Galicia resembles that in other jurisdictions: government initiatives, in the form of legislative bills, greatly outnumber parliamentary initiatives. The parliamentary groups have little influence, through their legislative proposals, over the legislation passed by the assembly. Over the first eight legislatures, out of a total of 346 laws passed, only 27, or 7.8 percent, were parliamentary initiatives. At certain times, the parliamentary groups have tabled numerous initiatives, even if only a few eventually became law. These initiatives can be summarized as shown in Table 3.1.

The main working and decision-making mode is debate. During debates, the spokespersons of the parliamentary groups first speak in support of the initiative, then against. Then spokespersons who are neither for nor against are given about fifteen minutes each to speak. The spokespersons have a right of a five-minute reply or rectification, and an extraordinary right to rebut allusions, for a maximum of three min-

Table 3.1
Parliamentary initiatives

| | Legislature | | | | | | |
	I	II	III	IV	V	VI	VII	VIII
Tabled	17	51	38	29	30	17	15	28
Passed	4	7	4	4	0	1	3	4

utes. There are three voting procedures: the vote by acquiescence; the ordinary vote, performed electronically or by show of hands; and the nominal vote.

Although the Parliament of Galicia is not involved in amendments to the Spanish Constitution, it plays a decisive role in the procedure for the reform of the Statute of Autonomy of Galicia. Last, the Galician Parliament maintains close interparliamentary relations, in particular through organizations such as the Conference of European Regional Legislative Assemblies (CALRE), the Conference of Speakers of Autonomous Spanish Parliaments (COPREPA), the Inter-Parliamentary Union, and the Spanish Association of Legal Advisors to Autonomous Parliaments (AELPA). In 2011, the Speaker of the Galician assembly chaired the COPREPA, in addition to the CALRE taskforce on regional institutional models–regional democracy in 2012.

SPECIFIC ASPECTS OF THE GALICIAN PARLIAMENT

The Galician Parliament formally constructed the autonomous community using the possibilities put in place by the Spanish Constitution of 1978 and given concrete expression by the Statute of Autonomy of Galicia of 1981. It achieved this mainly through its legislative work to establish the institutions and entities of the autonomous regime and define a framework for the implementation of its competences. However, in terms of substance, the Galician identity was also forged in other areas, such as culture and literature, and even politics, outside Parliament, although Parliament has always played a preponderant role in the process. In other words, the Galician Parliament has been one of the key players in the material implementation of the Galician identity, but not the only player. However this may be, the assembly has always played a leading role simply because it lies at the heart of the political system. Parliament makes Galicia's political autonomy possible, while ensuring that the democratic principle can be applied in reality – explaining the socio-political importance of everything that happens there and public interest in all its actions and deeds.

Contributions to the Consolidation of Autonomy

The political autonomy that the Spanish Constitution and the Galician Statute of Autonomy confer on Galicia has enabled the adoption of a set of norms to facilitate the exercise of its autonomy. Parliament has played an essential role in this task, in particular by using its legislative powers, which can be considered the key to the consolidation of autonomy. Parliament has, since its foundation, displayed a remarkable legislative vitality, which explains why the chamber of deputies achieved such a high level of institutional performance as it built the legal system,[11] giving full meaning to Galicia's political autonomy.

The scope of the legal corpus built up by the Galician autonomous community results from the need to regulate broad sectors of activity that, in many cases, are complex. The laws central to this process date back to the early years of the autonomous community.

For example, a first group of laws aimed to develop specific mandates under the Statute of Autonomy and institutions specific to Galicia (some established by the statute, others not). This legal corpus was mainly built up in the 1980s, starting with the six "basic development" laws under the Statute of Autonomy, which required an absolute majority vote: Statute 1/1983, regulating the Xunta and its president, amended by Statute 11/1988; Statute 3/1983, on linguistic normalization; Statute 6/1984, on the Valedor do Pobo (the Ombudsman of Galicia), amended by Statutes 3/1994, 1/2002, and 10/2012; Statute 6/1985, on the Consello de Contas (audit office), amended by Statute 4/1986; Statute 8/1985, on elections to the Parliament of Galicia, amended by statutes 15/1992 and 12/2004; and, last, Statute 1/1988, on popular legislative initiatives tabled before the Parliament of Galicia.

Other institutional laws include Statute 1/1982, determining the seats of institutions; Statute 4/1983, on recognition for Galicianism; Statute 5/1984, on the symbols of Galicia; Statute 9/1984, creating the radio and television corporation of Galicia; Statute 5/1988, on the use of Galician as the official language of Galicia by local communities; Statute 6/1995, establishing the Galician economic and social council; Statute 9/1995, on the Consultative Council of Galicia; Statute 2/2006, on civil law in Galicia; and Statute 1/2011, regulating the Galician Competition Council.

These laws contain key statutory provisions, such as those relating to the recognition of expatriate Galicians; the joint official status of the Galician and Spanish languages; the anthem, coat of arms, and flag of Galicia; the location of the most important entities in the autonomous community (Parliament, Xunta of Galicia, president of the Xunta, community departments, Superior Court of Justice); the electoral system and the related entities.

A second group of laws deals with financial matters, including, each year, the general budgetary statutes of the Autonomous Community of Galicia. These statutes highlight the community's growth, with large budget increases in the first years as competences were transferred to Galicia, especially in the education and health sectors. These levelled off in 1993. Also included in this group are other statutes on fiscal measures (Statute 15/2010), finance (Statute 14/2004), tax (Statute 6/2003), and savings banks (Statute 1/2004), which have been substantially amended in response to the current economic crisis.

The third group of laws that deserve attention are those that refer to the actual competences held by Galicia.[12] These more numerous statutes concern administrative organization (such as Statute 16/2010, on the organization and functioning of the general administration and autonomous public sector in Galicia); agriculture, fishing, hunting, and the environment (Statute 9/2001, the conservation of nature or Statute 11/2008, on fishing); tourism (Statute 7/2011); education (Statute 4/2011, on the coexistence and participation of the education community or Statute 11/1989, on the planning of Galicia's university system – a statute which is scheduled for replacement); health care (Statute 7/2003, on the planning of the health care system); police (Statute 8/2007, on police organization); urban planning and public works (Statute 8/2012, on housing, or Statute 9/2002, on urban planning and protection of the rural environment), etc.

This last group of normative statutes has played a necessary and indispensable role in determining the content, scope, and dimensions of Galician autonomy. The functions that may be exercised in Galicia belong to a series of specific domains, most of which are governed by this group of laws.

Similarly, this group can be extended to include the work performed by Parliament to defend competences through proceedings before the Constitutional Court, whose decisions have necessarily been taken into consideration to delimit, with precision, the competences of the Galician community.[13] Parliament, via its legal department, has intervened in a number of "unconstitutionality proceedings" (abstract application of laws) and "unconstitutionality questions" (concrete application of laws). Unconstitutionality proceedings have led to rulings such as Decision 48/1988, on the 1985 Galician statute on savings banks; Decision 47/2002, on the Galician fisheries statute; and Decision 47/2004, on the statute determining appeals for annulment in the field of civil law. In all three cases, certain principles were struck down. Unconstitutionality questions, in turn, have led to Decision 87/2012, on the 2002 Galician statute on urban planning and protection for the rural environment; Decision 152/2011, on the 1988 Galician statute on the civil service; and Decision 79/2011, on the pharmacy statute. These rulings have, in practical terms, adapted the extent and scope of the competences exercised by the Autonomous Community of Galicia.

Contributions to Identity and the Political Community

Parliament, the nerve centre of the Galician political system, has made an important contribution to consolidating identity profiles in Galicia but, as mentioned above, has not been alone in this process. Although the Spanish Constitution refers to the existence of nationalities, it does not specify which. The constitution has been interpreted in a way that includes Galicia, not only under the constitution's second transitional provision, which mentions the regions that had obtained a positive referendum result on their Statute of Autonomy in the past (under the Second Spanish Republic), but also on the basis of its historic and cultural features, which add up to a "differential fact." This question is part of a broader debate, encompassing a wide range of doctrinal positions that bring into question the state model for Spain's autonomous communities and could justify the existence of asymmetry between the communities. Although there is no doubt that the constitution itself is based on differences between Spain's regions, which explains why it provides for two ways to accede to autonomy (therefore establishing differences in the communities' legal and political processes), it is also true that over the years attempts have been made to equalize and homogenize the regions (on the basis of pacts in 1981 and 1992 between the two majority parties of the time in Spain – respectively the UCD and PSOE and the PSOE and PP). However this may be, it is clear that certain autonomous communities, like Galicia, have an identity-defining bonus in the shape of a language other than Spanish.[14]

The Galician Parliament has examined all these questions using its ordinary tools – legislative debates, committee meetings, debates on the state of the autonomous community, examinations, questions, inquiries, motions, etc. – and the repercussions on the public have been considerable, even to the point of influencing and forming public opinion. In general, also, as part of the government/opposition dialectic, both sides have resolutely defended the Galician identity, although not on the basis of the same principles and with different conclusions. Something similar occurred concerning the relationship with the Spanish state, although the differences could be considerable depending on whether the governing party was the same in Spain and in Galicia.[15]

The majority governments generally obtained by the PP were based on a moderate form of Galicianism, known as "constitutional Galicianism" because of its attachment to the 1978 Spanish Constitution. This moderate Galicianism was reflected in the actions of both the government and Parliament while the PP was in power, and the official discourse was characterized by loyalty to the Spanish constitutional project and solidarity with the other Spanish regions. In this connection, it is important to note the period under the Xunta president Manuel Fraga Iribarne (PP, 1990–2005), who imposed the moderate Galicianist model through his clear leadership within the centre-right. The PSdeG-PSOE also contributed to the moderate approach by defending the same constitutional and statutory framework, although the lack of stable party leadership did not allow it to enjoy a continuous period in power. In addition, the fact that the central state was always governed by the PSOE or the PP promoted and strengthened this moderate political approach. Both parties, then, had Spanish connections but in no way gave up on defending Galicia's interests and identity.[16]

Other political parties with a nationalist agenda and no ties to Spain were less present in Parliament, although they did influence its activities to a certain extent, and were in general part of the opposition. Although these nationalist Galician parties always held some seats, their presence was not as significant as in other Spanish regions, such as Catalonia and the Basque Country. As mentioned above, this situation can be explained by the fact that the PP maintained a Galicianist policy and that the clearly nationalist sector in Galicia had difficulties coordinating because of the presence of a range of movements and parties. Centre-right nationalism was represented (for example, the Coalición Galega) during the first few legislatures, until the arrival of Manuel Fraga Iribarne, who incorporated it into the PP. Left-wing nationalism was found mainly within the BNG, the most important party within the movement from a diachronic point of view. Its discourse became increasingly moderate, until it won 25 percent of the vote in 1997 (fifth legislature), making it the second largest party, although it continued to express its disagreement with the country's constitutional and statutory framework. In contrast, the new left-wing nationalist coalition AGE obtained more seats in the current ninth legislature of the Galician Parliament than the BNG, with nine seats compared to seven. In addition, the seventh legislature was led by a coalition between the PSdeG-PSOE and the BNG.

We review below a series of issues from parliamentary debates that can be considered to have forged the Galician identity and singularity.

THE STATUS OF THE CAPITAL

The debate was intended to determine where Galicia's political capital would be located. A large majority of deputies voted for Santiago de Compostela rather than A Coruña (sixty to eight), leading to the abovementioned Statute 1/1982, establishing the seat of the community's institutions. This was, in fact, the first statute discussed by parliamentarians. More recently, Statute 4/2002, on the status of the city of Santiago de Compostela as the capital, was passed unanimously by the deputies of the Galician Parliament.

LINGUISTIC NORMALIZATION

The assembly has promoted the Galician language as an essential cultural vehicle that had often been neglected. The related legislation was passed unanimously in 1983 thanks to the open-minded and flexible attitude displayed by all parliamentary groups. In addition, Parliament passed numerous measures to ensure equality between the Galician and Spanish languages.

ELECTORAL PROCEDURE

The regulation of elections for seats in Parliament is another topic that has been frequently debated. Although a key agreement was reached in 1985, the reform of 1992 was vehemently rejected by the opposition of the time. In 1992, the threshold for eligibility for the distribution of seats was raised from 3 percent to 5 percent, and stricter rules on incompatibility were introduced.

UNIVERSITY AGREEMENT

After a first unsuccessful attempt, the universities of A Coruña and Vigo were created by statute in 1989, joining the existing university in Santiago de Compostela.

DEVELOPMENT OF CERTAIN ASSUMED COMPETENCES

The key competences, from a quantitative point of view, are education and health. Parliamentary debates have also called for new competences and the transfer, by the Spanish state, of previously assumed competences.[17]

SELF-AWARENESS IN THE AUTONOMOUS COMMUNITY, OR
GOING BEYOND PROVINCIAL LIMITS

Parliament regulated local administration in Galicia based on its particularities (1989, 1997), leading to a socio-political result that combined local administration with the dimension of autonomy beyond provincial boundaries.

THE CREATION AND PROTECTION OF GALICIAN INSTITUTIONS

In the early 1990s, the institutions of Valedor do Pobo (Ombudsman of Galicia) and Audit Office began their operations; they had been provided for previously, but with no protection.

THE SINGLE ADMINISTRATION

One of the best-known proposals of the Fraga Iribarne era (1992), the idea was to simplify public administration by avoiding duplication, so that the only administration would be that of the autonomous community, rather than the central government, in historic communities, excluding the public treasury, social security, justice, and general security. If this had become a reality, Galicia would have taken over a larger number of competences from the Spanish state.

THE ROLE PLAYED BY EXPATRIATE GALICIANS

Large numbers of Galicians emigrated during the nineteenth and twentieth centuries. These Galicians, and their descendants, were the focus of several debates in Parliament, especially in terms of recognition and support. In addition, there were many different opinions, as divergent as they were numerous, about the way in which the votes of emigrants were regulated.

CIVIL LAW SPECIFIC TO GALICIA

On the basis of constitutional possibility and statutory competency (section 149.1[8] of the Spanish Constitution and section 27.4 of the Galician Statute of Autonomy), Galicia established its own civil law creating links with its historic past. The provision was passed unanimously in 1995, enacting a large part of the customary law.

THE ATTEMPT AT STATUTORY REFORM IN 2006

An ad hoc committee to study the reform of the Statute of Autonomy was established by Parliament, to define the grounds for proposals for amendments to the statute. After many different social and political stakeholders had been heard, the leaders of the three parties represented in Parliament were unable to reach an agreement and the reform was shelved (January 2007).[18]

DEFENCE OF GALICIA'S OWN FINANCIAL SYSTEM

The recent financial crisis created a need to review savings banks, in part because of the requirements of the EU and the Spanish State. The process was designed to preserve the interests of Galicia by setting up a new banking entity resulting from the merger and termination of the former regional savings banks. Their social involvement was also accorded specific protection.

Since many more examples could be cited – unfortunately not possible within the scope of this chapter – it is important for readers to note that this list covers only part of the subject. Also important is the fact that several political parties, despite their differing outlooks, have always displayed a willingness to defend the culture and identity of the Galician people, with sincerity and determination, throughout the debates and discussions.

EXAMPLES OF PARLIAMENTARY TEXTS

Five texts from the Parliament of Galicia are presented below: two are excerpts from statutes passed by Parliament, and three report comments made during plenary sessions of the assembly.

Preamble to Statute 3/1983 on Linguistic Standardization
The historic process of centralism has, over the centuries, had two profoundly negative consequences for Galicia: it prevented it from creating its own institutions, and it prevented it from developing its own culture at a time when printing was promoting the emergence of modern cultures.

The Spanish Constitution of 1978, in recognition of our right to autonomy as a historic nationality, has made it possible to implement a constructive process to fully recover our collective personality and harness its creative potential.

One of the fundamental factors in this recovery is language, given that it is the vital source for our creativity.

Language is the greatest and most original collective creation of the Galicians, and it is an authentic spiritual force from which our community draws its internal unity.

This Act ... guarantees the equality of Galician and Spanish as the official languages of Galicia and ensures the standardization of Galician as the language of our people.

Statute 5/1984, on the Symbols of Galicia
Section 1 The flag, coat of arms, and anthem of Galicia symbolize its identity as a historic nationality.

Section 2.1 The flag of Galicia, in accordance with the precept established in section 6 of the Statute, is white with a blue diagonal band which crosses it from the top left to the bottom right corner.

Speech given by Manuel Fraga Iribarne (PP) during the first two presentations of his governmental program as a candidate for the presidency of the Xunta of Galicia
Galicia is a human community whose characteristics are clearly de-fined by its geography, history, and economy, by its way of being and living, by its awareness of what it possesses ...
We are not aiming for a utopian form of self-determination but for an irreversible and definitive form of self-identification.[19]

Our government's actions will be marked by constructive Galician-ism, respectful of Spanish and European realities and open to new cultural trends, a Galicianism that will strengthen the Galician identity in agreement with Spanish and European ideas; this will be an open-minded, tolerant form of Galicianism.

We intend to achieve the stability necessary for our model of au-tonomy ... based on three fundamental premises: faithfulness to in-stitutions, the definition of the list of competences, and demands for institutional meeting-places where the autonomous communi-ties will be able to discuss shared problems and forge a new solidarity.

Democracy in Spain is possible, in particular thanks to a system of autonomous communities able to settle the centuries-old problem of its nationalities and regions; Galician autonomy is a consequence of Spanish democracy and the result of our country's attachment to a free, pluralistic, and European Spain.[20]

Speech by Emilio Pérez Touriño (PSdeG-PSOE) on 27 July 2005, when presenting his governmental program as a candidate for the presidency of the Xunta of Galicia
Our governmental action is founded on six essential aims: strengthen Galicia as a political and institutional reality, add a new dimension to Galicia's presence in Spain, raise the quality of our democracy, move toward swift, intense, balanced, and sustainable economic development, guarantee the quality and effectiveness of essential public services, and defend and promote the Galician language and the culture of Galicia.[21]

Galicianism, more than just a political position, is a movement whose roots are clearly cultural.[22]

Galicia needs to affirm its political autonomy ... Galicia wants and needs to be a place of coexistence, and a society of inclusion and cohesion.[23]

Speech given by José Manuel Beiras Torrado on 29 January 2003, at the beginning of the debate on the no-confidence motion tabled by the parliamentary group BNG (of which Beiras Torrado was the spokesperson)
An alternative approach to governmental political and legislative action that seeks to adapt and to respect identities ... must be based on postulates and ethico-political values that act as a foundation and guide, taking support from four axiological goals ... progress, well-being, freedom, and dignity.

Economic progress, which implies the existence of sustainable, self-centred development

Social well-being, without which it will be impossible for the fruits of economic progress to be converted into profit for the various layers of society and citizenship, and into moral and cultural progress for a community of individuals

Civic and democratic freedoms, without the exercise of which ... it would be impossible to envisage peaceful, serene social coexistence

Community-based and institutional dignity, given that, without dignity, peoples and individuals lose their identity[24]

CURRENT AND FUTURE ISSUES

The Parliament of Galicia is solidly founded on the set of powers of the Autonomous Community of Galicia. However, some questions remain that could substantially alter its operations. On the one hand are the aspects relating to the nature of the parliamentary assembly itself, and on the other are questions relating to the territorial model in effect.

In the first group, the Parliament must be updated on the basis of a new material legitimacy derived from the correct exercise of its functions, going beyond its simple formal legitimacy. In other words, besides its representativeness, it must look with more depth at the topic of the general interest and citizen preferences by seeking inclusive, deliberative forms of democracy. Three aspects of this problem serve to illustrate the work to be done.

First, the Galician Parliament, like many others, may be affected by the crisis of representativeness touching all institutions of its type because of the heterogeneous and polyhedral nature of the current political representative system. The new legitimacy drawn from the current ways of doing politics requires a capacity for self-representation that is hard to match with overly institutionalized modes of representation. A crisis of traditional representation in Galicia has also been mentioned. In this connection, the current Speaker of the Parliament of Galicia, Pilar Rojo, has stated that "the parliamentary institution is now, in the twenty-first century, at a crossroads," which will require the classic dimension of Parliament to take into account the new issues raised by the current context, among which she mentions the new modes of democratic legitimization.[25] Continuing in the same vein, Pilar Rojo also specified that it is important to avoid any kind of schism between "formal representation and material representation, by projecting an image to society as a general forum for meetings that encompasses the collective plurality."[26] In fact, the Galician Parliament has recently introduced a series of initiatives to increase its transparency, in particular using new technologies. The mechanisms of cyber-democracy have been implemented to add new dynamism to parliamentary life and functions. This goal of moving closer to citizens, based on an increasingly marked policy of transparency, seeks to raise their levels of trust, joint responsibility, and participation.

Second, it has also been suggested that the work of Parliament should become more fluid, for example, by reducing the delays inherent in formal questions and examinations, and that discipline and order should be improved from a technical standpoint. These questions, which would require a reform of the standing orders of the chamber, have not yet been addressed. On the other hand, following complaints, another aspect has been reformed: voting by pregnant deputies. On 2 August 2012, to guarantee equal treatment, article 84 of the standing orders was amended to allow delegated or distance voting for reasons of pregnancy, maternity, or paternity. The Office of the Parliament is the entity that gives authorization.

Third, it is important to note that the functioning of the public system has become more complicated in recent years due to the emergence of a multilevel reality and inter-institutional governance. The Galician Parliament has attempted to respond by taking part in various interparliamentary forums, whether national or international (mentioned previously).

Another set of questions relates to the Spanish territorial model, the future of which appears uncertain for two reasons. The current economic crisis has led, first, to a series of proposals for reforming political structures in the whole of the Spanish territory, which point to a shrinking of government in the autonomous communities and a decrease in their expenditure. The system of autonomous communities in Spain appears, over the last few years, to have been forced to move on to a new stage, which remains poorly defined, subject to hesitations (reformulation or reform?), and subject to strong political connotations. Clearly, the crisis has led to the formation of two antagonistic positions. The first, traditional, calls for autonomous communities with more competences, while the other calls for re-centralization. In other words, thirty years after the constitutional possibility of autonomous communities was introduced by the state, the problems have not been resolved; many questions concerning the Spanish territorial model – and therefore involving Galicia – have remained in suspense for the whole period. This situation calls for reforms to the system: whether the Senate is merely a duplication of the Chamber of Deputies without exercising the functions of a chamber of territorial representation; how to combine the principles of unity and solidarity with the principle of decentralization; how to implement constitutional as well as statutory reform; how to address the dialectic between symmetry and asymmetry in the governments of the autonomous communities; what to do about the duplication of administrative functions; how recognition by the European Union of a series of competences could alter the division of powers between the Spanish state and the autonomous communities, etc. Today, this crisis has led to calls to implement reforms and to rethink how the autonomous communities should be governed.

In addition, tensions between the central state and some autonomous communities – especially Catalonia – tend to have repercussions for the positions of other regions, leading not only to a hardening of political relations but also to the implementation of legal measures of supervision.

In fact, current perceptions among the Spanish population are not critical of the territorial power structure; rather, their concerns are focused on other topics, as reported in recent surveys by the Spanish Centre for Sociological Research.[27] We will pay special attention, in the near future, to the difficult question of territory in Spain, which appears hard to resolve in a way that will satisfy all players. On the other hand, there are no doubts about the stability of the Galician cultural and political identity, for which our Parliament rightly considers itself a stable reference and an institutional beacon that has come to play an indispensable role in the collective imagination of Galician politics.

All in all it must be said, with modesty, that the Galician Parliament does not appear to offer much in terms of originality. Possibly because of this, it is a useful object for scholars who concentrate on the logic and the procedures of parliamentary democracy. Nevertheless, the fact that the Partido Popular has obtained six absolute majorities in nine elections, in one of the three constitutionally recognized nationalities of Spain, deserves adequate recognition. The same remark applies to the kind of moderate Galician nationalism espoused by a political party such as the BNG. It remains to be seen to what extent the emergence of two new parties across Spain, Podemos and Ciudadanos, will have consequences for the Parliament of Galicia, for its institutions, and for the parties competing in its political environment.

NOTES

1 *Galleguistas*: political movements defending the Galician identity.
2 "The Constitution is based on the indissoluble unity of the Spanish Nation, the common and indivisible homeland of all Spaniards; it recog-

nizes and guarantees the right to self-government of the nationalities and regions of which it is composed and the solidarity among them all."

3 "The territories which in the past have, by plebiscite, approved draft Statutes of Autonomy and which at the time of the promulgation of this Constitution, have provisional self-government regimes, may proceed immediately in the manner contemplated in section 148, subsection 2, if agreement to do so is reached by the overall majority of their pre self-government higher corporate bodies … The draft Statutes shall be drawn up in accordance with the provisions of section 151, subsection 2, where so requested by the pre Self-government assembly."

4 The first draft statute, following the reforms carried out by the Constitutional Committee of the House of Deputies, was considered insufficient and referred to as the "estatuto do aldraxe" (statute of affront). The *Pact of the Hostal dos Reis Católicos* (which gained its name from the ancient building where it was signed in Santiago de Compostela) then restarted the process and led to a second draft statute, which was eventually passed.

5 For the historical and political background to this process, see R. Villares, "Contexto histórico político dos estatutos de autonomía de Galicia. Da utopía de 1936 á realidade de 1981," in *Galicia: Estatutos de Autonomía 1936 e 1981* (Parlamento de Galicia, 2011), 7 ff.

6 The current Speaker of Parliament, Pilar Rojo, has stated that Parliament has a duty to centralize the system as a whole and that "the passage of time has given Parliament an institutional dimension that makes it an icon of Galician public power and a guarantor, since it has become a instrument for perceiving citizens' concerns … making democracy an everyday experience," page 3, http://www.parlamentodegalicia.es/sitios/web/BibliotecaDiscursosPresidenta/Pleno%20Solemne,%2019-12-2011.pdf, accessed 29 December 2015.

7 In the other autonomous communities, and especially in Catalonia, electors tend to follow a different pattern, with many voting for a nationalist party in regional elections and then for a party with a similar ideology but a national vocation during general elections for the Spanish Parliament.

8 There has been criticism of the fact that the two least populated provinces, Lugo and Ourense, are over-represented compared to the more populous A Coruña and Pontevedra. This situation can, however, be justified in a social state, which is required to promote its least developed areas.

9 For more in-depth information, see X.A. Sarmiento Méndez, *Dereito parlamentario de Galicia* (Vigo: Edicións Xerais, 2001).

10 Statute 1/1988 regulates popular legislative initiatives, which require the signature of 15,000 electors in order to be tabled.

11 During the eight first legislatures, 346 laws were passed: forty during the first; forty-two during the second; forty-four during the third; forty-four during the fourth; thirty-two during the fifth; forty during the sixth; fifty-four during the seventh; and fifty during the eighth.

12 Concerning Galician's competencies, see J.J. Fernández Rodríguez and V.A. Sanjurjo Rivo, "Las competencias de la Comunidad Autónoma de Galicia. Perspectivas de reforma," in J.A. Sarmiento Méndez, ed., *Repensando o autogoberno: estudos sobre a reforma do estatuto de Galicia* (Vigo: Université de Vigo, 2005), 181 and following, or M.B. López Portas, *El sistema competencial de Galicia: autonomía y federalismo* (Santiago de Compostela: Escola Galega de Administración Pública, 2008).

13 With respect to the constitutional jurisprudence that has affected the autonomous community of Galicia, see X.A. Sarmiento Méndez, *O Estatuto de Galicia: 20 anos de Parlamento e xustiza constitucional* (Vigo: Xerais, 2003).

14 This discussion about difference and historic nationalities is more political and sociological than legal, although sometimes reduced to a question of party interests for the purposes of an election. Because of this, the – evasive – term "nation" is used widely in some debates. However, the constitution applies the term only to the "Spanish nation" (section 2). The Spanish Constitutional Court, in turn, stated in its decision 31/2010 that the only nation recognized by the Spanish Constitution is the Spanish nation, in relation to the people holding sovereignty (twelfth legal reason).

15 The political relationship with the central government depends on whether the parties overlap; if the same political party is in power in the autonomous community and in the central state, the opposition in the autonomous community criticizes the central government and also places responsibility (indirectly) on the regional government (for example, the case of the shipwreck of the oil tanker *Le Prestige* in 2002); if the two parties in power are different, the logic shifts; the government of the autonomous community, faced with criticism from the opposition, criticizes the central government and makes it responsible for the issue concerned (for example, funding for the autonomous community), referred to in the doctrine as "opposition to the opposition." R.L. Blanco Valdés, *A construcción da autonomía galega 1981–2007* (Santiago: Escola Galega de Administración pública, 2008), 35.

16 The situation differs from that in Catalonia or the Basque Country, where there are regional parties that have, on several occasions, played a key role in government, giving them a pole position in negotiations with the central power. See R.L. Blanco Valdés, "Nacionalidades históricas y regiones sin historia: Algunas reflexiones sobre las cuestiones de los nacionalismos en España," *Revista Parlamento y Constitución*, number 1 (Toledo: Cortes de Castilla-La Mancha, 1997), 33–7.

17 These discussions have gone as far as the Constitutional Court, which ruled that the transfer of services from the central state to the autonomous community could not be controlled by omission (see, for example, decisions 155/1990 and 209/1990).

18 The three divergent positions that could not be reconciled concerned the provisions on funding for autonomy, on language, and on the nation. In the latter case, the problem was whether or not to include the term "nation" in the reform to refer to Galicia. In the preamble to the draft reform, the PSdeG-PSOE supported the use of the word "nation," while the PP wanted to see the term "national feeling."

19 *Diario de Sesións do Parlamento de Galicia*, no. 3, 29 January 1990, 31.

20 *Diario de Sesións do Parlamento de Galicia*, no. 3, 29 November 1993, 53.

21 *Diario de Sesións do Parlamento de Galicia*, no. 2, 27 July 2005, 5 and 6.

22 Ibid., 15.

23 Ibid., 17.

24 *Diario de Sesións do Parlamento de Galicia*, no. 133, 29 January 2001, 10.242.

25 Pages 2 and 3 of http://www.parlamentodegalicia.es/sitios/web/Biblioteca DiscursosPresidenta/discursoSesionAperturaDonaPilarRojo.pdf, accessed 29 December 2015.

26 Page 10 of http://www.parlamentodegalicia.es/sitios/web/Biblioteca DiscursosPresidenta/Sesión%20Solemne%20de%20apertura%2004-12-2012%20(2).pdf, accessed 29 December 2016.

27 In November 2012, the barometer produced by the centre showed that only 0.1 percent of the people interviewed considered the statutes of autonomy to be Spain's main problem; and nationalism, in whatever form, was considered to be the main problem by 0.2 percent of respondents. http://www.cis.es/cis/export/sites/default/-Archivos/Marginales/2960_2979 /2966/Es2966.pdf

4

The Flemish Parliament
and Its Role in a Bipolar Federal System

MARTINE GOOSSENS AND MICHIEL ELST

On 7 December 1971, the day on which the precursor to the Flemish Parliament was sworn in, its temporary president, Leo Elaut, introduced the opening plenary as follows: "History never takes a step backward. All the signs indicate that the consequences of an event such as this, which is all about cultural federalism, shall be felt even more powerfully and at an accelerated pace, and that it shall continue even more intensely than ever."[1]

Over forty years later – the Flemish Parliament celebrated its fortieth anniversary in 2011 – we can fully appreciate the predictive value of his words. This becomes clear in the first part of this chapter, in which we go in search of the historical roots of the federalization process in Belgium. The second part focuses on the Flemish Parliament as an institution. On the one hand we describe its main institutional characteristics, and on the other we consider its present-day political composition and activities. In the third part attention turns to the achievements of this parliament throughout the forty years of its existence. How has it contributed to the creation of a Flemish federated entity in a federal Belgium and to what extent has it helped create the Flemish federated entity's own identity? Finally, in the fourth part, we look ahead. What are the prospects of the Flemish Parliament in the short, as well as in the longer, term?

BELGIAN FEDERALISM:
THE ORIGIN AND ESSENCE OF A COMPLEX SYSTEM

"The greatest specialists worldwide which I ... have consulted on this matter have told me that federalism with the two [linguistic groups] –

which is the only conceivable option for the Flemings – is a contradiction in terms. They tell me that a federalism with two entities is not federalism proper, that it is the juxtaposition of two nations which are moving in an opposite direction."[2]

These are the words of Leo Tindemans, at the time the minister of community relations, who in 1971, as he defended the very first state reform of Belgium in the heat of a debate in the Senate, addressed the heart of the problem, a problem that still exists more than forty years later. Is a bipolar federalism, in which the same two language groups find themselves pitched against each other at the negotiating table time and again, really possible? Is it sustainable in the long term or will it ultimately prove to be a suicide mission? The doubts expressed by Minister Tindemans and which he used to defend *sui generis* solutions for Belgium, would repeatedly surface during the following decades. Where do the origins of this bipolar federalism lie, and how has it managed to survive for over forty years, in spite of itself?

The Early Years

In order to understand the present we need to briefly, schematically even, examine the history of Belgium. Belgium was founded in 1830 following the secession of the Southern Provinces from the United Kingdom of the Netherlands. The latter had been founded in 1815 at the Convention of Vienna as a buffer state against France, which had been defeated at Waterloo.

The Southern Provinces did not appreciate the policies of the Dutch king, Willem I, in terms of religion, education, and the press. His language policy, which was aimed at preventing the decline of Dutch in Belgium, after it had been rejected as a language for administration, education, and justice under French rule, was a stumbling block for the Belgian French-speaking, liberal bourgeoisie and for the Catholic clergy, which considered Dutch to be the language of Protestantism. French was the language of the economic, political, religious, cultural, and administrative elite. It would go on to become the language of the Belgian revolution in 1830 and the only official language of an independent Belgian nation. The freedom of language, which was enshrined in the constitution, was interpreted by the French-speaking upper classes as the freedom to speak French throughout Belgium. The majority of the population, meanwhile, spoke a Dutch (Flemish) dialect.

In the newly independent Belgium, economic prosperity was unequally divided: Brussels and Wallonia especially reaped the fruits of nineteenth-century industrialization while Flanders had an agricultural economy, with widespread poverty and, in some years, famine. There were only two ways the Flemish population could climb the social ladder: find a job in Wallonia or try to get a job with the government or as a teacher. In both cases, however, it meant speaking French.

The inequality was also apparent at the political level. Only men had the right to vote, and only if they paid sufficient taxes or had a certain level of education. As a consequence, Dutch-speaking men could not be elected to the Belgian Parliament.

Evolution in Terms of Language, Politics, and the Economy

Soon after Belgium became independent, Dutch-speaking groups started to react against the dominant position of French in the newly founded state. A Vlaamse Beweging or Flemish Movement was founded. It made the recognition of Dutch as an official language a political bone of contention. As a result, the language struggle fuelled the Flemish pursuit of political recognition within the Belgian state.

Initially the language struggle was aimed at achieving equality for French and Dutch at the Belgian level. The struggle succeeded, albeit very slowly: successive linguistic laws acknowledged Dutch and French as two equivalent official languages in education, justice, the administration, and legislation. Flemish linguistic demands and struggles had a second, indirect effect: they provoked a Walloon counter-movement that feared that Wallonia would become bilingual. As a result, the Belgian territory was divided into four language areas: unilingual Dutch, French, and German[3] language areas and a bilingual area known as the Brussels-Capital area. The linguistic laws of 1962–63 finally demarcated the linguistic boundary, thus translating into law the long-standing dividing line between the Latin and the German cultures.

This marked the introduction of the territoriality principle in terms of language. The regional language would serve as the administrative language in these language areas. The emphasis would no longer be placed on the right of Flemish individuals to be served in their own language. Instead, the focus shifted to the right of a community to preserve and secure its cultural integrity, and as a result its linguistic borders. From then on it was blatantly clear that Belgium was not a homogeneous country; two cultural communities lived together in Belgium, each in its own contiguous territory. The unitary Belgium was doomed.

Furthermore, industrialization, with all its excesses, gave rise to a social movement that pursued equal social and political rights. In 1919, immediately after the end of the First World War – hardly a coincidence – universal suffrage for all men was adopted, paving the way for more adequate linguistic representation in the Parliament: for the first time there was a possibility that the French speakers would find themselves in the minority.

The political evolution finally gained momentum after the Second World War when a major economic shift occurred: Wallonia's outdated industrial economy dramatically and structurally declined whereas Flanders, because of its sea ports, its demographic evolution, and the improved level of education of its population, experienced a huge boom. In 1966 the Gross Domestic Product per capita in Flanders was higher than that of Wallonia for the first time. After losing its political and cultural-linguistic dominance, French-speaking Belgium now also had to forfeit its economic dominance and feared that a "liberated" Flanders would not be interested in the recovery of the Walloon economy.

At that precise instant all the ingredients were available to grant a form of autonomy to the language groups. The Flemish side hoped to achieve cultural autonomy, whereas the French-speaking side pursued economic autonomy. The federalization process would not be simple, however, because the language groups distrusted one another: the francophones distrusted a Belgian state dominated by the Flemish – *l'état belgo-flamand* – and feared that the Flemings would put an end to the solidarity with Wallonia, which had become the poorer region; the Flemings distrusted the francophones because they continued to claim Flemish territory every time they returned to the negotiating table.

The *territoriality principle* and the *solidarity principle* would thus become the framework within which the Belgian state would be reformed in the following decades, from a unitary state into a federal state.

Since 1970 six major state reforms have converted Belgium, which was a unitary state, into a federal state. In the past forty years, several generations of politicians have laboured tirelessly, hoping to strike compromises on the institutions of the federated entities, the devolution of powers, the development and the adjustment of the funding mechanisms, and the redefinition of the national institutions, resulting in several political crises and deadlocks. They did not follow a pre-set plan. Instead, after every political struggle and the ensuing heated debates, they struck pragmatic compromises. The result is a very complicated federal model.

During the first state reform, in 1970, important powers relating to language – a historical concern of the Flemings – and cultural matters were transferred to the newly created cultural communities: the Dutch-speaking and French-speaking cultural communities.

As a result of the state reform of 1980 the communities, in addition to their other powers, were granted important powers relating to so-called personal matters, e.g., youth protection and care for the elderly. The regions were established concomitantly.[4] Their powers related to territorial matters such as economic policy, urban planning, and the environment.

Following the third state reform of 1988, several important powers were devolved to the federated entities – including education, public works, and transport. The financial resources of the federated entities were also significantly increased as a result.

Only five years later, in 1993–94, the fourth state reform was enacted, undoubtedly the most radical to date. The federated entities were given new powers again – including international treaty-making power – and the financial resources of the federated entities were once again increased. The most important outcome of this state reform, however, was the direct election of the parliaments of the federated entities. Consequently, the Flemish Parliament was directly elected for the first time on 21 June 1995. This completed the transformation of the unitary state into a federal state, reflected in article 1 of the constitution, which now reads, "Belgium is a federal state composed of communities and regions." The fifth and sixth state reforms of 2001 and 2012–14 also transferred additional powers and financial resources to the federated entities, but the fundamental principles of the federal model, as it had been conceived in 1993, have never changed. The process leading up to the most recent state reform was especially laborious: the country was without a federal government for more than 500 days as the political parties tried to strike a compromise.

A Divided Country

One community, the Dutch-speaking community, lives in the densely populated north of the country, called Flanders (57.6 percent of the total population), and in Brussels, and constitutes the majority of the Belgian population. The other community, the French-speaking community, lives in the much less populated south of the country, Wallonia (32.2 percent), and in Brussels and is in the minority in Belgium. However, the roles are reversed in Brussels, the capital, where approximately 10.2 percent of the Belgian population lives and where francophones are clearly in the majority compared with the small Dutch-speaking minority (a ratio that is estimated to be 85 percent vs 15 percent).[5]

Increasingly the "Belgian model" faces the challenge of reconciling the divergent visions and wishes of two language communities, each living in its own territory. They do not regularly encounter each other in daily life, except in the capital; hardly ever watch each other's media or read each other's newspapers; and cannot even vote for each other's political parties. There are no longer any Belgian political parties; the three traditional unitary parties did not survive the rising community tensions and were divided into separate Flemish- and French-speaking parties as a result – the Christian-Democrats in 1968, the Liberals in 1972, and the Socialists in 1978. These parties, as well as all new parties that have emerged since 1972 (e.g., the Green Party), exclusively target public opinion in their own federated entity and no longer try to arrive at compromises across the language divide with their Christian democrat, liberal, or socialist soulmates. The lack of homogeneity, with the language divide, social-economic diversity, and ideological divisions largely following the same fault lines and reinforcing one another, undoubtedly is the main factor of instability in Belgium. The country's national identity is not very strong.[6] The Belgian federal system institutionalized this social bipolarity although, as we shall see, it is partly camouflaged by the complexity of this system; conversely, the institutional bipolarity also reinforces the two language groups' awareness of their individuality and identity. The disintegrating dynamic of the federalization process in Belgium has thus become both the cause and consequence of the progressive social division of its people. Instability and variability have become essential characteristics of the Belgian federal system.

THE BELGIAN COMPROMISE OF 2014 UNVEILED

What is the essence of the Belgian compromise? Not one, but two of Ariadne's threads are required to find a way through the Belgian institutional maze. The first thread is the neutralization of the linguistic majority at the federal and Brussels level; the second relates to the granting of far-reaching autonomy to the linguistic groups. And these threads are inextricably linked. On the one hand, the Belgian state would not be sustainable if the Flemings were to convert their demographic predominance into a preponderance of votes in the Belgian institutions and use their numerical majority to rule the francophones. On the other hand, the Flemings can only accept the neutralization of this demographic majority in exchange for far-reaching autonomy for Flanders.

The Neutralization of the Majority

The members of Parliament (MPs) and senators in the Belgian houses of Parliament are divided into two language groups. This shows that they do not represent the Belgian nation, as stated in the constitution, but their own language community. The Dutch language group is in the majority in the chamber as well as in the Senate. The Parliament of the Brussels-Capital Region is also divided into two language groups. Here the French-speaking group is clearly in the majority. The majority language groups could thus adopt legislation, each in their own assembly, which exclusively or mainly defends the interests of their language group.

However, democracy is not just a matter of demographics; it is also designed to protect minorities. Usually this fear of the tyranny of the majority gives rise to a catalogue of fundamental rights and judicial control of the constitutionality of legislation. This is also the case in Belgium. More importantly, however, majority rule as a decision-making method is radically neutralized here. This result is mainly achieved by the rule that the federal government and the government of the Brussels-Capital Region should have an equal number of Dutch-speaking and French-speaking ministers and that they have to make decisions by consensus. Belgium, in other words, is governed on the basis of a confederal principle: the two big language groups govern Belgium in parity in a federal government, which in effect is a permanent diplomatic conference between Flemings and francophones. The Belgian federal system has clearly opted in favour of a consensus and pacification model instead of the majority model.

The parity in the federal and the Brussels governments is significant for both the executive power and the legislative power. Governments are, after all, the driving force behind the legislative process: most legislation is enacted on the initiative of the government, in which the two language communities have equal representation. When the government submits a draft bill in Parliament, this draft already contains a compromise that the Dutch speakers and the francophones reached at the federal government level. In other words, in Belgium a law will hardly ever be adopted as a result of a vote of the majority language group against the minority language group. Moreover, the constitution states that a number of important institutional laws – so-called special-majority laws – can be adopted only by a two-thirds majority of the votes and a majority in each language group. Furthermore, the parliamentary procedure may be suspended on the demand of the minority group when a proposed legislative measure "is of such a nature as to seriously impair relations between the communities," i.e., the so-called "alarm-bell procedure." The measure is then referred to the Council of Ministers, which has parity and decides by consensus.

Finally, the members of the Constitutional Court and the highest courts of Belgium, as well as all senior positions in the federal administration, are equally divided between Dutch and French speakers.

Autonomy

The federated entities have in theory almost absolute[7] autonomy when it comes to exercising the powers they have been granted. The division of powers is based on the principle of exclusivity, meaning that one, and only one, government in principle has the power to take regulatory action for any problem in a given territory. The division of powers, moreover, is in accordance with the verticality principle, meaning that each federated entity has full legislative and executive power[8] to regulate the matters for which it holds responsibility. The powers granted to the federated entities relate to the internal and the external aspect, meaning that the federated entities may also sign international treaties pertaining to matters for which they are competent (*in foro interno, in foro externo*). In that sense Belgian federalism is unique.

Moreover, there is no hierarchy between the federal laws and the laws of the federated entities: the federal government cannot intervene in any way in the decisions made at the federated entity level; laws approved by the regions or communities cannot be pre-empted by the federal authorities. The only limitation as regards autonomy stems from the division of powers between the federal and federated authorities itself: the Constitutional Court and the Council of State can override any violations of this division of powers.

In some cases the exercise of a certain power by a federated entity presumes the conclusion of cooperation agreements with one or more federated entities and/or the federal authorities. These cooperation agreements are, in a sense, intra-Belgian treaties and constitute another confederal characteristic of the Belgian construct.

What makes the Belgian federal model unique, however, is the existence of two federated entity levels that overlap: the level of the communities on the one hand, and the level of the regions on the other.

The Flemish, French-speaking, and German-speaking communities are responsible for all personal matters such as language, culture, education, and a number of welfare matters, including health policy, assistance to the disabled, family policy, youth protection, and so on. They can exercise these powers within their own language area; the Flemish and French-speaking communities can also exercise this power vis-à-vis the institutions in Brussels, which are responsible for one specific community respectively.

There are also three regions: the Flemish Region, the Walloon Region, and the Brussels-Capital Region.[9] They are responsible for such *territorial matters* as the economy, urban planning, energy, the environment, agriculture, social housing, public works, local authorities, transportation, and employment.

This unique, two-dimensional structure provided the answer to the conflicting demands of the Flemings and the francophones. The Flemings wanted to form a cultural community of all the Flemings in the Dutch-speaking language area and in Brussels, probably also strategically inspired by the desire to not abandon the small Dutch-speaking minority in the predominantly French-speaking city. On the French-speaking side, the pursuit of autonomy was largely based on economic motives. In this frame Wallonia and Brussels were considered two separate regions, with their own individual issues. The compromise that was finally reached consisted of founding communities *and* regions.

The logical consequence of this two-dimensional institutional structure is that the communities and the regions each have their own parliament and their own government.

The constitution, however, facilitated a "tailor-made" approach. As a result the communities and regions may transfer powers to one another, but only under strict conditions. The Flemish chose to found a single Flemish Parliament and government, which exercise the powers of both the Flemish Community and the Flemish Region.[10] Flanders wants to make clear that the Flemings in Brussels are part of the Flemish Community by merging the community with the region.

On the other side of the language divide, however, the francophones established a separate parliament and government for the French Community alongside a Walloon Parliament and a Walloon Government. The result is a two-dimensional, asymmetric federal structure.

THE FLEMISH PARLIAMENT IN 2014:
INSTITUTIONAL CHARACTERISTICS, POLITICAL
COMPOSITION, AND ACTIVITIES

The Flemish Parliament has 124 members: six members are elected in the bilingual Brussels-Capital Region and the remaining 118 in the Flemish Region, which is subdivided into five constituencies in which the seats are defended according to proportional representation, with an electoral threshold of 5 percent. Elections are held every five years. The Parliament may not be disbanded any earlier.

The Flemish Parliament elects the Flemish government, which always consists of a coalition of various political parties. Parliament controls the activities of the government in debates, with questions and interpellations, in the plenary, in committees, as well as in commissions of enquiry. By adopting a motion of censure Parliament may force the government or an individual minister to resign, but so far this has never occurred. The most important means of control in effect is the approval of the budget. Next to this the Flemish Parliament also has legislative power: it adopts Flemish Parliament Acts (*decreten*) – usually by a simple majority of votes cast – in the various policy areas for which it is competent. Although individual members of Flemish Parliament (MFPs) can submit draft bills, most of the Flemish Parliament acts are enacted on the initiative of the Flemish government.

Every week, on Wednesday, the Flemish Parliament convenes in a plenary. Every plenary starts with a question period; the Parliament then discusses the draft bills, proposed legislation, and proposals for resolutions, and votes on these. The activities of the plenary are prepared in specialized committee meetings. Currently the Flemish Parliament has twelve committees of fifteen members each for various policy areas. In addition, there are a number of specific procedural committees, such as the Committee on Standing Orders and the Commission for the Control on Electoral Expenditure.

Parliament elects a bureau and a Speaker. The Speaker traditionally is elected from a majority party. When presiding over the plenary, the Speaker is responsible for ensuring proper conduct during the debates. As a result they may not express their personal opinion but this does not mean complete political neutrality: Speakers vote. The Flemish Parliament's building is in the centre of Brussels.

Judicial Control of Legislative Activities

There is a double judicial control of compliance with the division of powers in the federal Belgian state: a control *ex ante* and a control *ex post*. Before the Flemish government can submit a draft bill to the Flemish Parliament it has to seek legal advice from the legislation department of the Council of State, the independent judicial adviser of all Belgian legislative bodies. If the Council of State rules that the draft bill exceeds the Flemish powers, then the government will have to submit the draft bill to the Consultative Committee. The federal government and the governments of all the federated entities are represented in this political body, which can make a decision only by consensus. If no consensus is reached then the Flemish government can still submit the draft bill to the Flemish Parliament.

After publication of a Flemish Parliament act its validity can be challenged by stakeholders or by the other governments before the Constitutional Court for violation of the rules regarding the division of powers or for violation of fundamental human rights. This may lead to the annulment of the Flemish Parliament act.

Political Control of Legislative Activities

There is a second mechanism of control *ex ante*, this time of a political nature. A legislative assembly (e.g., the Walloon Parliament) may declare that a given legislative proposal or draft bill being discussed in another legislative assembly (e.g., the Flemish Parliament or the Chamber of Representatives) harms their interests, even though the proposal or draft bill respects the division of powers in Belgium. This is the so-called "conflict of interests procedure." As a result of such a declaration, the parliamentary discussion on the proposal or draft bill is temporarily suspended to allow delegations of both assemblies involved to exchange views on the matter. If parties fail to agree, the draft bill or legislative proposal shall be submitted to the Senate, which will send an opinion to the aforementioned Consultative Committee. After scrutiny by the Consultative Committee the suspension shall expire and the Flemish Parliament can continue to scrutinize the draft bill or legislative proposal, with or without taking into account the objections of the other assembly. In practice, this whole procedure seldom leads to real negotiations or the acceptance of amendments to the initial proposal.

The Absence of Structural Interparliamentary Consultation

The only mechanism of interparliamentary consultation is a negative mechanism, in the framework of the conflict of interest procedure. There is no positive mechanism of structural consultation with the federal legislative chambers or with the assemblies of the other federated entities when creating legislation.[11] The necessity of this was not recognized: in view of the fact that the powers are exclusive there is no need to consult with the other assemblies. This does not mean that there is no awareness that collaboration is useful, and in some cases even essential in various fields. But this cooperation is exclusively organized at the level of governments, which conclude (either mandatory or voluntary) cooperation agreements which are then adopted by the relevant parliament. The parliament can only adopt or reject the agreement – it cannot amend it.

The Political Composition of the Flemish Parliament in 2014

When a party has three or more elected MFPs they form a parliamentary group. Each group chooses a leader, who will act as a spokesperson for the party. Since the election of 25 May 2014 the Flemish Parliament consists of six political groups. The political groups of N-VA (nationalists, forty-three seats), CD&V (Christian democrats, twenty-seven seats), and Open VLD (liberals, nineteen seats) have delegated members to the government. The current Flemish Government is composed of nine ministers. Four are supplied by N-VA (including the minister-president), three by CD&V, and two by Open VLD. The opposition parties are SPA (socialists, eighteen seats), Groen (ecologists, ten seats), and Vlaams Belang (nationalists, six seats). There is one independent French-speaking MFP (Union des Francophones, UF).

THE FLEMISH PARLIAMENT'S CONTRIBUTION
TO THE ACQUISITION OF AUTONOMY AND
THE DEVELOPMENT OF A SELF-IDENTITY

As we have already seen in the historical overview, the Belgian federal system is the result of a devolutionary "centrifugal" process. It was set up by the centre, which at a certain time decided to gradually cede powers to federated entities, which were also established by this centre. The communities and regions owe their existence and powers to decisions made at the Belgian federal level. Legally, the federated entities do not have any input into the acquisition or extension of their own autonomy. This is all the more obvious given that the federated entities as such are not in any way involved in the procedure to amend the Belgian Constitution or other institutional laws.

The federalization process is not instigated by the parliaments of the federated entities but by the political parties, which are either Flemish or French speaking but never "Belgian." This does not mean, however, that the members of the Flemish Parliament have spent the last decades on the sideline waiting until a new load of powers fell into their laps like manna from the generous federal heavens.

Three Pathways to Greater Autonomy

We can identify three pathways which allowed the MFPs to have an impact on state reform, and which they have used: an institutional, a judicial, and a political pathway.

THE INSTITUTIONAL PATHWAY
In the period between 1971 and 1995 the members of the Flemish Parliament were not directly elected. The only elections organized were for the federal houses of parliament (the Chamber of Representatives and the Senate). The Dutch-speaking members thereof automatically became members of the Flemish Parliament (which had a different name at the time: the Cultural Council, subsequently renamed Flemish Council). In other words, they simultaneously held a federal mandate and a mandate of the federated entity. Even though the Flemish Parliament as such was not involved in the various state reforms during this period (1980, 1988–89, and 1993) the members of the Flemish Parliament, as members of the federal parliament, approved the required constitutional reforms and the special institutional laws. By supporting the reforms they did not express the Flemish Parliament's desire for autonomy. Instead, they voted as representatives of the political parties, which had arrived at an agreement at the federal level after drawn-out negotiations.

Since 1995 the members of the Flemish Parliament are directly elected by popular vote and are no longer members of the federal parliament. They no longer sit on the same benches as the French-speaking MPs, no longer hear their arguments in debates, and they can freely articulate their own dreams of greater autonomy for Flanders in their own Flemish Parliament. At the same time they can no longer realize these dreams themselves given that they no longer have a seat in this federal parliament. There was one major exception to this, however. The state reform of 1993 had also occasioned a reform of the Senate. Ten of the seventy-one senators would be appointed by and from the Flemish Parliament, ten by and from the Parliament of the French-speaking Community and one from the Parliament of the German-speaking Community. The aim was to transform the Senate into a meeting place where the federal and the federated entity levels convened. However, the logic was rather inconsistent. The ten senators of the Flemish Community were appointed by the various parties based on the electoral results of the directly elected senators. As a result, these senators did not necessarily reflect the balance of power at the Flemish level. Moreover, the political parties that endorsed the government at the federal level expected the community senators of their party to also do this. In practice the community senators did not really represent their community parliament (which, by the way, never gave them any instructions about this). Instead, they represented their party and played a majority or opposition role in the Senate depending on the federal government's political composition.

THE JUDICIAL PATHWAY
The Flemish Movement has cherished the dream of a far-reaching autonomy embodied by its own Flemish institutions for several decades. It will come as no surprise, then, that the Flemish Parliament started to exercise its new powers with great enthusiasm, every time new powers were transferred. Parliament repeatedly tested the boundaries of the division of powers, interpreting its own powers in the broadest possible manner. Whenever this was insufficient, the Flemish Parliament relied on its implied powers, i.e., powers not granted to the Flemish Region or Community, but the exercise of which is necessary in order to use in an effective way the explicitly devolved powers. In some cases, the Constitutional Court blew the whistle, but in other important cases it has repeatedly validated the broader interpretation of the powers of the communities and regions, e.g., in recognizing their power to establish administrative courts. In a sense this also was a latent state reform in favour of the federated entities.

THE POLITICAL PATHWAY
Throughout its forty-year history, the Flemish Parliament has repeatedly intervened in institutional debate even though it had no formal voice in the debates on successive state reforms. The Flemish Parliament positioned itself as the defender of the Flemish cause, thus broadsid-

ing the Flemish members of the Chamber of Representatives as well as
the Flemish senators. The members of the Flemish Parliament address
questions and interpellations to the members of the Flemish government; they adopt resolutions about vague provisions in the division of
powers and about initiatives of the federal legislative level, which they
consider a Flemish power. They also launch the conflict of interest procedure described above for draft bills of the Parliament of the French
Community aimed at promoting the French language and French-lan-
guage education in the municipalities around Brussels for the French-
speaking inhabitants, and so on.[12]

In addition to these incident-based actions, the Flemish Parliament,
albeit hesitantly from 1987 but resolutely from 1995 onward, took the
lead in formulating objectives and wishes for the next state reforms.
During the 1995–99 coalition period, Parliament even founded a special committee for state reform, in which it attempted to strike a consensus between the Flemish parties about future reform. As a result,
five resolutions were adopted on 3 March 1999.[13] These formulated the
Flemish wishes for a next state reform in elaborate detail. They were
reaffirmed in the next legislative period[14] and served as the political
guideline for successive Flemish governments:[15] time and again they
stated that these resolutions or an updated version thereof[16] would
serve as a benchmark to assess further (federal) progress in terms of
state reform. As of 2014 large parts of the demands formulated in these
resolutions have been complied with in the fifth and sixth state reforms.
This clearly shows that the Flemish Parliament has had a significant
political impact by adopting a position with the widest possible support, even though it does not have formal legal say in the further development of its own autonomy. As a result, the Flemish government
was politically obliged to also adopt this position and the majority parties supporting the Flemish government were politically forced to defend the same point of view at the federal level.[17] Interestingly, the
leading figures in some Flemish political parties, i.e., politicians with
considerable weight in their party when it comes to defining a position, abandoned the traditional, ultimate political ambition to become
the prime minister of Belgium and purposefully chose to focus on a
political career at the Flemish level. This, too, undoubtedly played a
role in this development.

Finally, the Flemish Parliament's interest as an institution in the pursuit of more autonomy can take still other forms. For example, in 2011
the Flemish Parliament organized an international scientific conference on federalism in Belgium, Germany, and the United Kingdom on

the occasion of its fortieth anniversary. The Flemish Parliament also maintains close contacts with other regional parliaments in Europe.

The Creation of a Self-Identity

Since its foundation in 1971 the Flemish Parliament has slowly but surely developed into a fully fledged parliamentary assembly. It has eagerly used its powers to set out its own policy, which is different from that of the other communities and regions. This policy is based on a Flemish societal model and identity and even influences it. Below are some examples.

THE PROTECTION OF THE DUTCH LANGUAGE

The historical overview has clearly shown that the most important motive for the Flemish Movement was the protection of the Dutch language and culture. The first matters for which Flanders acquired autonomous decision-making powers over forty years ago were culture, including broadcasting; the language used in administrative and educational matters; and labour relations. It will come as no surprise, then, that the protection and promotion of the Flemish language, as an element of a broader cultural policy, plays a prominent role in the Flemish Community's policy. Employers are required to use Dutch in their contacts with their employees; the community also invests heavily in a Dutch-speaking radio and television broadcaster, which, for example, is encouraged to broadcast Dutch-speaking music; a dense network of public libraries has been developed, in which at least 75 percent of all books have to be in Dutch, and so on. As the Flemish authorities acquired more economic powers, the explicit language policy that was aimed at the promotion of the Dutch language faded into the background somewhat. Currently, when new language-related measures are taken, they tend to focus more on the social aspect of language, as a way of promoting integration. This includes the creation of integration courses for immigrants, offering Dutch as a second language courses, and the obligation for candidate social housing tenants to demonstrate a rudimentary knowledge of Dutch in order to promote social integration and counter ghettoization. Some claim that the measures are in fact designed to counter the Frenchification of the Flemish municipalities around Brussels in order to protect the linguistic homogeneity of the territory.

THE SYMBOLS OF THE FLEMISH COMMUNITY

The Flemish federated entity has adopted the symbols of a nation state: it has its own flag, coat of arms, national anthem, and public holiday. Nation building is largely related to the way in which we look at the past and what is engraved in the collective memory.[18] In the choice of Flemish state symbols, historic events have also become instruments to create a collective identity and to express that the Flemish community has a common language as well as a shared history, connecting its inhabitants with each other and distinguishing them from the other communities.

CHOOSING A CAPITAL

The Flemish community also chose its own capital, Brussels. The choice of Brussels is charged with symbolism, but there is also a strategy behind it: political Flanders considers the largely French-speaking city of Brussels, the capital of Belgium and the European Union, which is also the capital of the French-speaking community, a Flemish city – historically speaking – which is surrounded by Flemish territory. Even though the Flemish have since become a small minority in Brussels, the Flemish political parties believe that it is important to emphasize the ties of Flanders with the Flemings in Brussels, as one Flemish community. Nor did Flanders wish to be accused of provincialism at a time when Brussels became the capital of Europe. The Flemish Parliament and the Government of Flanders chose to establish themselves in Brussels. The arguments for this choice may have evolved over time, and have been inspired by the economic importance and the international renown of that city.

THE FLEMISH PARLIAMENT AS A SYMBOL

In relation to the previous point, one cannot but remark that the Flemish Parliament rather "defiantly" chose a building across the road from the federal Parliament in which to hold their meetings. It adopted a modern and transparent image, with an assembly under a glass dome, designer furniture, and displays of works by Flemish contemporary artists. The committee rooms have all been named after old and somewhat less old Flemish master painters (Rubens, Brueghel, Van Dijck, James Ensor, and so on). Even though not explicitly stated, the symbolic message is clear: the Flemish federated entity is proud of its past while resolutely looking toward the future. Meanwhile, the federal parliament has to contend with a somewhat outdated image as the result of the very solemn decoration of its assembly rooms in a nineteenth-century building.

The Flemish Parliament also tries to contribute to reinforcing the identity of the Flemish federated entity with its own activities. It does this by, among other things, presenting medals to deserving Flemings every two years, organizing exhibitions of the work of Flemish artists in the Flemish Parliament, and selling "Flemish" products in the Parliament's store.

NO CONSTITUTION FOR THE FLEMISH COMMUNITY

The ultimate legal symbol for forming a political society with its own institutions, its own parties, its own public opinion, and its own identity would be the adoption of a constitution.[19] However extended the autonomy of the federated entities in Belgium may be, they still do not have constitutional powers. Since 1995 they do, however, have a limited number of so-called constitutive powers as regards the election, the composition, and the activities of the Flemish Parliament and the Flemish government. This category of powers has been exhaustively listed (for example, the power to regulate the right to submit petitions, to determine the constituencies for the Flemish elections, and so on). The Flemish Community has gathered all the relevant institutional provisions for which it is competent in one, single, special Flemish Parliament Act of 7 July 2006 on the Flemish institutions. There is no question of any autonomous power to determine the fundamental rules for the organization of their own political community, however. The election and the activities of the Flemish institutions remain largely determined by federal rules.

The Flemish political parties have repeatedly argued in favour of a proper constitution. In 1996 an academic competition was organized, asking participants to draft a Flemish constitution.[20] Recently, the majority parties in the Flemish Parliament submitted a draft resolution "on the Charter for Flanders."[21] This was a comprehensive political declaration, without judicial power but with the explicit ambition to (one day) constitute the groundwork for a real constitution. It contained institutional provisions as well as a comprehensive catalogue of fundamental rights, inspired by the European Union's Charter of Fundamental Rights and the Belgian Constitution. The charter by no means foreshadowed a constitution of an independent Flanders; in its first article the charter explicitly stated that Flanders is a federated entity of the federal state of Belgium. At the same time, the preamble to the charter stated that Flanders is a nation with its own language and culture. For political reasons, the draft resolution was not discussed before the elections.[22]

EVOLVING FROM THE LEGITIMACY OF FLEMISH POLICY TO A COLLECTIVE IDENTITY?

One may question whether any authority can contribute top-down to forming a common identity among the population. But if one accepts that it can, the adoption of collective symbols is not sufficient. What are needed are concrete policy decisions and actions in all the areas within its powers. This is no different for the Flemish government and Parliament. The economic stimulus measures, the construction of care homes and child-care facilities, the quality of the education funded by the Flemish government, the housing organized for socially vulnerable groups, the investments in road infrastructure, the support for scientific research, and so on will have to legitimate the existence of the Flemish federated entity.

From the state reform of 1980 onward the Flemish government and the Flemish Parliament explicitly hoped to develop a policy of their own, a policy different from the one conducted before at the level of the national Belgian state, and different also from the policy to be outlined by the other communities and regions. The first leader of the Flemish government, Gaston Geens, expressed this ambition in rather powerful terms in his motto: *Wat we zelf doen doen we beter (What we do ourselves, we do better)*. For most of the powers devolved to it since 1980 the Flemish authorities have effectively succeeded in developing their own policy and their own Flemish societal model. Unfortunately, we cannot elaborate on this in more detail in the framework of this chapter.[23]

It is certain, however, that as the powers of the Flemish federated entity expanded after each successive institutional reform, the population has noticed that the prohibition or permission to do something is issued by the Flemish government. By making daily decisions about matters that are directly visible in the lives of Flemish citizens, the Flemish Parliament and government are increasingly seen as the authority that governs them. This gradually pushes other policy levels to the background. Ultimately, the Flemish political institutions will become the reference for Flemish citizens, increasingly supplanting (the Flemish representatives in) the federal political institutions.[24]

WHAT WILL THE FUTURE BRING?

The sixth state reform became a reality with the adoption in 2012 and 2014 of an impressive number of amendments to the constitution and to a whole series of special majority laws, and an equally impressive number of amendments to ordinary laws. As we know from the past, a devolution process is not fully achieved with the adoption of all relevant laws. There are many transitional measures, some parts of the reform only enter into force in a few years' time, staff of the federal administration must be transferred to the administration of the regions and communities, some newly devolved powers may be exercised only upon conclusion of a cooperation agreement between all authorities involved, etc. Still we would like to formulate some observations about this state reform and the way in which it was realized, obviously without going into great detail.

A State Reform with Traditional Ingredients

As was the case for all previous state reforms, the sixth state reform entails the devolution of several powers to the communities and the regions: labour market policy, healthcare, family allowances, etc. Moreover, the tax autonomy of the federated entities is increased so that they will become largely responsible for acquiring the resources they need to fund their expenditures themselves.[25] The mechanisms for the federal funding of the federated entities also become more transparent. This greater autonomy, however, has led to an increase in the number of matters which can be regulated only with special-majority laws, requiring an overall two-thirds majority, combined with a majority in each linguistic group. As a result, the sixth state reform followed the classic pattern: more autonomy in exchange for the enhanced neutralization of the Flemish majority at the federal level.

The Reform of the Senate

An important novelty, however, is the reform of the Belgian Senate. From 2014 onward the powers of the Senate are significantly reduced: it will no longer exert any control over the federal government and at the legislative level its powers will become almost exclusively institutional (amendments of the constitution and of institutional legislation). This is also reflected in the Senate's changed composition: no senators are to be directly elected by popular vote. Apart from ten "appointed" senators, a large majority will be appointed by the parliaments of the federated entities (fifty overall, twenty-nine by the Flemish Parliament). The seats will be divided among the parties based on the electoral results for these parliaments. As a result, the Senate's composition will reflect the balance of power in the Flemish Parliament, the Walloon Parliament, and so on at a micro level. Perhaps this will enhance the ability of the Flemish Parliament to join in the decision-making process about future state reforms through its own senators. Continual demands for greater autonomy can thus be directly voiced at the federal parliamentary level. It is to be expected that the senators of the federated entities will position themselves more in the parliament of the federated entity than in the Senate, thus becoming emissaries of this parliament. The future will tell whether this will contribute to accelerating the defederalization process.

As already mentioned, state reforms traditionally originate in the consultations between the political parties supporting the federal government, possibly supplemented with one or more opposition parties prepared to lend their support. Once an agreement has been reached, the political parties count on the federal MPs of these parties to adopt the legislation that transposes the agreement, out of loyalty to the federal government and to the agreement made. This mechanism could now be disturbed because the senators at no time make a commitment to the federal government. As a result, they will not feel bound by a commitment to this government. Instead, the loyalty to their party and/or the parliament of their own federated entity will take priority. Especially in a situation in which the political composition of the federal government is different from the composition of the regional governments, the federated entities and their governments and parliaments will inevitably have to be involved more closely in the negotiations on the new state reforms.

Simultaneous Elections for the Federal and Federated Parliaments

The "risk" of different coalitions at the two levels (federal and federated entity), however, is reduced by another measure: as of 2014 the elections for the European Parliament, the federal Chamber of Representatives, and the parliaments of the federated entities will in principle take place on the same day. This means that voters will simultaneously decide by vote on federal and Flemish policy. Some fear that, when voting for the federal and the Flemish Parliament, voters will increasingly vote based on their opinion of the federal government and of federal policy, which attracts more media attention because of the discord, than on their approval or disapproval of the policies of the Government of Flanders. The risk is that the electoral results for the Flemish Parliament will be defined by campaigns that focus on federal themes, such as safety, justice, social security, or state reform and that the federated entity level will de facto be relegated to a subordinate role.

Dilemmas for the Flemish

The sixth state reform will probably not be the last state reform. Flanders' demands for more autonomy will not stop any time soon. This pursuit confronts Flemish political parties with a number of dilemmas or paradoxes. Here are a few:

1 The pursuit of cultural autonomy no longer has an object given that this autonomy is almost complete. Flanders' demand for additional powers today is almost completely inspired by economic motives. Flanders wants to have all the levers in hand, including tax levers, to safeguard and promote the prosperity of the Flemish region. In effect, Flanders advocates that the regions be strengthened, whereas, traditionally, it has argued in favour of the communities as much as possible. How can Flanders reconcile its pursuit of economic autonomy with the principle that Flanders does not want to leave the Flemish inhabitants of Brussels to their own resources?

2 A new state reform is often triggered by the observation that the political differences between the Flemish and the francophones in a given field are such that they give rise to constant blockages. Usually the solution is to transfer exclusive powers for this area to the federated entities so that they can exercise this power at their own discretion. As a result, the centrifugal dynamic of the federalization process is related to unwillingness or inability to work together and is thus aimed at isolation instead of cohesion.[26] However, the successive state reforms show that there is a trend toward combining the devolution of exclusive powers with the obligation to conclude a cooperation agreement between the federated entities about the exercise of these powers, or between the federated entities and the federal government. This certainly does not facilitate the exercise of these powers: prior to the devolution of these competences, the federal government exercised these powers. It would try to reach an internal consensus, bound as it is by the collective

desire to ensure that the government duly acquits itself of its tasks; after the devolution of powers, the exercise of these same powers becomes a matter of negotiation between governments, which do not necessarily want to reach the same social objective with these powers and which are not bound by a common project. The costs and time associated with the charting of a joint policy in negotiations with authorities that operate independently may completely cancel out the efficiency gains that the devolution of powers hoped to achieve: this is the so-called *joint decision trap*. In view of the devolutionary nature of Belgian federalism, accompanied by a lack of a sense of togetherness, cooperation between the federated entities or between the federated entities and the federal government in Belgium seems sometimes like a contradiction in terms.[27]

3 Various political parties and the Flemish government hoped to bring about a Copernican revolution during the sixth state reform, to achieve a change of mindset that would shift the balance of power to the federated entities. In legal terms, this Copernican revolution would give the federated entities residual, non-denominated powers[28] and would allow the federated entities to jointly agree which powers could still be exercised at the federal, or should we say confederal, level. The revolution did not take place. What the Flemish parties did achieve, however, was a traditional state reform, with important new powers and greater tax autonomy for the federated entities and more blocking mechanisms at the federal level. What else could the Flemish political elite expect? Belgium's institutional history of the past decades is largely determined by collective psychology, defined by the fundamental distrust between the major stakeholders in the federal state. Several generations of French-speaking politicians have been confronted with additional Flemish demands for autonomy. From their point of view these demands never seem to stop. They are paralyzed by the fear that Belgium will one day disappear under pressure of the Flemish. They see the Flemish demand for a Copernican revolution as the harbinger of Flemish independence, as a threat to the country and to the Walloon economy and prosperity. And yet the Flemish demands in effect reflect the preparedness of at least some major Flemish parties to clearly express themselves in favour of the survival of Belgium and to negotiate, not about the many conflicts which divide the two language groups, but about those matters which for reasons of solidarity or efficiency should be decided jointly at a Bel-

gian level. Even though this is pure speculation, it is not inconceivable that as soon as the francophones understand that this is a golden opportunity to put an end to the perpetual state reforms, the current process of reforms that are aimed at disintegration may take on a whole new dynamic leading to stability and pacification for a longer period of time.

The Unwritten Rules of a Bipolar Negotiation Process

The political agony that preceded the most recent state reform has also taught us something about the unwritten rules, the methodology of the state reforms. For this we need to remember the first of Ariadne's threads through the Belgian maze: Belgium is a state with a dual national identity, in which the Flemish majority cannot simply impose its views on the French-speaking minority. Conversely, however, the minority can impose its opinions on the majority in the sense that it can veto any demands for reform by the majority. In such a system, the majority finds itself in a minority position. Oddly, the Flemish federal majority will have to continually request more autonomy in order to achieve its own political projects as a majority.[29] If there is one thing that is really curious about the already complicated Belgian federalization process, it has to be the fact that the pursuit for greater autonomy emanates from the majority.[30] This, in a sense, is the opposite of federalism: was it not the French-speaking minority that feared the Flemish electoral majority? And isn't the best tactic for protecting the rights of geographically concentrated national or linguistic *minorities* to grant them autonomy?[31]

During the long political crisis between 2007 and 2011, the unwritten rules of the Belgian system were repeatedly flouted. The neutralization of the Flemish majority at the federal level can work only if the minority meets a demand by the majority with at least a willingness to negotiate. As soon as the minority uses its veto to refuse any real discussion with the majority, the whole legitimacy of the state is put to the test. Conversely, one can sympathize with the minority's veto when the majority is leaving the path of the gradual approach and choosing instead to bang loudly on the negotiating table at a time when this minority is in fact quite satisfied with the status quo and would not benefit in any way from reforms. In 2007 those Flemish political parties that campaigned in favour of a far-reaching extension of Flemish autonomy clearly won the federal election. The francophones refused from the start to negotiate: "on n'est demandeur de rien." Three years of great instability followed, without any institutional progress. This in turn led to a strong radicalization of the Flemish electorate during the early elections of 2010. The Flemish parties responded to the reluctance of the francophones to negotiate about a clear demand by the Flemish by refusing to form a federal government without first a political agreement on a new step in the devolution process. Sixteen months passed before such political agreement emerged and a new federal government was formed.

Concluding compromises is a condition sine qua non for the survival of Belgium. It is also the Achilles heel of this state.[32] The Belgian model can be sustained only if both communities correctly assess its dynamic: the compromise between running and standing still is walking. This compromise constitutes the essence of the system, as does the temporality of this compromise. The neutralization of the majority forces the majority and the minority to strike a compromise and to periodically return to the negotiating table. Anyone who no longer accepts the implicit rules (preparedness to negotiate, graduality, temporality), however, puts the system itself at stake.

The future will tell how long the mill of successive state reforms can continue to grind. Possibly the pursuit of autonomy in other European regions such as Catalonia and Scotland, and the reactions of national states and of Europe to this, will help shape the pursuit of Flemish autonomy and the Flemish Parliament's future role. So let us listen to their stories. Some of these stories are told in various chapters of this book.

NOTES

1 Parliamentary Proceedings of the Cultural Council for the Dutch Cultural Community, 1971–72, no.1, 7 December 1971, 2.
2 Parliamentary Documents, Senate, 7 July 1971, 2368.
3 The German language area consists of nine municipalities in the east of Belgium, which Germany was forced to cede to Belgium after the First World War in accordance with the Treaty of Versailles of 1919. In 2011 the area had 75,716 inhabitants (0.7 percent of the total population). This German-speaking Community will not be discussed in this chapter.
4 On the difference between the communities and regions, see further the discussion under the heading "Autonomy."
5 The authors abstract from the fact that due to migration Brussels is turning into a multilingual and multicultural city in a stunningly quick way.

6 W. Van Gerven, "Over Natiestaat en Burgerstaat, Federatie en Confederatie, België en Europa," in Herman Cousy et al., eds, *Liber amicorum Frans Vanistendael* (Herentals: Knops, 2007), 437.

7 This chapter elaborates on the major principles; the authors have chosen to leave the few exceptions to these principles out of consideration.

8 But not the judicial power: the organization of the courts remains within the federal power.

9 The specific, extremely complicated functioning of the Brussels-Capital Region will not be discussed in this chapter.

10 In legislative procedure, the bills submitted in the Flemish Parliament state clearly whether they regulate community or regional matters. The six MFPs elected in Brussels have no right to take part in votes on Flemish Parliament acts pertaining to regional matters.

11 Joint meetings may be held to discuss matters of common concern, but this is not part of the legislative procedure (see, e.g., the joint meeting of the Committee on Mobility and Public Works of the Flemish Parliament with similar committees of the Walloon and Brussels Parliament on 17 January 2013 on floods and water control, on the initiative of the president of the Flemish Parliament).

12 M. Goossens, *Dertig jaar Vlaams Parlement: historie en dynamiek van een parlementaire instelling 1971–2001* (Brussels, Vlaams Parlement: uitgeverij Pelckmans, 2002), 118–27, 168–78.

13 Parliamentary Documents, Flemish Parliament, 1998–99, nos. 1339 to 1343. See also D. Béland and A. Lecours, "Federalism, Nationalism and Social Policy Decentralization in Canada and Belgium," *Regional and Federal Studies* 17, no. 4 (2007): 405, 412; B. Maddens, *Omfloerst separatism? Van de vijf resoluties tot de Maddens-strategie* (Brussels: uitgeverij Pelckmans, 2009), 176; G. Pagano, *Les résolutions du Parlement flamand pour une réforme de l'État*, in *Courrier hebdomadaire*, Centre de recherche et d'information socio-politiques (CRISP), no. 1670–1671, 2000.

14 Parliamentary Documents, Flemish Parliament, 1999–2000, no. 59.

15 See, for example, the coalition agreement of Leterme I, Parliamentary Documents, Flemish Parliament, 2004, no.31/1, 22.

16 See the Octopus memorandum of 1/2/2008, annexed to the coalition agreement of Peeters-II, Parliamentary Documents, Flemish Parliament, 2009, no. 31/1, 107–14.

17 For more on the determinants of the positioning of parties on the question of territorial reform in Belgium in the past fifteen years, see K. Deschouwer, "Party Strategies, Voter Demands and Territorial Reform in Belgium," *West European Politics* 36, no. 2 (2013): 338–58.

18 O. Luminet et al., *België-Belgique. Eén staat, twee collectieve geheugens?*

(Heule: Snoeck Publishers, 2012), 192. In 2014–18, the centenary of the First World War will be commemorated, mainly in Flanders Fields. In 2015 the bicentenary of the Battle of Waterloo, a village in Wallonia, was commemorated. These historical events have had a decisive impact on Belgian history. Yet the preparation of these commemorative events is almost exclusively in the hands of the two communities. It will be interesting to examine how these two language groups will reflect on these episodes in the twenty-first century, and how their approaches differ.

19 C. Berx, "Een grondwet voor de Belgische deelstaten?, Lessen' uit het buitenland en de Europese Unie," in B. Peeters and J. Velaers, eds, *De Grondwet in groothoekperspectief. Liber amicorum discipulorumque Karel Rimanque* (Antwerp: Intersentia, 2007), 239–56.

20 The winning proposal was J. Clement, W. Pas, B. Seutin, G. Van Haegendoren, and J. Van Nieuwenhove, *Proeve van Grondwet voor Vlaanderen* (Brussels: die Keure, 1996).

21 Proposal of a resolution by Messrs Ludwig Caluwé, Kris Van Dijck, and Bart Van Malderen on the Charter for Flanders, Parliamentary Documents, Flemish Parliament 2011–12, no. 1643/1.

22 For more on the Flemish longing for a sub-national constitution, see P. Popelier, "The Need for Sub-national Constitutions in Federal Theory and Practice: The Belgian Case," in *Perspectives on Federalism* 4, no. 2 (2012): E–41–2, http://www.on-federalism.eu/attachments/133_download .pdf, accessed 29 December 2016.

23 The question to what extent the Flemish policies that were developed between 1970 and 2011 for the various policy areas were effectively genuine Flemish policies and different from the policies of the French-speaking Community and the Walloon Region is the theme of a book published in 2011 by the Flemish Parliament on the occasion of its fortieth anniversary: M. Van den Wijngaert, ed., *Van een unitair naar een federaal België: 40 jaar beleidsvorming in gemeenschappen en gewesten, 1971–2011* (Flemish Parliament/ASP, 2011). (Also available in French: *D'une Belgique unitaire à une Belgique fédérale: 40 ans d'évolution politique des communautés et des régions, 1971–2011*).

24 According to recent political research, the increasing political power of the regional governments in Belgium has not yet led to an increasing identification of the population with these regions and a declining identification with Belgium. This may be a consequence of the young age of the federation and of the circumstance that the dividing lines between the federal and regional policy levels hitherto are not very clear, not in the least because of the constant shifts of political personnel from one level to the other. See K. Deschouwer and D. Sinardet, "Identiteiten, com-

munautaire standpunten en stemgedrag," in K. Deschouwer, P. Delwit, M.Hooghe, and S. Walgrave, eds, *De stemmen van het volk* (Brussels: VUB Press, 2010), 81.

25 Traditionally, the federation largely funded the federated entities. The regions had limited power of taxation; the sixth state reform will enlarge this autonomous power of taxation significantly.

26 P. Popelier and Dave Sinardet, "Stabiliteit en instabiliteit in de Belgische federale staatsstructuur," in P. Popelier, D. Sinardet, J. Velaers, and B. Cantillon, eds, *België, Quo vadis?* (Antwerp: Intersentia, 2012), 9–11.

27 J. Vanpraet, *De latente staatshervorming* (Brussels: Die Keure, 2011), 33–4.

28 It is a typical feature of devolutionary federalism that the federated entities have enumerated powers and that all that is outside this list remains a matter for the federal authorities. The Copernican revolution, advocated by several Flemish political parties, would reverse this. In fact, the Belgian Constitution already states this reversal, but this provision has not yet been executed.

29 A. Alen, "Nationalisme, federalisme en democratie: het voorbeeld België," in *Nationalisme, federalisme en Democratie*, Cahiers Vakgroep Staatsrecht Groningen 4 (Groningen: Wolters-Noordhoff, 1993), 74.

30 The majority group, moreover, is economically stronger than the minority group. Some consider the pursuit of autonomy a mark of reduced solidarity with the weaker region.

31 S. Sottiaux, *De Verenigde Staten van België: Reflecties over de toekomst van het grondwettelijk recht in de gelaagde rechtsorde* (Mechelen: Kluwer, 2011), 64–5.

32 J. Velaers, "De crisis van de staat en de Achillespees van het staatsrecht," *Rechtskundig Weekblad*, 2011–12, 23–5.

5

The Parliament of Quebec:
The Quest for Self-Government,
Autonomy, and Self-Determination

FRANÇOIS ROCHER AND
MARIE-CHRISTINE GILBERT

In almost all countries there is a building whose primary purpose is to provide the people's representatives assembly with a physical and symbolic setting.[1] In Quebec, the body that best represents its citizens is parliament's National Assembly, housed in Quebec City's Parliament Building. Since the Assembly's inception in 1791, this parliament has been a theatre of political action and democracy in Quebec, a place where the most important issues pertaining to the affirmation and the promotion of the national community's unique features are debated. Having legislative authority, Parliament also participates in managing the state by creating, modifying, and repealing laws as well as by exercising governmental control. However, if changes in institutional practices were to diminish the latter role,[2] Parliament would remain a pluralistic political space where elected citizens could challenge institutions and contribute to the rules for achieving common good. It is in this sense " a forum where the nation takes its pulse."[3]

By looking back at Parliament's history and evolution, we demonstrate how over four centuries this political institution has played a central role in constructing, recognizing, and consolidating the Quebec nation. The first section briefly covers how the Legislative Assembly bore witness to many struggles that led to the establishment of "elective" institutions, which, however, fell short of French Canadian hopes in regard to the elective principle ensuring representation.[4] Today's recurring problem, if there is one, is that representation creates new challenges, particularly concerning the inclusion of women and individuals from the full range of social classes.

We tackle Parliament's place in Quebec's political system in the second part. Is it the incarnation of the people's sovereignty? Or is it subject to a greater set of norms? Finally, how does the combination of a federal state and a parliamentary form of government influence the Quebec Parliament's powers? We conclude by focusing on some of these features, in particular the institutional composition and operation behind the adoption of private members' bills.

The second section describes the Quebec legislature's main contributions to political struggles and debates leading to the defence, consolidation, and expansion of the nation's autonomy. Finally, we discuss the main challenges Parliament will face in the coming years.

PARLIAMENT'S HISTORY, EVOLUTION, AND ORIGINALITY

The Assembly as we know it today is the result of a history that spans over four centuries.[5] More specifically, the history of the Quebec Parliament does not begin with the Constitutional Act, 1791, as is often assumed. It begins earlier with those who wanted to build a house of representatives. The idea emerged after the turmoil of the British Conquest of New France and the Royal Proclamation of 1763, when the Lords of Trade[6] and Quebec merchants humbly petitioned their sovereign for a house of representatives.

The National Assembly is the result of many requests from business elites and, indirectly, a political and economic power play. Throughout this historic journey, we emphasize institutional changes, but also arguments and counterarguments regarding the transformation of the role and powers of the Legislative Assembly. In other words, we demonstrate that the creation of the Quebec Parliament dates back to the early colonial debates over the Legislative Assembly.

1763–91:
First Discussions of the Creation of a Legislative Assembly

In 1763, under the Great Seal of Great Britain, governors from different colonies were given the power and direction to call, once the colonies' state and circumstances permitted, general assemblies with the advice and consent of the Members of Council in London.[7] Although the proclamation mentions the possible convening of a general assembly – giving General James Murray, Governor of Quebec, the power to call general assemblies of freeholders and settlers – the meeting did not take place until 1791.[8] Murray, under the king's order, governed the colony with a privy council, combining legislative, executive, and judicial power, until other circumstances allowed the government to establish a legislative assembly.

The idea of creating an assembly was put back on the agenda a few years later when His Majesty's subjects were no longer happy with the political regime in place. Some were dissatisfied with judicial institutions; they demanded the return of French civil laws and felt bullied by being excluded from the public service because of their religion. Others wanted to enjoy the same privileges as all British subjects by having a legislative assembly.

On 22 June 1774, another opportunity arose to create a representative assembly with the Quebec Act. It was a failure. The act put in place a legislative council to enact laws, which, according to the metropolis, constituted a sufficiently representative body and served the community's sovereignty more or less adequately.[9]

After 1784, committees were formed to advance this common cause.[10] Under the leadership of Frederick Haldimand (1778–84), new rules of parliamentary procedure were implemented in the Legislative Council, but there would be no question of an assembly since "it is not yet ascertain'd that the people wish for a house of Assembly!"[11] Finally, in 1789, while the Third Estate (*tiers état*) met in the Salle du Jeu de Paume in Versailles to discuss the term "National Assembly,"[12] Quebec's inhabitants continued to advocate for a legislative assembly. And a war of attrition waged mainly by English traders in the province who wanted to create an English and Protestant assembly led to the establishment of local legislative bodies that truly represented Quebec.[13] It was ultimately the pressure of the Imperial Parliament Whigs, starting in 1786, that led to the adoption of a new constitution for Quebec and, consequently, a legislative assembly.[14]

1791:
A New Constitution and New Parliamentary Institutions

In general, history lacks enthusiasm when it comes to the Quebec Constitution of 1791. It did not represent, like its French equivalent of the same year, a success or a great consecration of past efforts; at most it was seen as a starting point. The Constitutional Act of 1791,[15] or more precisely the Act Repealing Certain Parts of the Quebec Act of 1774, was acceptable to the vast majority of the colony.[16] In fact, the true scope of the act was to divide the Province of Quebec into two separate political entities: Upper Canada and Lower Canada, each with its own representative assembly.[17] With the creation of this elective chamber, the colony was able to participate in the legislative and supreme state functions under new conditions of independence.[18] Therefore, the first Quebec Parliament dates back to 1791. It is not only one of the oldest legislatures in the world still operating, but it also has the second largest French-speaking majority in parliament in the history of modern democracy after the French National Assembly.[19]

The parliamentary institutions of Upper and Lower Canada were structured like Westminster.[20] The Parliament of Lower Canada was composed of three legislative bodies – a governor, the Legislative Assembly, and the Legislative Council. The governor was responsible for the executive function, which was assisted by an Executive Council whose members were appointed by London.[21] Until the early nineteenth century, the three branches of the legislature worked collegially, but the situation became complicated when Lower Canada members encountered the limits of their representative body within the colonial state.[22] The Legislative Assembly, which was elected, marked the legal recognition of the local population's new-found and collective sovereignty, but the governor continued to reflect the metropolitan government's traditional sovereignty. The opposition between monarchical and popular sovereignty seemed to offer a way, in Quebec, to meet the very different interests of the imperial government and the colony's local government.[23] But the system only appeared democratic. In reality, it was distinguished by different measures of centralization: confusing and overlapping powers concentrated within the executive branch, centralized authority, impunity of public administrators, and political domination of property owners.[24] The elected assembly had legislative power, but London and the colonial aristocracy held executive power over the government.[25] This is where the fight for ministerial responsibility – a true parliamentary democracy – and struggles over subsidies and language use in parliamentary debates began.[26]

1840–67:
Toward a Sovereign Quebec Parliament

In 1840, the Act of Union merged the colonies of Upper and Lower Canada under the new name "Province of Canada." The Parliament, still bicameral, had an elected Legislative Assembly where each former province was represented equally (despite Lower Canada's population being larger than Upper Canada's). It also included an upper house, the Legislative Council, whose members were appointed by the governor. In 1848, freedom of action and the governor's complete control of the Executive Council were limited by the principle of responsible government. However, political instability, the American Civil War, and pressure from major business interests forced the political class to consider a new constitutional formula and new parliamentary institutions. In 1867, the British North America Act (BNA Act, 1867) gave Quebec a parliament, but this time it was sovereign in its areas of jurisdiction. Parliament was made up of two houses: the Legislative Assembly, with sixty-five elected members (MPs), and the Legislative Council, with twenty-four members appointed for life by the lieutenant governor.[27] The federal state and the Canadian provinces did not break new ground politically: they faithfully copied the Westminster model.[28]

Consistent with the trend affecting most parliamentary institutions in liberal states, important changes were made to Parliament's structure and operation. For example, the lieutenant governor's and the Legislative Council's powers were reduced, while the executive gained greater control over legislative proceedings.[29] Gradually, the dominant presence of a prime minister and the executive's control over parliamentary business led to MPs being harnessed. In addition, the Executive Council's stranglehold on the legislative process and the strengthening of party discipline progressively reduced MPs' autonomy.[30]

In short, the Parliament of Quebec had its own distinct character: before 1867, it was shaped by the political, economic, and cultural colonial struggles. Later, the relationship between the central state and the province, and Quebec's particular national context within the federation, would somewhat alter the parliamentary institutions. Citizens' requests to play a larger democratic role eventually led the government to opt for an innovative project to bring the Citizens' Assembly together so that, through new technologies (online petitions, videoconferences, and public consultations), they could play a greater role in parliamentary proceedings.[31]

THE QUEBEC LEGISLATURE'S ROLE WITHIN THE NATION'S POLITICAL SYSTEM

In Canada, each province's state structure is composed of a parliament, government, and courts acting in accordance with a particular juridical system. The Parliament of Quebec or the National Assembly's role within the Canadian political system is typical of a British-inspired parliamentary system, a "soft" separation between the branches of government. More precisely, "the Parliament and the government both carry out legislative and executive functions."[32] The Quebec parliamentary system was based on two fundamental principles: first, the separation of powers and second, the relative independence of the bodies with executive or legislative power, enabling them to interact.[33] On the one hand, Parliament has a right to control government activity that may lead to the involvement of departmental responsibilities as well as the government's defeat in the house. On the other hand, the Executive Council (Cabinet) may send MPs before the electorate by exercising its right of dissolution, a consequence of ministerial responsibility.[34]

However, when this structure is used in multi-level governance, as is the case in the Canadian federation, it may be affected by executive federalism.[35] In this type of federalism, federal, provincial, and territorial cabinets are responsible for intergovernmental relations, so that intergovernmental agreements are directly negotiated and concluded by the executive MPs who are also members of the majority party in the house. Therefore, while ministers (or officials) make important decisions, parliamentarians are left to debate about the form of legislation and ratify the executive's decisions. The principle of parliamentary sovereignty is thereby diminished, to the extent that the executive's leaders select and define key issues beyond the Parliament's control.[36] Moreover, transparency, accountability, and citizen engagement are reduced.[37] Does this mean that parliamentary democracy and intergovernmental relations are incompatible? Not quite. Some believe that intergovernmental relations are better governed by rules:[38] that the provinces need to find the means to scrutinize agreements before they are negotiated in camera,[39] or that citizens participate in the decision-making process through advisory committees,[40] reducing the executive's monopoly and, consequently, rebalancing and restoring some of the Parliament's prerogatives.[41]

Parliament

The Parliament of Quebec, consisting of the lieutenant governor and the National Assembly, has one chamber.[42] The Assembly currently has 125 members, elected in general elections. The first-past-the-post system elects the candidate who receives the highest number of votes in a constituency. Although the party concept is central to the system, it is heavily diluted in the parliamentary process in that it no longer involves a political party, but instead a parliamentary group. However, not all

Table 5.1
Distribution of members of the National Assembly of Quebec, 40th Legislature, 2012, and 41st Legislature, 2014

Party	Party leader	Number of seats (%)		Number of men (%)		Number of women (%)	
		2012	2014	2012	2014	2012	2014
Parti Québécois (PQ)	Pauline Marois	54	30	37 (68.5%)	29 (78.4%)	17 (31.5%)	8 (26.7%)
Quebec Liberal Party (QLP)	Philippe Couillard	50	70	32 (64%)	52 (74.3%)	18 (36.0%)	18 (25.7%)
Coalition Avenir Québec (CAQ)	François Legault	19	22	14 (73.7%)	16 (72.7%)	5 (23.3%)	6 (27.3%)
Québec solidaire (QS)	Françoise David	2	3	1 (50%)	1 (33.3%)	1 (50.0%)	2 (66.6%)
TOTAL		125		84 (67.2%)	91 (72.8%)	41 (32.8%)	34 (27.2%)

Source: National Assembly, "members," available online at
http://www.assnat.qc.ca/fr/deputes/index.html, accessed 10 January 2013 and 27 August 2014

parties with elected candidates are considered a parliamentary group. As stated in the Standing Orders of the National Assembly, "only a party that qualifies under the rules of parliamentary procedure shall be considered a parliamentary group. Any member not having been returned under such a party will, once he or she has arrived at the National Assembly, join a recognized parliamentary group or sit as independent member."[43] A parliamentary group is any group of not fewer than twelve elected members of the National Assembly (MNA) of the same political party or any group of MNAs returned by a political party that has received not less than 20 percent of the vote in the most recent general elections.

Parliamentary group status is not insignificant, since it grants rights to its MNAs and provides them with numerous advantages associated with parliamentary proceedings. For example, during debates it enables them to have greater voice in the proceedings in the house and, consequently, to get their message across.[44] Finally, parliamentary groups have a research budget and MNAs who fulfill specific duties receive additional remuneration.

Political Party Representation

With respect to the representation of political parties in Parliament, the government has a majority when the parliamentary group forming the government holds the majority of seats. Otherwise, it is a minority, as in the case of the Parti Québécois (PQ), which came to power on 4 September 2012. The party was led by Pauline Marois, the first woman to become premier of Quebec. One of the defining features of this legislature was the significant increase in the number of seats won by women. In 2012, forty-one women were elected, nearly a third of the seats, which is a record in the history of Quebec. The results were less impressive in 2014, where only thirty-four women were elected.

Despite significant progress, there are even fewer women at the highest political levels. For instance, the Marois government failed to make innovations in the appointment process, appointing women as heads of only eight departments out of a possible twenty-three, most being ministers of state or in charge of social-oriented sectors. Strength in numbers alone does not yet enable women to rise to the top: their access to economic and, even more so, important missions is restricted.[45]

MNAs' Level of Education and Socio-Professional Experience

In the 1960s, there was a concern that Quebec MNAs were not representative of the general population. Most were part of the elite, and, therefore, were considered a minority.[46] During the 1980s, this finding remained valid, according Réjean Pelletier, who also observed that professionals in the fields of education and social sciences were replacing lawyers.[47] In 1981,[48] 83 percent of MNAs had a university education, a significant increase from 50 percent between 1960 and 1970.[49] Magali Paquin has shown that this proportion was similar for the PQ and Parti libéral du Québec (PLQ), while MNAs of the Action démocratique du Québec (ADQ) generally had less education.[50]

Even though a lack of mirror-representation (based on a similar or equivalent background for the overall population) has repeatedly been demonstrated,[51] we investigated whether this was still the case in 2013. To draw our own conclusions, we used data from MNA profiles, which can be found in the biographies posted online. However, some were missing at the time of writing this chapter.[52] According to our figures, Parliament has seven MNAs with a doctorate, thirty-seven with a master's degree, and thirty-four with a bachelor's degree. In other words, 38 percent of MNAs have a graduate degree and 29 percent have an undergraduate degree.[53]

With respect to their socio-professional profile, in 1980 Liberal Party MNAs had mainly economic backgrounds, while the PQ had primarily cultural backgrounds.[54] Similarly, in 2011, the PQ had greater representation in cultural and social fields, while MNAs with economic and administrative experience dominated the Liberal Party.[55] Meanwhile, MNAs of the ADQ had a more heterogeneous profile, due to the number of MNAs belonging to the middle class.[56] So, what is representation like today?

The data we collected showed an overrepresentation of MNAs of high social status. In addition, the presence of managers and executives (presidents, vice-presidents, etc.), representatives of the legal profession (lawyers, notaries, jurists), teachers, consultants, and policy advisers in the National Assembly is impressive. Cultural professions were also largely represented, especially in the PQ.

In conclusion, in 2008 an individual's education was a major factor in accessing leadership positions and those elected were mainly university educated.[57] However, partisan and ideological cleavages are less clear. The Coalition Avenir Québec (CAQ) and the Liberals continue to have a greater representation of groups with high social status or economic power, while the left parties – Québec solidaire (QS) and PQ – have more MNAs with cultural and intellectual professions. More generally, representatives do not mirror the Quebec population.

Overview of the Parliament of Quebec's Institutional Operation

As part of Quebec's parliamentary system, and under the National Assembly Act, Parliament has legislative power. This means that laws are adopted by the National Assembly and sanctioned by the lieutenant governor (LAN, art. 2 and 3 and art. 29). However, given that under the current system powers are not strictly separated between the executive and legislative branches of the state, the government also has legislative power. Therefore, the Assembly does not play an exclusive role in the law-making process.[58]

Most parliaments traditionally, and almost universally, are said to have three tasks: to legislate, control the government, and foster public debate.[59] Focus is usually placed on the first, despite its recent decline. In fact, the government controls the Assembly's agenda, since it determines each bill to be studied by the latter during a session.[60] Moreover, only the government can propose bills with a financial impact, which significantly reduces MNAS' power to introduce bills.[61] Today, the government submits most legislative pieces. Parliament now simply controls the legislative activity of government.[62]

Nevertheless, bills introduced by MNAs who do not sit on the executive council or the opposition can be considered useful mechanisms for citizens. Whether the bill passes or not, it creates discussion and motivates the implementation of various policies.[63] In relation to legislation, freedom of speech permits MNAs to openly criticize bills under consideration and to propose any amendments deemed appropriate.[64] Therefore, "it is by debating the major issues of the day, even if the discussion is not sanctioned by a vote, that Parliament can improve the quality of law-making in the future by influencing its development and directing it toward the general interest of citizens."[65] We discuss below how this form of critical debate has often fuelled Quebec's demands for autonomy and self-determination.

THE QUEST FOR AUTONOMY AND SELF-DETERMINATION

The Quebec Parliament against the Centralized Federalism of John A. Macdonald

To grasp the importance of Quebec's quest for autonomy and self-determination, we must remember the intentions of the Founding Fathers. The adoption of a federal system of government in 1867, ending the British colony of United Canada, was presented to the people of Canada East (today Quebec) as providing a range of protections that would allow them to pursue their national destiny. Some French Canadians in 1867 did not consider Confederation a threat, but rather a necessary step in building a predominantly French Catholic state in British North America. It was presented, defended, and evaluated based on the degree of autonomy it gave French Canadians. For many people of Lower Canada's former colony, Confederation granted them powers of a quasi-independent state and promised conditions that would guarantee their survival.[66] The 1867 Constitution exclusively devolved some powers to provincial governments (control over health, education, municipalities, marriage, property and civil rights, interprovincial trade, etc.).

However, Conservative prime minister John A. Macdonald's federal government quickly saw demands for autonomy emerge, since its constitutional and institutional arrangements favoured the central government.[67] The first claims for autonomy appear in Ontario premier

Oliver Mowat's speeches and those of Quebec premier Honoré Mercier (1887–91). For example, during a speech at the Quebec Legislative Assembly on 7 April 1884, the premier reminded the governor general that the 1867 Constitution had sanctioned the provinces' full autonomy, and the federal Parliament's frequent encroachments on the provinces' prerogatives were unacceptable. Subscribing to the doctrine newly articulated by Justice Loranger (1884), he also condemned the use of the power of disallowance. His interpretation of Confederation did not go without consequence: Prime Minister Macdonald would refuse to take part in the first interprovincial conference of 1887.[68]

Respect for provincial jurisdictions was repeatedly reiterated in the house, but in July 1917, it made room for a new challenge: the self-determination of the French-Canadian nation, more specifically, the adoption of the Military Service Act by the Canadian Parliament. French Canadians demonstrated in the streets, protesting their marginalization in this attempt to force them to fight in an imperial conflict.[69] In light of Prime Minister Sir Robert Borden's aversion to French Canada, which in 1917 had overwhelmingly voted against his party (Conservative), on 17 January 1918, Joseph-Napoléon Francoeur, Liberal MP for Lotbinière in the Legislative Assembly of Quebec, tabled the following motion: "This House is of the opinion that the Province of Quebec would be prepared to agree to break away from the federal pact set up in 1867 if, in the other provinces, it is felt that Quebec is an obstacle to the Union, and to the progress and development of Canada."[70] The motion was later withdrawn following Premier Lomer Gouin's speech (1905–20). Today, this can be interpreted as both an example of Quebec parliamentarians' exasperation with the treatment of French Canada, and as a symbol of the affirmation of the latter's rights with respect to other Canadians. It also marks the beginning of the struggle for provincial autonomy, which, since the twentieth century, has become a constant in Quebec politics and in provincial and federal governments' conflicting relationships.[71]

The Postwar Quebec Parliament:
Toward a Definition of Federalism in Quebec

Provincial autonomy became a recurring theme in politics, especially for Premier Maurice Duplessis, leader of the Union nationale (1936–39 and 1944–59). During the 1939 election, in the name of provincial autonomy, Duplessis opposed conscription, which was perceived as a threat: "we are asking the people of Quebec to stand up to the tyrants of Ottawa ... to rise up against them so that Quebec can live and breathe the air of freedom."[72] Like his predecessors, Duplessis insisted that provincial jurisdiction be respected. During the Second World War he denounced Ottawa's control over taxes and, later, the "federal spending power" that the federal government sought to justify by establishing the welfare state. Tensions over the creation of a family allowance program were another powerful indicator of his attitude.[73]

In order to understand the driving force with which provincial autonomy became a *leitmotif* for Duplessis and how the idea was deeply coloured by social and political conservatism, it is necessary to remember that Canada was then entering a period of economic and symbolic reconstruction following the severing of ties with the British Empire. Furthermore, the federal government spearheaded the creation of a modern and "national" state, guaranteeing all its citizens access to uniform social services across Canada.[74] Once again, Ottawa's intervention translated into the shrinking of provincial autonomy, to which Duplessis was strongly opposed. In fact, he would fight federal initiatives on taxation and social legislation.[75] He directly criticized the new federal funding of universities that began in 1952 and encouraged universities to refuse federal grants, out of respect for exclusive provincial jurisdiction over education, while they complained of underfunding. Nor did Duplessis stop there. Faced with the federal government's lack of regard for the sovereignty and autonomy of the provinces, and more particularly in an attempt to solve the constitutional problems, in 1953 Duplessis created the Royal Commission of Inquiry on Constitutional Problems, headed by Justice Thomas Tremblay. Despite Duplessis' decision in the end to ignore its advice, this parliamentary initiative was important because it illustrated how Quebec perceived Canadian federalism.[76]

Filed in February 1956, the commission's report covered the primary autonomist arguments developed by Justice Loranger in the nineteenth century and supported by all Quebec premiers since Honoré Mercier. The commission followed a classic "watertight compartments" definition of federalism. On the one hand, the focus was on the balance between unity and plurality trends and, on the other, the presence of two orders of equal and coordinated governments. Provincial governments were responsible for looking after the special interests of their political communities. The commission insisted that the role of each level of government be limited to the jurisdiction where it enjoys independence from the others. The principle of non-subordination has a prominent place in the construction of federal institutions. It is indeed "the system's primary and general idea, the one that applies to all authentic federal states."[77] This idea was reflected institutionally through the distribution of powers, the balance between the constitution (and rigidity to prevent it from being amended unilaterally, at least regarding the distribution of powers) and the supremacy of the courts. The proper functioning of the federation was guaranteed by the presence of a spirit of cooperation opposed to both an attitude of domination and unification from the central government and an attitude of independence and separatism from regional governments. Compromise and a spirit of partnership were required to prevent any disturbance of the "delicate and careful" balance in favour of one of the governments.[78] The report described the social federalism that was based on the principles of partnership, dialogue, consensus, and respect for human independence, and that would inspire society as a whole.[79] As Dominique Foisy-Geoffroy points out, "all the arguments developed in the report justify the autonomy of Quebec, in every proposed reform, based on the fundamental choice in favour of a spiritualist and personalist culture as part of the Christian West crisis."[80] In doing so, the report continued to present French Canada in its sociological dimensions and did not support the political nationalism that binds state and nation. Nevertheless, the province of Quebec needed to preserve its jurisdictional independence because it is the homeland, the political arena of French Canada and, in this respect, has a mission that distinguishes it from other provinces. Once the Tremblay Commission's report was filed, Premier Duplessis blacklisted it for being politically explosive.[81] However, in 1954 the commission would play a key role in the creation of provincial income tax since research at the time convinced Premier Duplessis that the electorate would support such an initiative despite opposition from the federal government, which capitulated in 1955.

The Quebec Parliament's Quiet Revolution: The Search for New Powers as an Affirmation of National Identity

The death of Premier Duplessis in 1959, but more particularly the election of a Liberal government led by Jean Lesage in 1960, marked a profound change in perception and strategy. Political autonomy was presented not as a means of limiting Ottawa's deleterious influence, but rather as a means of political, economic, and social restoration of the French-Canadian "people." The autonomous discourse thus took a new direction: the need to preserve French Canada's traditional character gave precedence to the need to affirm its national identity, which required defending the powers conferred upon the provinces, powers considered essential to the task of modernization toward which Quebec was striving. For Jean Lesage, constitutional amendments were not absolutely necessary to obtain a particular status for Quebec. In practice, administrative arrangements could have resulted in fostering such a distinct status: "To the extent that the other provinces are not working toward the same objectives, Quebec will move toward a particular status that will reflect both the specific characteristics of its population and the more extensive role it wishes to assign to its government."[82] The federal government expressed its openness to these claims. In 1964, Lester B. Pearson's Liberal government adopted cost-sharing programs (particularly for hospital insurance, social welfare, unemployment relief, etc.) and gave all provinces the right to opt out of these programs, with financial compensation, so they could put their own programs in place. Quebec was the sole province to take advantage of this opportunity.

However, Jean Lesage decided to take a different course of action in light of the debates centred on the federal government's proposal to patriate the Canadian Constitution and propose an amending formula. The discussion of a new distribution of powers and the inclusion of Quebec prevailed over the constitutional mechanics, namely, the patriation and the amending formula. The amending formula, proposed by Ottawa and first accepted by the Quebec Liberal government, was perceived as a "straitjacket" and closed the door on any future expansion of provincial powers. With the Parliamentary Committee on the Constitution of Canada, which sat from 1963 to 1968, the constitutional question took a new turn. The various officials who served as members recommended not merely a series of amendments to the constitution, but rather a rewrite based on recognizing the two-founding-peoples thesis.[83]

If the Quiet Revolution's state nationalism gradually led many Quebecers to demand a distribution of powers, it also witnessed the emergence of a political movement that increasingly advocated Quebec sovereignty. Daniel Johnson, who became head of the Union nationale in June 1966, had already raised this possibility without ever adjudicating in its favour.[84] He proposed recognizing the equality of the two founding peoples. The logical outcome was the use of the constitution as a tool to establish equality between French and English Canadians, the two primary "nations" on which Canada was built: "A new constitution should be designed so that Canada is not solely a federation of ten provinces, but a federation of two nations equal in law and in fact."[85] This meant equality of the two groups on a national scale, which could only be made possible by increasing Quebec's constitutional powers in such areas as social security, international relations, education, and culture. Nevertheless, Johnson thought it impossible to revise the 1867 Constitution because it was obsolete. Instead, he decided to try the more radical approach of writing a new constitution. After failing to reach a satisfactory agreement, Johnson argued that Quebec would have no choice but to opt for independence. However, the ultimatum of independence sometimes referred to the French-Canadian nation and sometimes only to the Quebec territory. It was not Johnson who would resolve this ambiguity, but René Lévesque, the first PQ leader, who opted without question for the adoption of a new political status for Quebec.

Since the 1960s, political discourse around "the nation" has always drawn on the past, but it is projected differently in the future. The BNA Act brought together existing political communities, and the National Assembly was the legitimate voice for the entire national community's aspirations and needs. Therefore, it played a distinct role within the federal Parliament where French Canadians (and, by extension, Quebec) were a minority. Beginning in the late 1960s, constitutional talks were no longer limited to the issues of patriating the constitution and a domestic amending formula but, in an effort to modernize and clarify the fundamental law, they also touched on revising the distribution of powers. These talks also sought to limit growing federal government intrusions in areas of provincial jurisdiction (whether it be in education, health, municipal affairs, natural resources, social assistance, etc.) and increase the Quebec government's jurisdiction over areas such as communications, radio broadcasting, workforce training, social security, culture, etc. As emphasized by law scholars and political scientist Marc Chevrier, "in the view of Quebec governments, the reform of the division of powers came before any other reform. The issue was the coherence of tools needed to offer integrated and comprehensive public policies to the population of Quebec."[86] Quebec also believed it should have a right of veto over constitutional reform to reflect that it was the birthplace of one of Canada's founding peoples. In short, the BNA Act adopted a federative form of the state to account for the fundamental truth that it could not be modified without the participation and consent of Quebec.

The Quebec Parliament:
Recognizing and Exercising the Right to Self-determination

The 1976 election of the PQ profoundly changed the political dynamic. It affirmed the authority and established the legitimacy of the National Assembly as the only place where the political and constitutional future of Quebec could be defined. Therefore, in June 1978, the National Assembly passed a referendum bill, an umbrella act on referendums, under the title "Referendum Act" in order to fully exercise its right to self-determination. Among other things, the act defined the consultation process, identifying the mechanisms controlling spending during a referendum campaign and creating a Conseil du référendum (Referendum Council).[87] The federal government responded with concurrent legislation. In response to a framework law tabled by the federal Parliament in 1978, on 4 May 1978, the PQ voted on the following motion: "that the members of the Assembly unequivocally and firmly reiterate their commitment to the principle that Quebecers alone are entitled to decide their constitutional future, in accordance with the rules and dispositions the Assembly wishes to adopt."[88]

In 1980, 60 percent of Quebecers rejected the PQ's referendum on sovereignty-association with Canada. Taking advantage of this defeat, the federal government took steps to patriate the Canadian Constitution without provincial consent. The National Assembly adopted a resolution on 21 November 1980 demonstrating its opposition to the unilateral federal approach. It affirmed that the Canadian Constitution must be renewed in accordance with the principles of federalism, recalled the fact that the constitution, since 1867, defined the rights of Quebec as a founding member of the Canadian federation and, consequently, requested negotiation between the two orders of government.[89] The Quebec Liberal Party (PLQ) did not support this initiative. On 2 October 1981, after the Supreme Court of Canada released its decision on the constitutionality of unilateral patriation of the Canadian Constitution, all Quebec political parties, with the exception of nine members, supported a resolution tabled by the PQ that would reject any action that could prejudice the rights and affect the powers of the National Assembly.[90] In November 1981, the federal and provincial first ministers announced a constitutional agreement that led to the patriation of the Constitution in April 1982. Only the Quebec government refused to ratify it.

On 17 December 1981, the National Assembly, for the second time, adopted a resolution – which members of the PLQ voted against – to reiterate "the right of the people of Quebec to self-determination" and the "historical right of being a full party to any change to the Constitution of Canada which would affect the rights and powers of Quebec" and to identify the conditions needed for Quebec to accept the plan to patriate the constitution. The first condition was recognition "that the two founding peoples of Canada are fundamentally equal and that

Quebec, by virtue of its language, culture and institutions, forms a distinct society within the Canadian federal system and has all the attributes of a distinct national community."[91]

Throughout these memorable times in Canadian and Quebec politics, the National Assembly was never able to speak with one voice with respect to the federal government's initiatives that led to the adoption of the Constitution Act, 1982. Another result would have been unlikely insofar as those who supported a Quebec within Canada and those who favoured independence were strongly represented in the National Assembly.

After the 1984 election of Brian Mulroney's Progressive Conservative Party, while taking note of the federal government's new openness toward Quebec, Robert Bourassa's provincial Liberal government, elected in 1985, put forward five conditions for Quebec to sign the 1982 Constitution: recognition of Quebec's unique character, a constitutional veto, control of federal spending power, increased provincial powers with respect to immigration, and provincial input in the appointment of Supreme Court judges from Quebec. Negotiated by all the premiers in 1987, the Meech Lake Accord met most of these conditions. On 23 June 1987, with a majority in the National Assembly, the PLQ approved the accord by way of resolution, despite the PQ's opposition. However, the constitutional agreement failed to obtain the support of all provincial legislatures – Manitoba and Newfoundland decided against the accord – and as a result was not ratified. In a speech to the National Assembly on 22 June 1990, Premier Bourassa recalled the efforts made by the Quebec government to submit requests for constitutional amendments deemed "reasonable" by the government party, and in response to the failed agreement, solemnly affirmed that "since 1985, the question has been: '*What does Canada want?*' And we're still waiting for Canada's answer to that question. Mr President, English Canada must clearly understand that, regardless of what is said or done, Quebec is today and always will be a society that is distinct, free and able to assume its destiny and development."[92]

In the wake of this failure, on 4 September 1990, the National Assembly voted unanimously in favour of the bill creating the Commission on the Political and Constitutional Future of Quebec. The commission submitted its report on 27 March 1991. After summarizing the debilitating effects of the Constitution Act, 1982, it recommended either holding a referendum on Quebec sovereignty, or creating a "special committee of the National Assembly with a mandate to assess all offers for a new constitutional partnership made by the Government of

Canada."[93] In response to these recommendations, Mr Bourassa's government submitted Bill 150 to the National Assembly, an Act Respecting the Process for Determining the Political and Constitutional Future of Quebec. It contained three main components: the establishment of two parliamentary committees, one on federal offers, the other on sovereignty; a referendum on sovereignty in June or October 1992; the reiteration of the principle of the National Assembly and the government's leeway. The act was adopted on 20 June 1991 (for, sixty-five; against, twenty-nine). The PQ did not support the bill because it provided a way to renew federalism and preserved the government's flexibility, enabling it to contravene the obligation to hold a referendum on sovereignty. The two committees created by Bill 150 would complete their work separately. The first did not file a report, but rather a draft report prepared by the committee's staff. The second committee's work was completed while the PQ members were absent. The PLQ and the PQ even voted in the National Assembly to reject the committee's report before studying the federal offers.

New constitutional discussions took place between 1990 and 1992. Several parts of the failed Meech Lake Accord were revived as part of a new agreement finalized in Charlottetown in August 1992. Once again, the National Assembly had to make a decision. Premier Bourassa amended Bill 150 to avoid the requirement of holding a referendum on sovereignty if Canada's offers do not meet Quebec's demands based on the assessment made by political actors. On 4 September 1992, after suspending some rules of parliamentary procedure and limiting the duration of debate to two hours (including one hour for opposition members), the Assembly adopted Bill 44, which obligated the Quebec government to hold a referendum on the Charlottetown Accord. The Assembly also adopted the wording of the referendum question approved by the House of Commons. The opposition voted against the government's proposal.

Canadian and Quebec citizens, the latter under Quebec's Referendum Act, were invited to comment on the Charlottetown Accord. It was subsequently defeated by voters in Quebec (56.7 percent voted No) and in five other provinces. In total, 54.3 percent of Canadians rejected the agreement. In September 1994, Jacques Parizeau's PQ government was elected, followed by a second referendum on sovereignty held on 30 October 1995 and a narrow victory for supporters of a united Canada, who won only 50.58 percent of the vote. This would result in a federal initiative to limit the National Assembly's power to determine Quebec's political future.

Quebecers' Right to Decide Their Political and Constitutional Future for Themselves

The 1995 "No's" narrow victory fuelled considerable criticism, mainly from English Canada, over the referendum strategy led by politicians to keep Quebec within Canada. As part of a set of legal and political measures meant to prevent a third referendum, the federal government called on the Supreme Court of Canada in September 1996.[94] In response, on 21 May 1997, the National Assembly unanimously adopted a resolution reaffirming the primacy of Quebec laws and challenging the entire political class, targeting in particular Ottawa's members of Parliament. The resolution read as follows: "That the National Assembly demands that the men and women politicians of Quebec recognize the will, democratically expressed by Quebecers in the referendum of October 30, 1995 held in compliance with the *Referendum Act*, thus acknowledging the fundamental right of Quebecers to determine their future pursuant to this Act."[95] In the House of Commons, the federal minister of intergovernmental affairs announced that Quebecers' right to decide their future for themselves did not exist.[96]

In late August 1998, the Supreme Court of Canada released its *Reference re Secession of Quebec*. It claimed that the Canadian Constitution, as well as international law, did not allow Quebec to unilaterally withdraw from the federation. However, while a unilateral secession is illegal, secession can still be achieved through negotiations conducted in good faith. The novelty of the reference was the obligation to negotiate provided that the question asked as well as the majorities obtained were clear. To give effect to the reference, the federal Parliament adopted the Clarity Act (Bill C–20) in June 2000. The act consists of only three articles. The first states that the Canadian government will decide on the clarity of the question before a referendum on secession is held and discredits the questions asked in the 1980 and 1995 referendums. The second article focuses on the Canadian government's power to assess, after a referendum has been held, if the results are sufficiently clear to undertake negotiations. The third prohibits the use of a unilateral declaration of independence and reiterates that the independence of a province shall be subject to a constitutional amendment. The principle at the heart of Bill C–20 is that the Canadian government, and more particularly the party in power, is the sole judge of what constitutes a "clear" question and majority.

In response to this attempt to harness the authority of the National Assembly, in December 2000, Bill 99, An Act respecting the exercise of the fundamental rights and prerogatives of the Québec people and the Québec State, was adopted despite opposition from members of the PLQ. In the National Assembly, Quebec's premier criticized the federal initiative in these terms:

> The federal Bill C–20 is a head-on collision with the democratic values that are dear to Quebecers. The federal government is seeking to impose a series of legislative padlocks to block the future of Quebecers. On the pretext of clarity, the federal government is acting as if it were seeking to give itself the means to evade the obligation of negotiating in good faith following a referendum favourable to sovereignty, as prescribed by the Supreme Court, advice the federal government itself sought. We subscribe to the obligation of clarity, but we maintain that it is a responsibility only the National Assembly can and must assume.[97]

The bill strongly reiterated several principles: the right of the Quebec people to self-determination; that the Quebec state's legitimacy is derived from the will of the people inhabiting its territory; territorial integrity; and that the will of the people can be expressed only through the National Assembly. The bill was adopted on 7 December 2000, with a sixty-nine to forty-one vote. The Liberals were opposed, fearing that the bill would open the door to challenging the constitutionality of the Quebec law. They would have preferred the adoption of a motion that would have recognized the legitimacy of the Supreme Court of Canada's conclusions, while reaffirming that only the National Assembly can determine the conditions surrounding the referendum process on Quebec's political future.

Recalling these important moments in Quebec's political history serves to emphasize three major concerns. The first was the need to recognize and accept the principle of provincial autonomy. From Premier Honoré Mercier to Maurice Duplessis, it was necessary to respect the powers devolved to the provinces, particularly Quebec, under the BNA Act. Federal initiatives, sometimes interpreted as intrusions in and overlaps of provincial prerogatives, were openly criticized. The second concern was the Quebec government's increased capacity to intervene. This issue became pre-eminent in the 1960s and up until the patriation of the constitution in 1982. Moreover, constitutional negotiations at the time did not permit successive Quebec governments to revise the division of powers, as they had hoped. Instead, the Constitution Act, 1982 was adopted without Quebec's consent. The National Assembly particularly criticized the federal government for not granting Quebec a veto over future constitutional amendments that could directly affect its powers, but also for the adoption of measures concerning English minority-language education in Quebec, nullifying certain provisions of the Charter of the French Language. A final concern has more recently emerged and pertains to the need to protect the National Assembly's power to represent the Quebec people and be the place where they express their will. The Clarity Act assumes both the status and the power to determine the process through which Quebecers will decide their fate. The federal policy initiatives following the 1995 referendum helped to restrict the autonomy of Quebec. They forced the National Assembly to reaffirm the principles presented by Honoré Mercier, at the expense of the emancipatory dynamic that characterized the political struggles after the 1960s.

The Struggles and Symbols of National Identity

The National Assembly has over time spearheaded the defence of provincial autonomy and Quebec's right to self-determination; the debates that took place there and the many laws passed sought to consolidate and promote a singular national identity. Sometimes these actions were symbolic in nature. At other times, they resulted in legislation that focused on specific national identity components. These initiatives attempted to strengthen both the subjective and objective dimensions of national identity. According to Boudon, the former refers to common interests and representations, and to a sense of sharing a common destiny that is different from that of other nations. This destiny is shaped by a shared past, overcoming hardships, founding heroes, and a collective plan for the future. In this sense, "the nation is not only a given, it becomes an ideal, the desire to continue to live together, by overcoming new hardships."[98] The objective dimensions, in turn, are based on tangible and verifiable criteria such as language, religion, ethnicity, habits, and customs, etc.[99] Finally, for the nation to exist, it should have some form of political organization giving it a local presence, institutions, and a basis in the consent of the people.

The Quebec Parliament was one of the main theatres for affirming this type of national identity. A sense of belonging was created through the need to assert a francophone identity in an America dominated by the English language. Therefore, it is important, from the very beginning, to document the first language legislation adopted by Quebec members of Parliament. One member, Armand La Vergne, was instrumental in getting the legislation passed unanimously by the Legislative Assembly in May 1910. It came into force in January 1911. The legislation amended the Quebec Civil Code, forcing public utility companies (railway, shipping, telegraph and telephone, electricity, etc.) to print their contracts in both languages.[100]

After Confederation, there were numerous tensions and conflicts between the two founding national communities in Canada (it being recognized that Aboriginal nations were completely ignored). These divides were clearly present after the 1885 execution by hanging of Catholic Métis leader Louis Riel on the grounds of treason. Riel and the Métis fought against the illegal appropriation of their lands. Refusing to reduce the sentence, Canadian prime minister John A. Macdonald stated, "he shall hang though every dog in Quebec bark in his favour."[101] For Quebec, the hanging of Riel was not of a "rebel," but of a leading figure of French Catholics in the West. This sense of injustice was further exacerbated by restrictions of French Catholic educational rights in Manitoba in 1890 and in the Northwest Territories in 1892. After 1885, reflecting the deterioration of French Catholic status in the province, the Ontario government would convert unilingual French Catholic schools, tolerated up to that point, into bilingual schools. Requests to abolish the separate school systems in the province continued to intensify in the years that followed, eventually leading to the adoption of Regulation 17 in 1912.[102]

The Legislative Assembly passed numerous motions supporting French Canadians' struggles and invited provincial governments to show understanding and respect for their French Catholic minorities.[103] Member of Parliament Armand La Vergne even filed a motion "that it is in the interest and for the well-being of the Dominion, and in accord with the spirit of the federal pact of 1867, that the French language, which in virtue of the Constitution is official, be placed on a footing of equality with the English language in all public matters – for instance, in the coinage of moneys and in the administration of postal affairs."[104] The debate on the rights of French Catholic minorities outside Quebec was indicative of the rise of nationalism among English-speaking Protestant Canadians during the same period.[105] It also represented their impatience with French Catholics, impatience that was quickly perceived as a threat in Quebec given their weak position within the federation.

A review of the discussions that have taken place in the Assembly highlights, implicitly and explicitly, the identity issues that have written the history of the institution since its creation. But if a single public policy should symbolize this approach, it would arguably be the Charter of the French Language, ratified by the National Assembly on 26 August 1977 (Bill 101). The adoption of the charter played a role in creating a collective awareness of the French language's status in the public arena. This issue was particularly pre-eminent during the Quiet Revolution. For instance, in the 1960s, this new way of looking at language led the Royal Commission on Education in Quebec (Parent Commission) to tackle head-on the phenomenon of under-education of French-speaking Quebecers, a concern also expressed through the creation of the Commission of Inquiry on the Situation of the French Language and on Language Rights in Quebec (Gendron Commission) established under the Union nationale government of Jean-Jacques Bertrand in December 1968. Language conflicts in the late 1960s led the Liberal premier Robert Bourassa (elected in 1970) to adopt, in July 1974, the Official Language Act (Bill 22). In the preamble, the French language is presented as "a national heritage, which the body politic is in duty bound to preserve, and it is incumbent upon the government of the province of Quebec to employ every means in its power to ensure the preeminence of that language and to promote its vigour and quality." This legislation required, most notably, that French be the language of commercial signage, that businesses that wanted to deal with the state adopt francization programs, that English school access be restricted to students who had sufficient knowledge of the English language, that French be the language of public administration, and that priority be given to French in legislation. However, the charter's adoption in 1977 broke away from the institutional bilingualism still present in Bill 22. It was based on four principles outlined in the White Paper tabled by Camille Laurin, the minister responsible for cultural development: (1) The French language is not just a means of expression but a medium of living; (2) the state has to respect minorities, their language, and their culture; (3) it is important to learn languages other than French; and (4) the status of the French language in Quebec is a matter of social justice.[106] Moreover, the first statement in the preamble clearly ties together language and identity.[107] Thus, the charter addressed three dilemmas facing Quebec society. It tackled the institutionalization of bilingualism in Quebec; the consequences of the anglicization, especially in public school, of Quebec immigrants (first or second generation); and, finally, the francization of the economy and the workplace. It attempted to transform power relationships in favour of the francophone majority in an effort to stabilize the French language in North America.[108]

We mentioned earlier the National Assembly's numerous debates and struggles to, first, recognize and respect the autonomy of Quebec political institutions and, second, expand their scope. The 1918 Francoeur Motion was prepared in response to animosity between the constituent nations of Canada. The discussion continued with many exchanges between Ottawa's and Quebec's legislative assemblies. In October 2003, the House of Commons, then dominated by the Liberal Party of Canada, refused to vote in favour of a motion proposed by Bloc Québécois (BQ) member Yves Rocheleau, recognizing the Quebec nation while placing the federal government in a binding legal framework that gave Quebec the right to opt out with compensation when new federal programs were created in areas of provincial jurisdiction. The vote had consequences in Quebec. On 30 October 2003, the National Assembly unanimously adopted, and without debate, a motion stating, "the people of Quebec form a nation."[109] Also in response to a motion proposed by the BQ, in November 2006, the House of Commons finally adopted, although in convoluted terms, a motion of recognition introduced by Conservative prime minister Stephen Harper.[110] Then a few days later, the National Assembly also unanimously adopted a motion introduced by Liberal premier Jean Charest, mirroring the federal parliamentary initiative:

> That the National Assembly: takes note of the fact that the House of Commons approved, last 27 November, by a wide majority and with the support of the leaders of all the political parties represented in the Canadian Parliament, the motion moved by the Prime Minister of Canada, which reads as follows: "That this House recognizes that the Québécois form a nation within a united Canada"; recognizes the positive nature of the motion carried by the House of Commons and that it proclaims that this motion in no way diminishes the inalienable rights, constitutional powers and privileges of the National Assembly and of the Québec nation.[111]

Although the contours of the Quebec identity are being redefined throughout history, there are two moments that illustrate this evolution. In 1936, Premier Duplessis hung a crucifix above the chair of the Speaker (now known as the President) in the Legislative Assembly, symbolizing the alliance between the Church and the state, and strengthening the Catholic Church's influence over education, health, and social services.[112] The political elite always considered the Catholic religion to be an important component, along with language, of national identity.

Things have changed significantly since then. On 22 May 2008 at 12:30 p.m., the Consultation Commission on Accommodation Practices Related to Cultural Differences released its report. The same day, the National Assembly held a debate on the basis of Quebecers' common values. Members voted unanimously in favour of a joint motion presented by Jean Charest, Mario Dumont, and Pauline Marois.[113] The premier announced the action his government intended to take, which predicted "a strengthened francization of immigrants before their arrival in Quebec by requiring immigration applicants to sign a statement acknowledging their agreement to respect the common values of our society, a mechanism that will help policy makers to address accommodation issues in accordance with our secular institutions."[114] The assembly then supported a definition that incorporated the objective and subjective dimensions of identity, referring to the sociological, normative, and legal referents that Quebec is a free, democratic, pluralistic society based on the rule of law, equality between women and men, governed by the Charter of the French Language and the separation of Quebec's political and religious powers. Moreover, these aspects are featured in the proposed Quebec Charter of Values, submitted by the PQ government in September 2013, and later on Bill 60, entitled Charter Affirming the Values of State Secularism and Religious Neutrality and of Equality between Women and Men, and providing a framework for accommodation requests. The charter intends to amend the Quebec Charter of Rights and Freedoms in order to include the state's religious neutrality and the secular nature of public institutions, to articulate a duty of confidentiality and neutrality for state employees (restriction on wearing religious symbols that are ostentatious), to require that persons have their face uncovered when giving or receiving services of public bodies, and to establish an implementation policy to ensure religious neutrality and facilitate religious accommodation requests within state agencies.[115] With the defeat of the PQ government in 2014, this bill was never adopted.

CONCLUSION: REFLECTIONS ON KEY ISSUES

Parliament, as a place to express and exercise power, has played a central role in the struggle to build, recognize, and consolidate the Quebec nation. The contours of the nation were converted as one outcome of the conflicts that took place throughout Quebec's social and political history. The debates, resolutions, and legislation adopted by the Legislative Assembly, followed by the National Assembly of Quebec, reflect this history. Parliament had the same political and economic cleavages, expressed the same priorities and, often, the same conflicting views as the people and the nation. Rarely were people unanimous in their desire. More often, parliamentarians, by the very nature of the institution, pitted themselves against each other. Nevertheless, the Parliament of Quebec's work played a powerful role in defining the political parameters and representing the Quebec nation and its identity. This work was often influenced by the dynamics of the relationships between the initially conquered minority nation and the dominant national group.

The Assembly's history began with its quest for representation, autonomy, and legitimacy. From 1763, the elites of the former New France wished to have representative institutions. Three decades later this wish was fulfilled with the creation of Lower Canada and the establishment of a representative assembly in 1791. Fifty years later Canada achieved real responsible government under the Act of Union in 1848. And, in 1867 the BNA Act (1867), adopted by the Westminster Government in London, created the Legislative Assembly as we know it today.

The federal form of government allowed the provinces to develop their own state structure. However, the place then occupied by the Parliament of Quebec in the Canadian political system was part of a tradition established by the United Kingdom, characterized by a flexible separation between the legislative and executive branches of the state. This remains an essential feature and should be stressed since it explains the important role played by the premier and the members of cabinet. Even though the Assembly designates its members, they have considerable flexibility when they control the Assembly in a majority government. When Parliament "speaks," that is to say when it adopts legislation, it is usually the parliamentary majority that imposes its views. This majority reflects imperfectly the electorate's political preferences because the first-past-the-post system, also inherited from the United Kingdom, usually brings to power a parliamentary group (known as a political party) holding an absolute majority of seats, while a majority of voters voted against them. The 1989 provincial election was the last time a party, in this case the PLQ, raked in an absolute majority of votes. With the increase in third parties, the probability of this happening again is dwindling.

If Parliament, as a whole, were to allow different interests, options, ideologies, and political preferences to be expressed and heard, the parliamentary group with executive authority would not represent the majority opinion. Similarly, the Assembly, made up of members with a general education and socio-professional status, better represents the middle-class professionals or entrepreneurs in Quebec than the working class and average wage earners. The Legislative Assembly has never represented, either yesterday or today, the complexity of the social fabric of Quebec.

That said, the Parliament of Quebec, as holder of the supreme authority of the Quebec government, not only actively participated in political struggles to define, defend, and sometimes strengthen Quebec's autonomy but also often served as the primary location where terms used in the political arena were defined. From the point of view of the representatives involved, these struggles took place within the imaginary boundaries of Quebec according to the institutional and ideational limits imposed by the central government. Indeed, the Legislative Assembly, later the National Assembly, was both confronted and questioned by the federal Parliament. This dual effort was and will continue to be significant for Quebec's future.

Thus, the political struggles for the nation's autonomy are informed by three dynamics. The first is resistance, which is characterized by the need to recognize and respect the principle of autonomy. Since the late nineteenth century, Quebec's premiers have chosen this particular issue in an effort to mitigate the Parliament of Canada's tutelary power over the Quebec Legislative Assembly's powers and prerogatives. This fight coloured most notably Premier Duplessis' leadership, but fell within the approach adopted by most government leaders who preceded him.

The second is the need for emancipation. The Quiet Revolution differed from previous periods in that it took action not only to protect and enforce Quebec's autonomy but also to broaden its scope. These concerns have led to a growing constitutional debate and expanding political options. Quebec's nation-building project was developed at a time when the Canadian political society revised its own identity references while establishing the welfare state and international migration flows and severing political and symbolic ties with the British Empire. The symbols and political institutions representing this new "Canadian-ness" also required adjustments. The struggles between competing political projects, built around the principle of Canadian citizenship for some, Quebec for others, would be shifted to the field of constitutional politics. The expansion of the Quebec state's powers, such as the independence project supported by a large number of Quebecers, would have to face Ottawa's centralized power.

The third is the need for recognition and self-determination (within or outside Canada). The 1960s through the mid-1990s was a period marked by three referendums (1980, 1992, and 1995) as well as by the patriation of the Canadian Constitution in 1982. During this time, the National Assembly led efforts to ensure the recognition of two central dimensions of its political life: Quebec's national character and its right to self-determination, two dimensions that have been jeopardized by the federal government. More specifically, the defeat of the sovereignist coalition in the 1995 referendum led the Canadian Parliament to impose limits on Quebec's use of its right to self-determination. The Clarity Act performed this binding function, reducing the National Assembly's ability to determine the political future of Quebec.

At the same time as these political struggles often pit Canadian and Quebec parliaments against each other, the National Assembly has helped to change how the "nation" is perceived, characterized, and defined. Consequently, the Assembly was heavily involved in a dynamic of internal affirmation. Language legislation and, more particularly, the adoption of the Charter of the French Language, but also control over the immigrant selection process, often harrowing debates over "common values" and the adoption of national identity symbols – all these have confirmed the central role played by the National Assembly in this dynamic.

The parameters defining the scope and limits of the nation's autonomy are themselves the subject of fierce struggles. Issues surrounding Quebec's inclusion in Canadian society and the compatibility of Quebec and Canadian identities are far from being resolved. For some, the powers held by Quebec in the current Canadian federal framework meet the needs of Quebecers. For others, the degree of autonomy should be increased to ensure that, on a global level, Quebec's distinct features with regard to language, culture, and essential solidarity among minority nations can continue to have a significant presence in North America. In this regard, the Parliament of Quebec will continue to be a theatre of important political competition that presents conflicting – and often irreconcilable – projects relating to the very foundations of the nation.

At the heart of Quebec's identity is the fact that it is the heir of the encounter in the Americas of two great state and juridical traditions of Western modernity: the French and British traditions. Operating essentially in French, claiming French-based civil law as one of its key jurisdictions, Quebec's Parliament has inherited and adapted the British parliamentary customs and practices. This allows the Parliament to establish major cooperation relations with the parliaments of La Francophonie and those of the Commonwealth. This is not an insignificant presence on the world stage.

NOTES

1 Gilles Gallichan, "Nos parlements: une histoire mouvementée," *Cap-aux-Diamants: la revue d'histoire du Québec* 30 (1992): 14.

2 Jean-Charles Bonenfant, *La réforme du travail parlementaire au Québec* (Québec: Assemblée législative du Québec, 1964); Denis Vaugeois, *L'Assemblée nationale en devenir: pour un meilleur équilibre des institutions* (Québec: Assemblée nationale, 1982); Réjean Pelletier, "Les fonctions du député: bilan des réformes parlementaires à Québec," *Politique* 6 (1984): 145–64; Assemblée nationale du Québec, *Journal des débats, le jeudi 7 décembre*, 2000, http://www.assnat.qc.ca/fr/travaux-parlementaires /assemblee-nationale/36-1/journal-debats/20001207/9425.html (accessed 20 January 2013); Marie-Christine Gilbert, "L'impact de la Loi sur l'administration publique sur le contrôle parlementaire," master's thesis, Université Laval, 2009, 175.

3 Jean-Charles Bonenfant, "Le parlementarisme québécois," in *Réflexions sur la politique au Québec* (Québec: Les Presses de l'Université du Québec, 1970), 24.

4 Henri Brun, *La formation des institutions parlementaires québécoises 1791–1838* (Québec: Les Presses de l'Université du Québec, 1970).

5 Michel Bonsaint, *La procédure parlementaire du Québec*, 3rd ed. (Québec: Bibliothèque de l'Assemblée nationale, 2012), 1.

6 In the National Archives there are passages referring to an *Assembly* shortly before the Royal Proclamation of 1763. For example, in a letter to George Dunk, Earl of Halifax, dated 4 October 1763, the Lords of Trade wrote: "That it will be expedient for His Majesty's Service, and give Confidence and Encouragement to such Persons as are inclined to become Settlers in the new Colonies, That an immediate and public Declaration should be made of the intended permanent Constitution and that the power of calling Assemblies should be inserted in the first Commissions, We have therefore drawn the Proclamation agreeable to this Opinion, and have prepared the Commissions accordingly; and we humbly hope Our Conduct herein will meet with His Majesty's approbation, as we conceive, that any temporary Power of making Ordinances and Regulations, which must of necessity be allowed to the Governors and Councils before Assemblies can be called, as well as the mode of exercising that Power, will be better inserted in the Instructions, which we are now preparing" (Adam Shortt and Arthur G. Doughty, eds, *Documents Relating to the Constitutional History of Canada 1759–1791*, 1918, http://archive .org/stream/documentsrelatino1publuoft#page/156/mode/2up, accessed 23 September 2013).

7 Shortt and Doughty, *Documents Relating to the Constitutional History of Canada 1759–1791*, 165.

8 Bonsaint, *La procédure parlementaire du Québec*; Brun, *La formation des institutions parlementaires québécoises 1791–1838*. Brun explains the process with a legal argument: "the king could have chosen when to abolish his prerogative, but once he became involved, he could no longer go back. To escape the royal prerogative marked, for a colony, the emergence of a local legislature. The first British institutional principle (the participation of an elective chamber in legislation) should be applied, in relation to the colony, on the local level and not only at the imperial level. The Imperial Parliament's legislation was sufficient to ensure compliance, in all practical cases, but it should have been institutionally possible to also obtain the same respect in the colony" (5).

9 Bonsaint, *La procédure parlementaire du Québec*, 14–15.

10 Shortt and Doughty, *Documents Relating to the Constitutional History of Canada 1759–1791*, 495; Bonsaint, *La procédure parlementaire du Québec*, 15.

11 Finlay to Napean, Québec, 22 October 1784, in Shortt and Doughty, *Documents Relating to the Constitutional History of Canada 1759–1791*, vol. 1, part 2, 739.

12 Michel Ameller and Georges Bergougnous, *L'Assemblée nationale* (Paris: Presses universitaires de France, 1994), 3.

13 Brun, *La formation des institutions parlementaires québécoises 1791–1838*, 9.

14 Ibid., 12.

15 1791, 31 Georges III, c. 31 (R.-U.) (reproduced in L.R.C. (1985), app. II, no 3).

16 Henri Brun, "La Constitution de 1791," *Recherches Sociographiques* 10, no.1 (1969): 37.

17 Bonsaint, *La procédure parlementaire du Québec*, 15–16.

18 Brun, "La Constitution de 1791," 38.

19 Réjean Pelletier, "Le parlementarisme québécois : une copie (trop?) fidèle au modèle de Westminster," in Éric Montigny and François Gélineau, eds, *Parlementarisme et Francophonie* (Québec: Presses de l'Université Laval), 33–4.

20 Magali Paquin, *L'Assemblée nationale du Québec* (Ottawa: Groupe Canadien d'étude des parlements, 2011), 4; Brun, "La Constitution de 1791," 38.

20 Pelletier, "Le parlementarisme québécois," 34.

21 Paquin, *L'Assemblée nationale du Québec*.

22 Bonsaint, *La procédure parlementaire du Québec*, 19.

23 Brun, *La formation des institutions parlementaires québécoises 1791–1838*, 16–19.

24 Paquin, *L'Assemblée nationale du Québec*, 12.

25 Philippe Boudreau and Claude Perron, *350 mots de science politique* (Montréal: Chenelière/McGraw-Hill, 1998), 2.

26 Bonsaint, *La procédure parlementaire du Québec*; John Hare, *Aux origines du parlementarisme québécois, 1791–1793. Étude et documents* (Sillery: Les Éditions du Septentrion, 1993), 85; Pelletier, "Le parlementarisme québécois," 34.

27 Paquin, *L'Assemblée nationale du Québec*, 4–5.

28 Pelletier, "Le parlementarisme québécois," 35.

29 Louis Massicotte, *Parlement du Québec, de 1867 à aujourd'hui* (Québec: Presses de l'Université Laval, 2009), 113–81; Paquin, *L'Assemblée nationale du Québec*, 6.

30 Paquin, *L'Assemblée nationale du Québec*, 7.

31 Pelletier, "Le parlementarisme québécois," 44–5.

32 Bonsaint, *La procédure parlementaire du Québec*, 50.

33 Jean-Maurice Arbour, "Axiomatique constitutionnelle et pratique politique: un décalage troublant," *Les Cahiers de Droit* 20, no. 1–2 (1955): 118.

34 Ibid., 118–19; Henri Brun, Guy Tremblay, and Eugénie Brouillet, *Droit constitutionnel* (Cowansville: Éditions Yvon Blais, 2008).

35 Ronald Watts, *Comparing Federal Systems* (Montreal & Kingston: McGill-Queen's University Press, 1998); Kathy Brock, "Executive Federalism: Beggar Thy Neighbour?", in François Rocher and Miriam Smith, eds, *New Trends in Canadian Federalism* (Peterborough: Broadview Press, 2003), 67–83; Daniel J. Savoie, *Breaking the Bargain: Public Servants, Ministers and Parliament* (Toronto: University of Toronto Press, 2003); Guy Laforest and Éric Montigny, "Le Fédéralisme exécutif: problèmes et actualité," in Réjean Pelletier and Manon Tremblay, eds, *Le Parlementarisme canadien* (Québec: Les Presses de l'Université Laval, 2006), 345–73; Arthur Benz, "Multilevel Parliaments in Canada and Europe," *International Journal* 66, no. 1 (2011): 109–25.

36 Laforest and Montigny, "Le Fédéralisme exécutif: problèmes et actualité," 353–4.

37 Donald J. Savoie, *Governing from the Centre: The Concentration of Power in Canadian Politics* (Toronto: University of Toronto Press, 1999).

38 Joanne Poirier, "Intergovernmental Agreements in Canada: At the Cross-Roads between Law and Politics," in Peter J. Meekison, Hamish Telford, and Harvey Lazar, eds, *Reconsidering the Institutions of Canadian Federalism* (Kingston: Institute of Intergovernmental Relations, 2004), 425–62; Joanne Poirier, "Les ententes intergouvernementales dans les régimes fédéraux: aux confins du droit et du non-droit," in Jean-François

Gaudreault-Desbiens and Fabien Gélinas, eds, *Le fédéralisme dans tous ses états: Gouvernance, identité et méthodologie* (Montréal/Bruxelles: Carswell/Bruylant, 2005), 441–74.

39 Richard Simeon and Amy Nugent, "Parliamentary Canada and Intergovernmental Canada: Exploring the Tensions," in Herman Bakvis and Grace Skogstad, eds, *Canadian Federalism: Performance, Effectiveness, and Legitimacy* (Toronto: Oxford University Press, 2008), 89–112.

40 Meekison, Telford, and Lazar, eds, *Reconsidering the Institutions of Canadian Federalism.*

41 Richard Simeon and David Cameron, "Intergovernmental Relations and Democracy: An Oxymoron if ever There Was One," in Bakvis and Skogstad, *Canadian Federalism: Performance, Effectiveness, and Legitimacy*, 278–95.

42 The Parliament of Quebec is indeed composed of only one chamber: the National Assembly's Blue Room. As highlighted by Éric Montigny and Réjean Pelletier, "the Legislative Council, whose function was relatively similar to the Senate, was abolished in 1968. The Red Room, now used by major parliamentary committees, at one time housed the Legislative Council" (Réjean Pelletier and Éric Montigny, "Le pouvoir législatif: le Sénat et la Chambre des communes," in Pelletier and Tremblay, *Le parlementarisme canadien*, 293). Edmond Orban explained that in Canada "the largest province, Ontario, and the other western provinces deemed this system useless. Manitoba had an elected upper house between 1870 and 1876, Prince Edward Island abolished its house in 1893 at almost the same time that its neighbour New Brunswick did. Finally, Nova Scotia, a rather traditional province, abolished its Legislative Council in 1928. It was Canada's oldest and was very difficult to abolish. As for Quebec's Legislative Council, it was the last upper house to be dissolved in Canada. It survived until 1968." Edmond Orban, "Le bicaméralisme québécois: rétrospective comparative," *Revue d'Histoire de l'Amérique française* 25, no. 2 (1971): 194.

43 Bonsaint, *La procédure parlementaire du Québec*, 174–5.

44 Ibid., 173–5.

45 Manon Tremblay and Sarah Andrews, "Les femmes nommées ministres au Canada pendant la période 1921–2007: la loi de la disparité progressive est-elle dépassée?," *Recherches féministes* 23, no. 1 (2010): 148–57.

46 Robert Boily, "Les hommes politiques du Québec 1867–1967," *Revue d'histoire de l'Amérique française*, 21, no. 3a (1967): 599–634; Paquin, *L'Assemblée nationale du Québec.*

47 Réjean Pelletier, "Le personnel politique," *Recherches sociographiques* 25, no. 1 (1984): 100.

48 However, Réjean Pelletier clarifies that these data do not necessarily reflect an official educational credential, but rather a level of education attained by the member, whether the schooling has been sanctioned by a
diploma or not. See Pelletier, "Le personnel politique," 87n13.

49 Paquin, *L'Assemblée nationale du Québec*, 25.

50 Magali Paquin, "Un portrait des Députés québécois, 2003, 2007 et 2008,"
Politique et Sociétés 29, no. 3 (2010): 21–37.

51 Boily, "Les hommes politiques du Québec 1867–1967"; André Gélinas,
Les parlementaires et l'administration au Québec (Québec: Les Presses de
l'Université Laval, 1969); Pelletier,
"Le personnel politique"; Réjean Pelletier, "Les parlementaires québécois
depuis cinquante ans: continuité et renouvellement," *Revue d'histoire de
l'Amérique française* 44, no. 3 (1991): 339–61; Réjean Pelletier, "Le
personnel politique québécois: un bilan," in Robert Boily, ed., *L'année
politique au Québec 1997–1998*,
http://www.pum.umontreal.ca/apqc/97_98/pelletie/pelletie.htm, accessed
22 January 2013; Paquin, *L'Assemblée nationale du Québec*.

52 If we consider the percentage according to the level of education attained, without graduation, this figure is higher, 88 percent or 104 of 117.
Informally, we conclude that in 2012 the PQ elected fifty-one members,
two with a doctorate, eleven with a master's degree, and twenty-three
with a bachelor's degree, while twelve had a DCS and three completed
studies not sanctioned by a diploma. Among the forty-seven Liberals
who have posted their profiles, there are five with a doctorate, eleven
with a master's degree, fifteen with a bachelor's degree, nine with a DCS,
and seven completed studies not sanctioned by a diploma. For the nineteen caucus members, two received a master's degree, seven a bachelor's
degree, and five a DCS or a high school diploma, while two do not have a
degree. Québec solidaire members have a bachelor's degree and a doctoral degree (medicine). In short, in 2012, 66 percent of Quebec members
have a bachelor's or graduate degree (seventy-eight out of 117).

53 More specifically, the PQ has 49 percent of members who completed
graduate studies, while the PLQ has 34 percent. This number is even lower
for the CAQ at only 10 percent, whereas, 21 percent of PQ representatives
and 32 percent of PLQ representatives have an undergraduate degree. In
the CAQ, 36 percent of members have an undergraduate degree. Québec
solidaire has one member with a graduate degree and another with an
undergraduate degree.

54 Pelletier, "Le personnel politique," 90.

55 Paquin, *L'Assemblée nationale du Québec*, 24–6.

56 Paquin, "Un portrait des Députés québécois, 2003, 2007 et 2008."

57 Ibid., 23.

58 Bonsaint, *La procédure parlementaire du Québec*, 50; Brun, Tremblay, and Brouillet, *Droit constitutionnel*, 591–2, 598.

59 Philippe Séguin, "L'Évolution du rôle des parlementaires," *Les Cahiers de droit* 42, no. 3 (2001): 356.

60 Bonsaint, *La procédure parlementaire du Québec*, 414.

61 Bonsaint also noted, "the statistics in this regard are also revealing. During the 34th Parliament, the Assembly adopted 369 public bills from the government and only 7 from members; during the 35th Parliament, the Assembly adopted 308 public bills submitted by the government and 11 by members. During the 36th Parliament, 305 public bills from the government were adopted and 13 from members. During the 37th Parliament, 167 public bills from the government were adopted and only 5 from members. Finally, during the 38th Parliament, 72 public bills were adopted from the government and two from members, even though it was a minority government." Bonsaint, *La procédure parlementaire du Québec*, 414n3.

62 Séguin, "L'Évolution du rôle des parlementaires," 357.

63 David Forbes, "Les projets de loi d'initiative parlementaire sont-ils encore utiles?" *Revue Parlementaire canadienne* 35, no. 4 (2012): 6.

64 Bonsaint, *La procédure parlementaire du Québec*, 415.

65 Séguin, "L'Évolution du rôle des parlementaires," 358.

66 Arthur Isaac Silver, *The French-Canadian Idea of Confederation, 1864–1900* (Toronto: University of Toronto Press, 1997).

67 The federal government uses its powers to subordinate the provinces by rejecting provincial legislation. It can appoint lieutenant governors and federal court judges, as well as use its residual power to exercise any powers not explicitly assigned to provincial legislatures.

68 Thomas-Jean-Jacques Loranger (1823–1885) was a minister in the Macdonald-Cartier ministry. At the time, he stated that Confederation was the result of an agreement between the provinces and the Imperial Parliament, and that the Parliament of Canada could not encroach on the powers of the provinces, and, hence, they exercised their full sovereignty in areas under provincial jurisdiction. In this way, the provinces could not in any way be dependent on the federal government. Justice Loranger defended the idea of absolute equality between the two. Joseph Octave Pelland, *Biographie, discours, conférences, etc. de l'Hon. Honoré Mercier* (Montréal, s.n, 1890), 397–404.

69 *Canadian Encyclopedia*, "Military Service Act," http://www.thecanadianencyclopedia.ca/fr/article/military-service-act/, accessed 28 August 2014.

70 Quoted in Réal Bélanger, Richard Jones, and Marc Vallières, *Les grands*

débats parlementaires 1792–1992 (Québec: Presses de l'Université Laval, 1994), 25. This is why he insisted at the time on filing the motion to the Legislative Assembly on the failure of Confederation. In his words, "all our struggles have aimed to exclusively defend what we consider to be the expression of the Constitution. Impartial history will witness that French Canadians remained above all Canadians! In some neighbour-hoods, it is difficult to understand this mentality. If this struggle considers us to be a plague on Confederation, an obstacle to a united Canada, to progress and to development of this country, it can only lead to one result: the rupture of the federal pact." Quoted in Philippe Thérien, *Les grands discours de l'histoire du Québec* (Québec: Presses de l'Université Laval, 2010), 190–1.

71 Please note the interventions by Liberal premier Lomer Gouin on the weakness of federal transfers and the province of Quebec's inability to adequately fulfill its obligations and, similarly, those of his successor, Louis-Alexandre Taschereau (1920–1936), who, in the Speech from the Throne on 18 January 1928, reiterated that he "believes the factor that will best ensure Canadian unity and save Canada's future, lies in respecting provincial autonomy and in the fidelity to the spirit and the letter of Confederation" (*Speech from the Throne*, available at http://www.archives politiquesduquebec.com/discours/p-m-du-quebec/louis-alexandre-taschereau/discours-du-trone-quebec-18-janvier-1928/, accessed 17 August 2014).

72 Quoted by René Durocher, "Maurice Duplessis et sa conception de l'autonomie provinciale au début de sa carrière politique," *Revue d'histoire de l'Amérique française* 23, no. 1 (1969): 33–4.

73 François-Albert Angers, "Les relations fédérales-provinciales sous Duplessis," in Alain-G. Gagnon and Michel Sarra-Bournet, eds, *Duplessis: Entre la grande noirceur et la société libérale* (Montréal: Les Éditions Québec/Amérique, 1997), 231–43.

74 Louis Balthazar, *Bilan du nationalisme au Québec* (Montréal: Éditions de L'Hexagone, 1986).

75 Bernard Saint-Aubin, *Duplessis et son époque* (Montréal: Les Éditions La Presse Limitée, 1979); Gérard Boismenu, *Le duplessisme* (Montréal: Les Presses de l'Université de Montréal, 1981); Richard Jones, *Duplessis and the Union Nationale Administration* (Ottawa: Canadian Historical Association, 1983).

76 François Rocher, "La dynamique Québec-Canada ou le refus de l'idéal fédéral," in Alain-G. Gagnon, ed., *Le fédéralisme canadien contemporain* (Montréal: Les Presses de l'Université de Montréal, 2006), 93–146; Gérard Boismenu, "Politique constitutionnelle et fédéralisme canadien: la vision

de la Commission Tremblay," *Bulletin d'histoire politique* 16 (automne 2007): 17–29.

77 Québec, *Rapport de la Commission royale d'enquête sur les problèmes constitutionnels* (Québec: Commission royale d'enquête sur les problèmes constitutionnels, 1956), 98.

78 Québec, *Rapport de la Commission royale d'enquête sur les problèmes constitutionnels*, 107.

79 Marc Chevrier, "La conception pluraliste et subsidiaire de l'État dans le rapport Tremblay de 1956," *Cahiers d'histoire du Québec au XXe siècle* 2 (été 1994): 45–58.

80 Dominique Foisy-Geoffroy, "Le Rapport de la Commission Tremblay (1953–1956), testament politique de la pensée traditionaliste canadienne-française," *Revue d'histoire de l'Amérique française* 60, no. 3 (2007): 266.

81 René Durocher and Michèle Jean, "Duplessis et la Commission royale d'enquête sur les problèmes constitutionnels, 1953–1956," *Revue d'histoire de l'Amérique française* 25, no. 3 (1971): 337–63.

82 Speech by Jean Lesage to the Empire & Canadian Club, Toronto, 16 November 1964, 3–4, and to the Sainte-Foy Chamber of Commerce, 14 December 1965, 5.

83 François Rocher, "Pour un réaménagement du régime constitutionnel: Québec d'abord!," in Robert Comeau, Michel Lévesque, and Yves Bélanger, eds, *Daniel Johnson: Rêve d'égalité et projet d'indépendance* (Québec: Presses de l'Université du Québec, 1991), 211–36.

84 François Rocher, "'Retour vers le futur': de Daniel Johnson à Daniel Johnson," in Michel Sarra-Bournet, ed., with the collaboration of J. Saint-Pierre, *Les nationalismes au Québec du XIXe au XXIe siècle* (Québec: Les Presses de l'Université Laval, 2001), 133–44.

85 Daniel Johnson, *Égalité ou indépendance: 25 ans plus tard à l'heure de Meech* (Montréal: VLB Éditeur, 1990), 124.

86 Marc Chevrier, *Le fédéralisme canadien et l'autonomie du Québec: perspective historique* (Québec: Ministère des Relations internationales, 1996), 9.

87 Henri Brun and Guy Tremblay, "Consultations populaires québécoises et référendums fédéraux," *Les Cahiers de droit* 20, no. 1–2 (1979): 140.

88 Québec, *Positions du Québec dans les domaines constitutionnel et intergouvernemental de 1936 à mars 2001*, Secrétariat aux affaires intergouvernementales canadiennes, 2004, 51.

89 Ibid., 58.

90 Ibid., 326.

91 Benoît Pelletier, "Les rapports de force entre les majorités et les minorités de langue officielle au Canada," *Revue de droit de l'Université de Sherbrooke* 24, no. 2 (1994): 262.

92 Québec, *Positions du Québec dans les domaines constitutionnel et intergouvernemental de 1936 à mars 2001*, 76.

93 Alain-G. Gagnon and Daniel Latouche, *Allaire, Bélanger, Campeau et les autres: Les Québécois s'interrogent sur leur avenir* (Montréal: Les Éditions Québec/Amérique, 1991), 602.

94 Daniel Turp, *La nation bâillonnée: Le plan B ou l'offensive d'Ottawa contre le Québec* (Montréal: VLB éditeur, 2000).

95 Québec, *Positions du Québec dans les domaines constitutionnel et intergouvernemental de 1936 à mars 2001*, 102–3.

96 For example, on 10 February 1998, the federal minister Stéphane Dion stated, "What is at issue is the claim by the current Quebec government that, under the international law … they have the right to proclaim themselves the government of an independent state as a result of a referendum process they alone would have defined and interpreted. We believe there is no such right." House of Commons, 1998, http://www.parl..gc.ca/HousePublications/Publication.aspx?Language=E&Mode=1&Parl=36&Ses=1&DocId=2332761&File=0, accessed 27 August 2015.

97 Briefing notes for a speech by Quebec premier Lucien Bouchard, at the time of the tabling of the bill respecting the exercise of the fundamental rights and prerogatives of the Québec people and the Québec state, Québec National Assembly, 15 December 1999, 1.

98 Boudon, quoted in Philippe Boudreau and Claude Perron, *350 mots de science politique*, 84.

99 Ibid.

100 Marcel Martel and Martin Pâquet, *Langue et politique au Canada et au Québec: Une synthèse historique* (Montréal: Boréal, 2010), 87.

101 George F.G. Stanley, "Louis Riel," *Revue d'histoire de l'Amérique française* 18, no. 1 (1964): 14–26; John Michael Bumsted and Marie-Hélène Duval, *Louis Riel c. Canada: les années rebelles* (Saint-Boniface: Éditions des Plaines, 2005).

102 Fernand Harvey, "Le français menacé: Le Canada français et la question linguistique," in Hélène Duval, Pierre Georgeault, and Michel Plourde, eds, *Le français au Québec: 400 ans d'histoire et de vie* (Québec: Conseil de la langue française, 2000), 124.

103 Martel and Pâquet, *Langue et politique au Canada et au Québec*, 86.

104 Ibid., 87.

105 Silver, *The French-Canadian Idea of Confederation, 1864–1900*, 185.

106 Jean-Claude Corbeil, *L'embarras des langues: Origine, conception et évolution de la politique linguistique québécoise* (Montréal: Les Éditions Québec/Amérique, 2007), 231–3.

107 Indeed, the preamble stated most notably the following elements: "the

distinctive language of a people that is in the majority French-speaking, is the instrument by which that people has articulated its identity," in respect of diversity to the extent that "the National Assembly of Québec recognizes that Quebecers wish to see the quality and influence of the French language assured, and is resolved therefore to make of French the language of Government and the Law, as well as the normal and everyday language of work, instruction, communication, commerce and business" and where it "recognizes the right of the Amerindians and the Inuit of Québec, the first inhabitants of this land, to preserve and develop their original language and culture" (*Charter of the French Language*, L.R.Q., c. C–11).

108   Guy Rocher, "Les dilemmes identitaires à l'origine de la Charte de la langue française," *Revue d'aménagement linguistique*, Hors-série (automne 2002): 17–24.

109   Québec, "Journal des débats, le jeudi 30 octobre," Assemblée nationale du Québec, 38 (19), 2003, http://www.assnat.qc.ca/fr/travaux-parlementaires/assemblee-nationale/37-1/journal-debats/20031030/2499.html#_Toc55374071, accessed 20 January 2013.

110   The English version of the motion opts for a sociological definition of the nation, which refers to French language citizens using the term "Québécois" rather than "Quebeckers," which helps to limit the political significance: "That this House recognize that the *Québécois* form a nation within a united Canada" (House of Commons, 2006, http://www.parl.gc.ca/housepublications/Publication.aspx?Docid=2528725, accessed 27 August 2014).

111   Québec, "Journal des débats, le jeudi 30 novembre," Assemblée nationale du Québec, 39 (65), 2006, http://www.assnat.qc.ca/fr/travaux-parlementaires/assemblee-nationale/37-2/journal-debats/20061130/2991.html#_Toc152746599, accessed 20 January 2013.

112   Jacques Rouillard, "Le crucifix de l'Assemblée nationale," *Le Devoir*, 27 janvier 2007, A7.

113   The motion reads: "That the National Assembly reiterate its desire to promote the language, history, culture and values of the Québec nation, foster the integration of each person into our nation in a spirit of openness and reciprocity, and express its attachment to our religious and historic heritage represented particularly by the crucifix in our Blue Room and our coat of arms adorning our institutions." Note that throughout the discussions, there was never any mention of the crucifix. Québec, 2008, http://www.premier-ministre.gouv.qc.ca/actualites/communiques/details.asp?idCommunique=812, accessed 27 August 2014.

114 Québec, "Journal des débats, le jeudi 30 novembre," Assemblée
       nationale du Québec, 40 (87), http://www.assnat.qc.ca/fr/travaux-
       parlementaires/assemblee-nationale/38-1/journal-debats/20080522/3183
       .html, accessed 20 January 2013.
115 Québec, *Parce que nos valeurs, on y croit* (Québec: Gouvernement du
       Québec, 2013).

6

The Scottish Parliament

MICHAEL KEATING

The United Kingdom of Great Britain was created in 1707 by the Acts of Union passed in the parliaments of England and Scotland, which replaced the two parliaments with a new Parliament of Great Britain. English historians, jurists, and politicians have seen this new body as the continuation of the old English Parliament, inheriting all its prerogatives and, in the form of the Monarch-in-Parliament, incarnating absolute sovereignty. Scottish doctrine has tended to the view that this was a new parliament, which could not possess absolute sovereignty since the old Scottish Parliament had made no such claims. For most of the last three hundred years, this has remained a matter of arcane debate, without practical implications, although a judgment of the Court of Session in 1953 did uphold the "Scottish" interpretation.[1]

Another feature of the union was that it preserved separate legal systems in England-and-Wales and in Scotland. It was common practice in many fields, including criminal justice, civil law, education, health, housing, and local government, to pass parallel laws for the two jurisdictions, or include Scottish clauses in British (or United Kingdom) bills.[2] Scotland also preserved its own court system and hence case law. During the late nineteenth century, as the state expanded its role, there was a tendency to set up separate administrative arrangements, gradually consolidated in the Scottish Office (established 1885) under a Secretary (of State) who was by convention a Scottish parliamentarian of the ruling United Kingdom (UK) party. It was often noted then that Scotland possessed two of the classic branches of government (executive and judiciary) while lacking the third (legislative).

Administrative devolution was gradually extended, partly for reasons of administrative efficiency but also to buy off periodic bouts of Scottish nationalism (discussed below). It was part of a wider strategy of accepting the plurinational nature of the UK polity while not conceding real power to the periphery. The strategy was supported by the two parties of state, Labour and Conservative, who dominated UK government from the First World War onward; the third British party, the Liberals, was in principle in favour of a form of federalism known as Home-Rule-All-Round but always gave priority to Ireland.

The system had a number of negative effects. It meant that English majorities could impose their will on all legislation, even when they did not constitute the Scottish majority. There was not even the safeguard of rebellions within the ruling party, which have sometimes held legislation for England in check, since English MPs would never rebel on Scottish matters, but instead provided reliable "lobby fodder." In the 1980s, for example, the UK government was able to impose a series of reforms in Scottish local government finance, culminating in the notorious poll tax (tried out first in Scotland) without a single rebellion. Another effect of the Scottish Office system was weak ministerial control, since the civil servants were in Edinburgh while the ministers spent most of the week in London (in Parliament) and had wide spans of responsibility. There was a further deficit of accountability within Scotland since various policy enclaves had retained a degree of autonomy both from Westminster (which was not interested in them) and from wider Scottish society (in the absence of a Scottish legislature). This applied particularly to the Scottish legal system.

While unionism was dominant in the main political parties during the twentieth century, it was regularly challenged by nationalists and autonomists. There were strong Home Rule mobilizations in the 1880s, before and after the First World War, after the Second World War, during the 1970s, and during the 1990s. In every opinion poll ever conducted and in every election at which a party presented home rule in its manifesto, a majority of Scots supported autonomy. The two main parties, however, resisted. Conservative unionists feared that home rule would inevitably lead to separation. Labour politicians shared this fear and also worried about working class unity and, from the 1940s, the unitary welfare state. At times of *relative* economic depression (the 1930s, 1950s, 1980s), support for home rule fell and unionists argued that Scotland could not maintain itself. At times of relative prosperity, support for home rule increased. Support also rose when Scotland was ruled by a party for which it had not voted.

During the 1970s, under severe electoral pressure from the Scottish National Party (SNP), Labour returned to its historic home rule traditions and agreed to set up a Scottish Assembly with legislative powers.

This was hampered by divisions within the Labour Party, the loss of the party's majority during the passage of the legislation, and a requirement imposed by Parliament requiring a referendum and support by a majority of those voting, but only if they represented at least 40 percent of the entire electorate. The Conservative Party campaigned against, after giving a solemn promise that a Conservative government would introduce a better bill, as did a significant section of the Labour Party. Independent and Liberal voters (the historic home rule party) were put off by the insistence that the assembly would be elected by the first-past-the-post system, practically ensuring a Labour majority in normal times but also raising the prospect of a future SNP majority. The result was a YES majority, but it fell well short of the 40 percent threshold and depended on the Labour heartlands in Scotland's industrial Central Belt.

During the 1990s, revived national feeling and opposition to a Conservative government whose support in Scotland was steadily shrinking served to power the longest and most sustained home rule campaign. A Scottish Constitutional Convention was established to bring together the political parties and civil society around an agreed scheme. In practice, it was dominated by Labour and the Liberal Democrats, after the Conservatives and Scottish National Party decided not to participate, and provided a vehicle for them to make compromises. It also enlisted support from local government, the churches, the voluntary sector, the trade unions, and a small section of the business community. The commitment to devolution was enshrined in the Labour manifesto, although subject to a referendum.[3] The incoming Labour government in 1997 held the referendum within months and, after a three-quarters majority, with broad support across all regions, set up the new parliament to start work in 1999.

THE SCOTTISH PARLIAMENT

The Constitutional Convention agreed on some general principles for the new parliament, intended to be more powerful than the assembly offered in 1979, but the need to defer to Labour meant that its recommendations were rather cautious.[4] There was to be proportional representation, but the devolved powers were to be specified, with residual powers remaining at the centre.

The bill produced when Labour returned to power, however, was rather more radical. The Scottish Parliament is given a general competence, with primary legislative power over all matters not expressly reserved to Westminster. The main reservations concern defence and foreign affairs, macro-economic and monetary policy, social security, and taxation. This gives it wider and more exclusive legislative competences than any other state legislature in Europe, but a very weak power of taxation. A new law, the Scotland Act (2012) extends its taxation power to include half of income tax and some minor duties; municipal taxation is already devolved. The extensive legislative competence is accompanied by extensive exclusive administrative competences for Scottish ministers, since no UK minister can act or spend money in Scotland except in pursuance of a specific reserved power. Hence there has been no equivalent of the federal spending power debate in Canada.

Under the doctrine of parliamentary sovereignty, Westminster still claims the right to legislate in devolved fields but there is a convention that it will do so only with the consent of the Scottish Parliament expressed in a Legislative Consent Motion. This convention has never been breached and, indeed, if Westminster did legislate in a devolved field, the Scottish Parliament could repeal the offending law the following day unless Westminster were to change the Scotland Act itself, which is regarded as constitutional legislation.[5] The Parliament is also subject to European Union law and the European Convention on Human Rights, which can be used by the courts to strike down legislation – this latter is in contrast to Westminster, where Parliament has the last word. In practice, almost the only challenges to the competences of the Scottish Parliament have come under these two European provisions. Challenges about competence issues can be made in any court, but eventually pass from the Scottish court system to the UK Supreme Court. The UK government has never challenged a Scottish law in the courts and only a few successful challenges have been made under the European Convention.

The highest court in Scotland is the Court of Session in Edinburgh but appeals in civil (but not criminal) cases have historically been allowed to the Judicial Committee of the House of Lords (now the UK Supreme Court).[6] Cases where a matter of competence is involved (a "devolution issue") can, however, be pursued to the Supreme Court and this includes cases where the European Convention has been invoked. This has led to some criminal cases going to the Supreme Court, a matter of some controversy within Scotland. As a result, the SNP government commissioned a review from Neil Walker of the University of Edinburgh, who recommended that the old division between criminal and civil cases should be replaced by one between matters of Scottish and UK jurisdiction, with the latter but not the former being appealable to the Supreme Court. Nothing has been done about this and nothing is likely to come of it.

The new parliament was intended to address both "democratic deficits" – the subordination of Scotland to Westminster – and the lack of participation and accountability of Scottish institutions to Scottish society. During the debates in the 1990s there was a lot of talk of "new politics" and of breaking with the conservative Westminster "gentlemen's club" way of working.

The "new politics" has always been a rather vague concept, with a number of quite distinct strands. One was to change the balance between executive and legislature in favour of the latter and a weakening of party dominance. The parties in the convention agreed that there should be proportional representation using the additional member list system as in Germany. This was essential to gain Liberal Democrat support but had the added advantage to the unionist parties of making an SNP victory apparently impossible. The Conservatives opposed proportional representation although they have in practice benefited from it. Having lost all their Scottish Westminster MPs in 1997 and gained only one in subsequent elections, they have a solid presence as a minority party in the Scottish Parliament.

There are 129 members of the Scottish Parliament (MSPs) of whom seventy-three are elected in constituencies and fifty-six on regional lists for a four-year term. In the elections of 1999 and 2003 the Labour Party won a plurality of seats and formed a coalition with the Liberal Democrats. In 2007, the SNP came narrowly ahead of Labour and formed a minority government. In 2011 the SNP gained an absolute majority. The next elections will take place in 2016.

However, while proportional representation has meant that, until 2011, no one party could dominate the Parliament, it has served to increase the power of parties as a whole, as they maintain a tight grip on candidate selection. For the first elections, the Labour leadership blocked a number of prominent candidates, including sitting MPs, and eventually the list of people eligible to seek candidacies was only slightly higher than the number of seats available. At the second election, the SNP left candidate selection in the hands of the activists, with the result that a number of prominent MSPs lost their position or were demoted on the lists. One of these, Margo MacDonald, ran as an independent in the added-member·section (and was re-elected in 2007 and 2011); Labour

MP Denis Canavan, sidelined by his party in 1999, did the same. Traditionally, Labour has not allowed candidates to present themselves both in a constituency and on regional lists, arguing (disingenuously) that a candidate who has been defeated in a constituency could have no legitimacy (although list MSPs are actually elected by a larger number of people). This was a transparent effort to undermine SNP MSPs, most of whom have come in on the lists.[7] It backfired on Labour in 2011 when, losing most of their constituency seats, they saw their leadership devastated.[8]

The second elections, in 2003, seemed briefly to herald an era of multi-party politics, helped by proportional representation. Seven Greens were elected, along with six members of the leftist Scottish Socialist Party and a handful of independents. This, however, turned out to be an exception, caused by a temporary decline in the SNP vote, leading electors to seek other outlets. Turnout for Scottish elections has consistently been below that of UK elections, averaging about 50 percent although UK turnout has also declined over recent decades, with a low in 2005, when it was similar to Scottish levels. There is, on the other hand, only limited evidence that voters treat Scottish elections as "second order," using them to cast a verdict on the Westminster government. The nationalists persistently do better at Scottish elections and, oddly enough, the Conservatives also gain more constituency seats then. Labour, on the other hand, is persistently well ahead in Westminster elections, making a serious miscalculation in 2011 in thinking that their big victory in 2010 (at the Westminster general election) would carry them through to the Scottish election. The Liberal Democrats in Scotland are historically entrenched in a number of constituencies in the Highlands, the North East, and the Borders and actually benefited from first-past-the-post in Westminster elections, regularly gaining more seats with fewer votes than the SNP or Conservatives (although in 2005 they did come second in the popular vote). In 2011 they suffered drastically from the rise of the SNP and, in a second order effect, from the consequences of their entry into coalition with the Conservatives at Westminster, the Scottish Liberal Democrats (who are a distinct, federated party) having failed to dissociate themselves from the coalition.

Low turnout may reflect a view that in devolved elections the stakes are lower but it does not indicate a lack of support for the institution. Confidence in political institutions in the UK, as elsewhere, is in decline, although the Scottish Parliament appears to do reasonably well, with the Scottish Social Attitudes Survey showing it persistently ahead of Westminster when it comes to voter confidence.

The strength of party politics is a determining feature across the whole spectrum of issues in relation to the working of the Parliament. At a time when parties are becoming disconnected from civil society across the Western world, they are ever more dominant in political recruitment and control of governments. Scotland is no exception.

REPRESENTATIVES

Another theme in the new politics was a better representation of the various sectors of the population. In the work of the Constitutional Convention, the issue of gender was prominent. While there was no agreement on statutory gender equality, the parties pledged to do their best. In the event, Labour succeeded, achieving broad parity, both in the constituency and the list sections. The SNP did less well and the Liberal Democrats did surprisingly poorly. The Parliament has also adopted family-friendly working hours of 9 to 5, in contrast to the late-night practice of Westminster. The outcome was that, at least in the early years when Labour was dominant, the Scottish Parliament had one of the most equal gender balances in the world. The proportion of women, however, fell from 40 percent in 1999 to 34 percent in 2007 and 2011.

It has performed much less well in relation to class representativeness. In the postwar era, Scottish MPs were closer to their party norms than those in England; Labour MPs were more working class and Conservative MPs more upper class.[9] This persisted into the 1990s, with a convergence in both parties on a middle class norm, but more slowly in Scotland. Devolution marked a steep change, with the virtual disappearance of working class politicians from the Labour benches, so that the Scottish Parliament was dominated even more than Westminster by the professional middle class. The move to gender equality even exacerbated this, as female MSPs are even more middle class than are males. The Scottish Parliament has also seen the rise of the professional politician, who leaves university, works in a politics-facilitating occupation (usually for a politician or think tank), and then gains electoral office at an early age, without other career experience of the old apprenticeship kind, working their way up.[10]

Visible minorities have been under-represented, with three MSPs of Asian origin elected (two for the SNP and one for Labour). On the other hand, people born in other parts of the United Kingdom (nearly all in England) were over-represented in relation to their share of the whole population until 2011. As of 2011 the proportion of MSPs born outside Scotland appears to be a little below that of the population as a

Table 6.1
Scottish Parliament results, 1999–2011

	Year	Constituency	Regional	Total MSPS	% of seats	% Constituency votes	% List votes
Labour	2011	15	22	37	28.7	31.7	26.3
	2007	37	9	46	35.7	32.1	29.1
	2003	46	4	50	38.8	34.6	29.3
	1999	53	3	56	43.4	38.7	33.6
SNP	2011	53	16	69	53.5	45.4	44.0
	2007	21	26	47	36.4	32.9	31.0
	2003	9	18	27	20.9	23.8	20.9
	1999	7	28	35	27.1	28.7	27.3
Liberal Democrat							
	2011	2	3	5	3.8	7.9	5.2
	2007	11	5	16	12.4	16.2	11.3
	2003	13	4	17	13.2	15.4	11.8
	1999	12	5	17	13.2	14.2	12.4
Conservative	2011	3	12	15	11.6	13.9	12.4
	2007	4	13	17	13.2	16.6	13.9
	2003	3	15	18	14.0	16.6	15.5
	1999	0	18	18	14.0	15.5	15.4
Green	2011	0	2	2	1.6	0	4.4
	2007	0	2	2	1.6	0.1	4.0
	2003	0	7	7	5.4	0.0	6.9
	1999	0	1	1	0.8	0.0	3.6
Scottish Socialist Party/Solidarity							
	2011	0	0	0	0	0	
	2007	0	0	0	0	0	2.1
	2003	0	6	6	4.7	6.2	6.7
	1999	0	1	1	0.8	1.0	2.0
Others	2011	0	1	1	0.8	1.1	5.5
	2007	0	1	1	0.8	0	10.1
	2003	2	2	4	3.1	3.4	8.9
	1999	0	1	1	0.8	1.9	5.7

Source: Scottish Parliament

whole.[11] This is not because of the advance of the SNP since in both periods they were the party with the highest number of non-Scottish-born members.

EARLY TROUBLES

The early years of the Parliament were marked by a systematic campaign by sections of the media to discredit and delegitimize the devolution settlement, effectively reviving the battle which they had lost in 1997. Coverage of parliamentary affairs was trivialized, scandals which anywhere else would be seen as minor were magnified out of proportion, and the Scottish government was consistently portrayed as worse than that at Westminster.

Partisan politics within the Parliament exacerbated the issue as politicians sought to destroy each other, in contrast to the visions of the "new politics." After First Minister Donald Dewar's sudden death, his successor, Henry McLeish, was brought down over a minor issue of the use of his Westminster constituency office in the days before devolution.[12] Conservative leader David McLetchie was forced to resign for claiming a couple of hundred pounds of taxi fares on party business. The fourth Labour leader, Wendy Alexander, resigned over a trivial matter of contributions to her leadership campaign from someone based abroad. In fact, rules in the Scottish Parliament are so tight that there have been no serious cases of corruption and the MPs expenses scandal a few years ago had no counterpart in Edinburgh[13] – and certainly nothing like the effective selling of peerages in return for contributions to funds as has happened at Westminster.

Another major challenge in the early days was over the repeal of Section 28/ 2A, a provision inserted into legislation across Great Britain as a whole under the Conservative government which prohibited schools and local authorities from "promoting" homosexuality as a normal way of life. The Conservative Party has since officially apologized for this law and, indeed, schools in England are now rather obliged in the opposite direction but its repeal after Labour won the 1997 UK election was the cause of a major row, especially in Scotland, where the issue is devolved and the churches play a larger role in public affairs and had been on the pro-devolution side. The Catholic Church led the campaign against repeal, with the Scottish cardinal at one point saying that it discredited devolution as a whole. Protestant fundamentalist transport tycoon Brian Souter (who had donated to the SNP) put up a million pounds for a private referendum against repeal. In the event, the main parties (Labour, Liberal Democrat, and SNP) held firm for repeal, but the experience was damaging for home rule morale. When the issue of civil partnerships came along soon after, the governing Labour/Liberal Democrat coalition passed the issue to Westminster through a Leg-

Table 6.2
Educational background (%), 2011

	Scottish MPS	English MPS	Scottish Labour MPS	English Labour MPS	MSPS	Labour MSPS	SNP MSPS
State school	91.0	58.1	94.7	76.6	84.9	86.7	88.0
Private school	8.9	39.0	5.3	21.9	15.1	13.3	12.0
Oxbridge	1.7	29.2	0.0	20.5	1.6	0.0	2.9
Other HE	77.6	52.8	75.0	59.5	68.5	72.7	63.7
Other FE	13.8	9.1	12.5	12.1	13.7	21.2	11.6
None	8.6	9.4	12.5	8.4	16.9	6.1	21.7

Table 6.3
Formative occupation (%), 2011

	Scottish MPS	English MPS	Scottish Labour MPS	English Labour MPS	MSPS	Labour MSPS	SNP MSPS
Professions	42.4	33.2	46.3	32.5	33.1	36.1	35.7
Business	6.8	28.3	4.9	7.3	17.7	0.0	25.0
Politics-facilitating	33.9	28.5	34.1	40.8	28.2	36.1	30.4
Blue/white collar	6.8	5.4	9.8	9.4	9.7	19.4	8.9
Miscellaneous	10.2	4.9	4.9	8.4	11.3	8.3	16.1

islative Consent Motion. Matters have since changed radically as Scotland has now legalized same-sex marriage, with the support of all the parties.[14] The Section 28/ 2A incident, while scarring the Labour politicians involved, probably served to strengthen the Parliament by demonstrating its ability to stand up to populist pressures, the Catholic Church, and moneyed interests.

The media also made a huge issue over the parliament building, as a way of undermining the institution itself. The 1997 White Paper suggested that, if no new building were erected but an old one converted, the job could be done for about £40 million. Options were the old High School, which had actually been adapted for the proposed Scottish Assembly in 1979 but was now considered inadequate, and the temporary quarters in the chamber lent by the Church of Scotland and used for their annual General Assembly.[15] Instead it was decided to invest in a new building and Catalan architect Enric Miralles won the competition, for an imaginative building whose cost was estimated at £195 million.

As with all public works in the UK, the building was late and over-budget, costing in the end some £420 million; Miralles died during the process and therefore did not see the end of it. The press seized on this figure and compared it with the £40 million to suggest, quite mendaciously, that the building's budget was tenfold, rather than just over double, the original figure. By comparison, the public cost of the London Olympic Games tripled from £3 billion to £9 billion but the press tell us that it came in within budget – because each time the cost went up the budget was increased proportionally! This story is important because the fixation on the building was used systematically to discredit the Parliament up until and after the inauguration of the building itself.

The building is a highly modernist design, set at the foot of the Royal Mile, on the site of an old brewery and opposite the royal palace of Holyrood. UK rules post-9/11 required the building of a massive security barrier (a significant reason for the added cost) and there are restrictions on movement around the building, but otherwise the idea is to emphasize openness. The general public can enter freely, circulate in the lobby area, and use the café. The chamber is formed as a hemicycle to avoid the confrontational layout of Westminster and members refer to each other by name rather than, as at Westminster, "the honourable member for (constituency)." Light and open spaces and little touches symbolize access by the public. It is, however, a world apart in the way the temporary quarters were not.

The Parliament was also marked in the early years by conflicts and rivalries between constituency and list members. While all MSPs are formally equal, winning a constituency is seen to provide greater status and legitimacy so that list members will often seek to move over (although Labour Party rules make it difficult). Members have complained of list members "poaching" cases and complaints within their boundaries, a grievance exacerbated when SNP list members were involved. Less has been heard of this since the SNP has the largest number of constituency members and Labour depends heavily on list MSPs.

PARLIAMENT AND EXECUTIVE

Scotland has a parliamentary system in which government is chosen from parliament and therefore tends to dominate it. The original legislation gave the title Scottish Executive to the government, to indicate a lesser status than the UK Government but, on coming to power, the SNP simply changed the name, a move later endorsed in the Scotland Act (2012) whose main aim was to implement the Calman report.

There is provision for the election of a First Minister (unlike at West-minster) who then nominates ministers from among MSPs. There were some suggestions in the 1970s that the proposed Scottish Assembly should be organized in the way that local government then was, with-out a strong executive and working through committees.[16] This, indeed, was the original model for the National Assembly for Wales, but it rap-idly evolved into a parliamentary system, with a Welsh Government re-sponsible to the assembly. The Scottish model was parliamentary from the start.

Proportional representation might be expected, by depriving any one party of a majority, to enhance the importance of the Parliament but there is little evidence of this in practice. In the first two terms, there was a coalition between Labour and the Liberal Democrats, who nego-tiated their program at the beginning of each term and then worked their way through it, leaving little scope for parliamentary initiative. The minority SNP government between 2007 and 2011 might also have given more scope for Parliament, but did not. The Parliament has a fixed term of four years, with dissolution possible only by qualified majority, and in the case of twenty-eight days expiring without choosing a first min-ister. This deprives the government of the threat of dissolution and a snap election but a first minister ahead in the polls and facing parlia-mentary obstruction can still threaten to resign and refuse renomina-tion for twenty-eight days, thus effectively forcing an election. This was exactly the threat employed by Alex Salmond when the opposition par-ties sought to pick off individual ministers by tabling no confidence mo-tions in them. Only when the SNP lost its opinion poll lead did the opposition parties effectively force out one minister and she was de-moted rather than removed altogether. There was one defeat on the budget one year but this was reversed a week later after a bit of haggling and thereafter the SNP were able to cut deals with one or other of the par-ties for a very small price. The general understanding, indeed, is that if the opposition parties are not prepared to give the government its budg-et they are obliged to bring it down and form an alternative coalition themselves, something that would be difficult, given their differences.

The minority government also enjoyed the extensive executive pow-ers which, as ministers of the crown, they had inherited from the old system. Thus, much was done without resort to legislation. Majority gov-ernment since 2011 has not led to relaxed discipline. Executive domi-nance has been strengthened by the party discipline, both in candidate selection and within the Parliament. There are few backbench rebellions and few of the independent-minded MPs who are a regular, if minority,

feature at Westminster. Malcolm Chisholm, a Labour MSP who has the
singular distinction of having resigned from both the UK and Scottish
governments, stands out as an exception. The only significant split in
the SNP occurred when the party accepted NATO membership, provoking
two of its MSPs to leave the party and sit as independents.

PARLIAMENTARY PROCEDURE

One feature in the design of the new Parliament was a system of committees which were intended to be more powerful than at Westminster
and to combine legislative and investigatory roles. Some of these are
mandatory while others are created to shadow ministerial portfolios.
Membership is proportional to party size in the Parliament and the
chairs are also allocated proportionally. Committees have suffered from
a high turnover, with few members being able to develop expertise in
the relevant field, and it has not been easy to combine the investigative
and legislative roles. In the early years, the large quantity of legislation
left less room for the former. At the same time, some of the Westminster select committees have grown in knowledge and authority, especially where they have a strong chair, often a former minister or a senior
politician passed over for high office, and more so since the choice of
chairs was seized away from the party whips. So the Scottish committees, in which so much hope was invested, can now come off the worse
from the comparison.

The legislative process was also designed to differ from Westminster,
where much time is spent on repetitive debates on general principles.
There is a pre-legislative investigatory stage, in which evidence is taken
and outside interests are consulted; but the process as a whole is still
dominated by the parties, so that few amendments genuinely originate
from parliamentary discussion or are carried against the wishes of the
executive. Only during the period of minority government were con-
cessions made to the opposition parties, and these tended to be on matters of detail.

Parliament has also found it difficult to make a real input to the
budgetary process. In part this is because to date there has only been a
spending process, with the overall level of taxation set by Westminster
and, until the crisis, more money than could be spent, discouraging a
debate about the best use of resources. The finance committee does
have an academic advisor but there is a lack of good data and of Scottish economic and financial models that it might use to project alternative scenarios.

LEGISLATIVE OUTPUT

The early days of the Scottish Parliament saw a large increase in Scottish legislation, including a backlog of matters which had never made the agenda at Westminster, such as land reform and poinding.[17] The number of Scottish bills increased from an average of six between 1979 and 1999 to fifteen and sixteen respectively in the Scottish Parliament's first and second four-year terms, falling off again under the SNP minority government. Much of the early legislation closely mirrored that at Westminster, often including identical or very similar clauses.[18] Gradually, the Scottish Parliament has steered its own course, with less resort to "photocopy" legislation, especially since the arrival of the SNP in government.

Provision was made at the outset for non-government legislation, which can be sponsored by backbench or opposition members (members' bills) or committees (committee bills). Unlike at Westminster, there was provision for support for members' bills but the pressure of demand led to some restrictions of their numbers. The number of committee bills has also been very small.[19] Most legislation is government-sponsored, with the proportion of backbench members' bills at just 12 percent between 1999 and 2007, much the same proportion as at Westminster.[20]

EUROPEAN MATTERS

The European Union (EU) has played into the debate on devolution in Scotland as it has in other parts of Europe. Many of the competences of the Parliament, including in agriculture and fisheries, environment, and economic development, are shared with the EU, while European competition policy affects a wide variety of matters. Scotland is also responsible for distributing European structural funds, although it has no influence over the amount of these.[21] European directives in devolved fields have to be transposed in Scotland although the Parliament can choose to transpose itself or leave the matter to Westminster. A European (currently Europe and External Affairs) committee is one of those mandated by the Scotland Act, with a wide-ranging role. In practice, like the other committees, it has suffered from high turnover and a failure to build up knowledge and networks. Under Labour, and even under the SNP, there was a general indifference as to whether European directives should be transposed by the Scottish or UK parliament. Scottish ministers are invited to form part of the UK delegation to the Council of Ministers where devolved competences are at stake, and the Scottish representative office in Brussels is treated as part of the "UKREP family" (United Kingdom Permanent Representation), giving its members diplomatic status, practices which have continued after the SNP arrival in government. Yet parliamentary accountability has been weak because Scottish ministers cannot dissent in public from the UK line and the Scottish Parliament is not always apprised in time of issues coming on to the agenda. Following the Lisbon Treaty, with its "early warning system" allowing the Committee of the Regions and national parliaments to indicate reservations on upcoming policy initiatives, a system has been put in place in the Scottish Parliament to try to monitor upcoming issues, but it is not always effective.

CONSTITUTIONAL CHANGE

The devolution settlement has continually been challenged by nationalists, who want to go all the way to independence, and others who see devolution as a process with a long way to go before it is complete. The main challenge was posed by the SNP's victory in the 2007 elections, followed by the absolute majority of 2011, which ensured a debate on independence and the referendum of 2014. Opinion coalesced around three broad options: a modified version of the status quo; independence; and a third way usually referred to as "devolution max." In practice these options have tended to converge as advocates of the status quo were obliged to promise (albeit in vague terms) more and nationalists retreated to something known as "independence lite." It is striking, comparing this to processes elsewhere, that the Scottish Parliament was not the main focus for these debates and the parties were not able to come together to defend a common minimum interest in the Parliament being an actor in itself, with institutional interests to defend. The reaction of the unionist parties to the victory of the SNP was to set up a commission (the Calman Commission), which started from a resolution of the Scottish Parliament (in which the unionist parties had a majority) but was immediately effectively taken over by the Westminster government (led by Scottish MP Gordon Brown), with a UK civil servant as secretary. The corresponding Scottish parliamentary committee, chaired by a Labour MSP and with a unionist majority, then appointed the same civil servant as their advisor. So partisan alignments trumped any idea of an institutional interest in the Parliament itself. The Labour Party position on the whole issue continued to be subject to London's limitations. This unionist front continues to hold, with parties moving together in their response to the referendum demand, at first denouncing it as unwanted, then belatedly declaring it illegal, and then daring the SNP to have it as soon as possible. The negotiations leading to the Edinburgh agreement, which legalizes the referendum by legislation in both parliaments, were strictly government-to-government and first minister to prime minister with no involvement of either parliament. Since then, committees of both houses of the UK Parliament have been very active on the unionist side, there being no SNP members in the House or Lords and no SNP member participating in the House of Commons Select Committee on Scottish Affairs.[22] Consequently the committees of both parliaments were used during the long referendum campaign more for rehearsing partisan arguments than for dispassionate analysis. After the 55–45 percent victory of the No side, the UK parties announced a rapid timetable for introducing more devolution, with negotiations among the political parties, including both sides in the referendum debate. It is notable that the Scottish Parliament was not the focus of this debate.

OVERALL ASSESSMENT

The Scottish Parliament has represented a huge enhancement of accessibility, accountability, and legitimacy for government in Scotland, compared with the old system. If it did not exist, the UK government formed in 2010 (with only one Conservative MP in Scotland) would have faced a constitutional crisis, confronting not just the SNP as it currently does, but the majority of Scottish political and civil society. It has not, on the other hand, settled the Scottish constitutional issue. Those who said that devolution would kill nationalism stone dead and those who argued that it was a one-way street to separation have both been proven wrong. Survey evidence consistently shows that most Scots now see the Parliament as the centre of political life and want it to have greater powers, but do not support independence.[23]

At the outset, expectations were extremely high, with large majorities thinking that it should and would have the most influence over how Scotland is governed. This rapidly changed after the Parliament came into being, with majorities continuing to think it *should* have most power but a minority thinking it actually did. Gradually, opinion has moved back again, with a more realistic appreciation of what the Parliament (which respondents do not usually distinguish from the government) can do. The arrival of the SNP, which was less inhibited about emphasizing Scottish differences and more assertive of its prerogatives, led to an increase in confidence in the Parliament.[24] The percentage believing that the Scottish Parliament had most influence over how Scotland is governed increased from 13 percent in 2000 to 38 percent in 2011, although 73 percent said that it should do so.[25] Surveys over the years have shown that most people do not believe that devolution has made much difference to policy, which was perhaps understandable when Labour-dominated governments were in office at both levels, and such policy differences as existed were downplayed. The arrival of the SNP has raised the number thinking that devolution does make a difference and surveys consistently show that those who think services have improved over the years tend to attribute this to the Scottish rather than the UK parliament, a tendency that has increased in recent years.[26]

Neither the establishment of the Parliament nor the arrival in power of the SNP seems to have shifted constitutional preferences, apart from a falling away to negligible proportions of those who would prefer no parliament at all. The achievement of the Scottish Parliament, however, has been to become a local version of Westminster, or other European parliaments, rather than a new type of body. The small size of the country and the spirit of devolution make it more accessible than Westminster, a finding confirmed by research among Scottish interest and advocacy groups.[27] Actors like the business community, who initially thought to bypass it because of their strong links into London, have been obliged to play the Scottish political game;[28] but this has not fundamentally altered the balance of power between the executive and the legislature.

NOTES

1 This was the case of *McCormick vs the Lord Advocate*, concerning the use of the title Queen Elizabeth II in Scotland, when neither Scotland nor Great Britain had had an Elizabeth I.

2 Since 1800 the state is the United Kingdom of Great Britain and Ireland (since 1922 Northern Ireland). It is correct to distinguish this wider United Kingdom (UK) from Great Britain.

3 Tony Blair, as his memoirs show, was no home ruler but was given no choice.

4 Around 1983 I had advised Labour's devolution committee that the new body should be called a parliament, that it should be elected by propor-

tional representation, that the reserved and not the devolved powers should be specified, and that the European Convention on Human Rights should be incorporated in the legislation. All four suggestions were rejected at the time but eventually featured in the 1998 Scotland Act.

5 Constitutional legislation is by convention taken on the floor of the House of Commons and there is an emerging convention that major changes in devolution or electoral systems will be subject to referendum. Any UK parliament ignoring this would invite a constitutional crisis.

6 This was not provided for in the Acts of Union but emerged afterward as the Lords accepted such cases.

7 Labour in Wales actually legislated for this, using their Westminster majority, in an amendment to the devolution act.

8 Exceptionally, one Labour constituency MSP was allowed to run on the list in 2011 as boundary changes had made her seat nominally Liberal Democrat. In fact, she lost to the SNP but came in on the list.

9 Michael Keating, "The Role of the Scottish MP," doctoral diss., Glasgow College of Technology and Council for National Academic Awards, 1975.

10 Michael Keating and Paul Cairney, "A New Elite? Politicians and Civil Servants in Scotland after Devolution," *Parliamentary Affairs* 59, no. 1 (2006): 1–17.

11 I have not been able to research the 2011 figure exhaustively and this is a minimum figure since some of those not mentioning their birthplace may have been born outside Scotland.

12 McLeish had sublet part of the office building to Labour-associated groups such as trade unions and welfare rights lawyers, ploughing the proceeds back into the maintenance of the building. This was seen as mixing public with party moneys. Although McLeish paid the sum back from his own pocket, he had miscalculated the number of lets and was forced out on this technicality.

13 Labour's third leader, Jack McConnell, was at one point obliged to declare the value of a painting he received as a Christmas present from his wife.

14 How far things have changed can be seen from the fact that the Scottish Conservative leader herself is in a same-sex relationship.

15 The General Assembly chamber had the advantage that MSPs, including ministers, had to cross the Lawnmarket, a major pedestrian area in Edinburgh's Old Town, to reach their offices, thereby mingling with the crowd. Politicians also frequented the Old Town pubs, although each party had its preferred watering hole.

16 In 1978, indeed, I wrote a Fabian Society paper advocating the parliamentary model.

17 This was a mechanism whereby the property of debtors could be sold off at auction, which mainly affected poor families.

18 Michael Keating, Linda Stevenson, Paul Cairney, and Katherine Taylor, "Does Devolution Make a Difference? Legislative Output and Policy Divergence in Scotland," *Journal of Legislative Studies* 9, no. 3 (2003): 110–39.

19 Jim Johnston, "The Legislative Process: The Parliament in Practice," in Charlie Jeffery and James Mitchell, eds, *The Scottish Parliament, 1999–2009: The First Decade* (Edinburgh: Luath Press Limited, 2009), 29–36.

20 Chris Carman and Mark Shephard, "Committees in the Scottish Parliament," in Jeffery and Mitchell, *The Scottish Parliament, 1999–2009*, 21–8.

21 In fact, due to UK Treasury rules and the workings of the non-additionality principle, Scotland received nothing from an increase, and loses nothing from a decrease, in its structural fund allocations. They merely affect the way the budget is allocated within Scotland.

22 As membership is proportional to the whole House, the SNP initially had no member until the Conservatives volunteered to give up one of their places (which are all held by English MPs in any case). After an argument with the chair, a rather aggressive Labour unionist, the SNP member then withdrew from participation.

23 Rachel Ormiston and Susan Reid, *Scottish Social Attitudes Survey, 2011: Core Module – Attitudes to Government, the Economy and Public Services in Scotland* (Edinburgh: Scottish Government Social Research, 2012), http://www.gov.scot/Publications/2012/06/9925/4, accessed 15 February 2016.

24 Ibid.

25 Ibid.

26 Ibid.

27 Michael Keating, Paul Cairney, and Eve Hepburn, "Territorial Policy Communities and Devolution in the United Kingdom," *Cambridge Journal of Regions, Economy and Society* 2, no. 1 (2008): 51–66.

28 Michael Keating, *The Government of Scotland: Public Policy Making after Devolution*, Edinburgh, Edinburgh University Press, 2010.

7

The Assembly of Northern Ireland:
Hope and Constraint

GUY LAFOREST

On the occasion of a major speech in Belfast in the summer of 2013, American president Barack Obama talked about the exemplarity of Northern Ireland for the world. He found it profoundly edifying and promising that this troubled theatre of one of the most intractable conflicts of the twentieth century (and of all kinds of political drama in previous eras) had also seen the emergence of a movement toward peace and intercommunity dialogue culminating in the Good Friday–Belfast Agreement of 1998 (leading to the British Northern Ireland Act of the same year) and the St Andrews Agreement of 2006 (leading to modifications of the Northern Ireland Act). Although he believed that much work remained to be done in the institutional consolidation of the peace process and in the development of a corresponding political culture of cross-community respect and cooperation, he congratulated the people of Northern Ireland for instilling an ingredient of hope for themselves and for the global politics of our times.[1] Thus, André Lecours and I have included the Assembly of Northern Ireland in this comparative examination of the parliaments of autonomous nations with regard to their roles in securing and enlarging political autonomy on the one hand, and affirming and preserving a distinct identity on the other.[2]

For those of us living in Quebec and elsewhere in Canada, the history of Ireland as a whole, and particularly that of Northern Ireland, bears many resemblances to our own history. Our respective histories are linked to that most formidable of medieval political cathedrals, the British state, whose post-1997 renovation by the Labour government led by Tony Blair in the era of devolution included the Good Friday–Belfast Agreement of 1998, which led to the re-establishment of an autonomous parliament in Northern Ireland.[3] Our shared history includes conquests, failed rebellions, and wars, but also compromises and breakthroughs. With the great famine of the nineteenth century, which brought many Irish people to Quebec and to the rest of Canada; with the civil wars before and after the partition of 1920 which separated the six Northern Irish counties from the rest of the island; and with the Troubles that emerged at the end of the 1960s following almost five decades of discrimination against Catholics by the Protestant-led Northern Irish Stormont Parliament, it is undeniable that the history of Northern Ireland has included much more violence and tragedy than our own.[4] Nevertheless, as Canadian political scientist Garth Stevenson has recently argued, our paths have been parallel and we have much to learn from each other.[5]

CONSOCIATIONALISM AND DEVOLUTION IN 1998

According to the pioneering work of Arend Lijphart, consociational democracy requires, first, extensive power-sharing by all relevant stakeholders agreeing to an executive coalition in a severely divided society; second, the wide use of proportional representation; third, the provision of segmented autonomy for the various parts of the community; and fourth, veto rights to protect the partners from being overpowered in matters that they deem essential to their very survival or existence.[67] All essential aspects of the model were present in the brokered deal that changed politics in Northern Ireland from 1998 onward.[8] In a complicated history that witnessed many setbacks between the advent of the Troubles and the reaching of, first, the Good Friday-Belfast Agreement of 1998 and later the St Andrews Agreement of 2006, all relevant political forces in the Unionist-Protestant and Nationalist-Catholic-Republican communities of Northern Ireland, without forgetting the governmental and political authorities of Britain and of the Republic of Ireland, and with considerable outside help from the United States but also from Canada, finally agreed to a way toward peace and the re-establishment of a form of political normalcy in the late 1990s.[9] This way passed through the application to the local circumstances of the four principles of consociational democracy. The following lengthy quote from Garth Stevenson ably summarizes the compromises that led to the resurgence of parliamentary life in Northern Ireland:

> The agreement [1998 Good Friday–Belfast Agreement] imposed
> significant modifications on three political systems: the United

Kingdom, the twenty-six county Irish state, and the six-county state of Northern Ireland. The United Kingdom promised to repeal the Government of Ireland Act of 1920. Northern Ireland would remain part of the United Kingdom until a majority of its people voting on a poll decided otherwise ... The Irish state agreed to amend its constitution to remove articles 2 and 3, which stated a claim to the whole island although acknowledging that the state's authority de facto extended only to the twenty-six counties. In their place, new articles would affirm the entitlement of anyone born anywhere in Ireland to be part of the Irish nation, as well as the will of the Irish nation "to unite all the people who share the territory of the island of Ireland, in all the diversity of their identities and traditions, recognizing that a united Ireland shall be brought only by peaceful means with the consent of a majority of the people, democratically expressed, in both jurisdictions of the island ... " For Northern Ireland itself, the agreement prescribed a new regime based on the principles of consociational democracy. There would be an assembly of 108 members elected from the 18 existing Westminster constituencies by the single transferable vote method of proportional representation. Committee chairs, committee membership and the ministerial portfolios would be allocated in proportion to party strengths, so that all significant parties would share in power. Cross-community (unionist and nationalist) support would be required for all "key decisions," including election of the speaker, the first minister, and the deputy first minister, standing orders and budgetary allocations.[10]

ELECTIONS IN NORTHERN IRELAND, POLITICAL PARTIES, AND THE PHASES OF DEVOLUTION

In the post-1998 Good Friday–Belfast Agreement era, democratically and openly contested elections in Northern Ireland have taken place in 1998, 2003, 2007, and 2011.[11] The next election will take place in May 2016 at the latest. A summary of the results of these elections is presented in Table 7.1. This summary includes only the five major parties that have been present at all elections since 1998 and are all involved in the formation of the executive of the government of Northern Ireland:

• Ulster Unionist Party (UUP), the traditionally dominant party of the Protestant community, hegemonic during the whole era of the Stormont Parliament between 1921 and1972, close to the British

Conservatives, led by David Trimble during the crucial talks prior
and up to 1998, and currently by Peter Nesbitt;

- Democratic Unionist Party (DUP), founded by Ian Paisley and promoter of a more radical brand of unionism. The party became the
dominant party in the Protestant community in 2003 and it played
a key role in the restoration of the devolved parliament, making
key compromises with Sinn Fein at St Andrews in 2006, and is currently led by the First Minister Peter Robinson;
- Social Democratic Labour Party (SDLP), close to the British Labour
Party and the European social democrats, led by John Hume and
Seamus Mallon in the crucial years leading to the breakthrough of
1998. The party represents the moderate voice in the nationalist
and Catholic community, and it is currently under the leadership
of Alasdair McDonnell;
- Sinn Fein (SF), meaning We Ourselves, the more radical and vocal
promoter of an all-Ireland republic within the nationalist Catholic
community, always a key player in the road toward peace under the
leadership of Gerry Adams. Because of its links with the Irish Republican Army, it was successful in displacing SDLP as the dominant
party in the Catholic community after the 2003 elections, with
Martin McGuinness emerging as a key figure in the context of his
election to the office of Deputy First Minister following the restoration of the devolved parliament in 2006–2007;
- Alliance Party (AP or Alliance), the cross-community party whose
elected members in the Assembly of Northern Ireland define themselves as "Other" for the purposes of the weighted votes in the legislature. It was led at the time of the Good Friday–Belfast Agreement
by Lord Alderdice, who became the first Speaker of the Assembly
between 1998 and 2004, and it is currently led by the Minister of
Justice, David Ford.
- A key characteristic of the political system in Northern Ireland is
the absence of an official opposition in the assembly. All five major
parties in the legislature partake in the operations of the executive.
From 1998 to 2011, parties outside of the executive never have had
more than twelve members in the Assembly (as matters stand in
March 2016, they have six members).

Despite all its complexities and the imaginative contours of its institutional network, the Good Friday–Belfast Agreement left many issues
unresolved. In the early years, the devolved assembly faced the key challenges of providing greater security for everyone by monitoring the
reciprocal decommissioning of arms and establishing a police force en-

Table 7.1
Election results, 1998, 2003, 2007, 2011

	Party	Number of seats	% of voting preferences
1998	UUP	28	21
	DUP	20	18
	SF	18	17.7
	SDLP	24	22
	Alliance	6	6.4
2003	UUP	27	22.7
	DUP	30	25.7
	SF	24	23.5
	SDLP	18	17
	Alliance	6	3.7
2007	UUP	18	14.9
	DUP	36	30.1
	SF	28	26.2
	SDLP	16	15.2
	Alliance	7	5.2
2011	UUP	16	13.2
	DUP	38	30
	SF	29	26.9
	SDLP	14	14.2
	Alliance	8	7.7

joying the respect of both communities. The difficulties associated with these tasks caused many disruptions in the operations of the legislature, none graver and longer than the re-establishment of British direct rule from 2002 to 2007.[12] Four phases have marked the life of the Assembly since the early days of 1998:

Phase 1 Pre-Devolution (July 1998–December 1999)
Phase 2 Devolution I (December 1999–October 2002)
Phase 3 Direct Rule (October 2002–May 2007)
Phase 4 Devolution II (May 2007–April 2015)

IMAGINATIVE POLITICAL CONFIGURATIONS

Before exploring the powers, functions, and overall operations of the Assembly, I wish to emphasize that Northern Ireland is involved in an extraordinarily complex web of collaborative institutions and inter-parliamentary and intergovernmental structures, in Ireland as a whole, in the United Kingdom, and at the European level. Starting with the

networks between parliamentarians, one must mention a Northern
Irish branch of the Commonwealth Parliamentary Association. Since
2001, members of the Assembly of Northern Ireland are also represented in the British-Irish Inter-Parliamentary Association. As a further
proof of the normalization of politics at this level of institutional life,
one must mention the emergence in 2012 of the North-South Inter-
Parliamentary Association. This provides a forum for formal discussion
twice a year to the members of the Assembly of Northern Ireland and
to those of the two houses of the Republic of Ireland's Parliament
(Oireachtas) on issues of mutual concern.[13] As peoples, communities,
and their representatives learn to collaborate and work together with
less mistrust and toward greater, albeit tentative, reciprocal trust, this
initiative is one among many steps in the right direction since the Good
Friday–Belfast Agreement of 1998. This political agreement was also an
international treaty between the Republic of Ireland and the United
Kingdom. Not only were Catholics and Protestants, Nationalists and
Unionists, politically and legally encouraged, indeed technically com-
pelled, to collaborate in the power-sharing system of Northern Ireland;
they were also obliged to collaborate institutionally with the Republic
of Ireland in the North-South Ministerial Council, with both the Republic of Ireland and the United Kingdom in the British-Irish Intergovernmental Conference, and with these two partners as well as with
the other devolved jurisdictions (Scotland and Wales) and crown de-
pendencies of the United Kingdom in the British-Irish Council. I briefly
examine the roles of these three bodies below. Intergovernmental affairs in the case of Northern Ireland also implicates the Joint Ministerial Committee, which operates between the UK government and the
devolved governments of Northern Ireland, Wales, and Scotland, to
provide a framework for efficient, respectful, and regular intergovernmental activity between the UK government and its three devolved partners on domestic as well as on European policy.[14]

The North-South Ministerial Council (NSMC) brings together ministers from the executive of Northern Ireland and from the government
of the Republic of Ireland for the purposes of consultation, cooperation,
and action on matters of mutual interest. The NSMC has met in plenary
forms seventeen times since 1999 and it has a permanent secretariat in
Armagh. It is directly accountable to the full governments of both partners and to their legislative bodies. It accomplishes its work in six areas
of cooperation: agriculture, education, environment, health, transport,
and tourism, including Tourism Ireland. The regularity of its meetings
is a positive sign, and interparliamentary forums have suggested ex-

panding the areas of cooperation. The current areas of cooperation find life in a variety of implementation bodies. I mention only two here: one deals with the protection of the Irish language and of Ulster Scots, the other with the relationships of the partners with the European Union (Special European Union Programs Body). The creation of the NSMC suited the desires of Catholics and Nationalists for greater proximity with the southern Republic, and Protestant and Unionist political leaders have honoured their engagement to participate in this institution.[15]

The British-Irish Council (BIC), as stated earlier, brings together two states, three devolved governments including the Executive of Northern Ireland, as well as the governments of the Isle of Man, Guernsey, and Jersey. Its twenty-second plenary meeting took place in Guernsey in June 2014. It is established to encourage practical relationships, cooperation, and consultation between members. Its areas of work include demography, environment, housing, energy, education in the early years, social inclusion, transport, and indigenous, minority, and lesser-used languages.[16] The great regularity in the meetings of the BIC is one more positive sign of current political normalization, and everything indicates that Nationalists and Catholics, who prefer greater linkages with the Republic of Ireland, have been trustworthy in their relationships with their partners from all UK jurisdictions in the BIC. The permanent secretariat of the BIC is in Edinburgh.

The British-Irish Intergovernmental Conference, like thee institutions just described, stems from the Good Friday–Belfast Agreement. It met regularly between 1999 and 2006, and one of its main goals was to provide a forum in which the Republic of Ireland could be consulted in matters affecting Northern Ireland, even when these matters had not been devolved by British authorities. Between 1999 and 2006, eighteen plenary meetings took place, dealing with issues such as security, immigration, European Union issues and international relations, education and social affairs, and fiscal matters including fraud. The permanent secretariat of the conference is in Belfast. The fact that it has not held plenary meetings since 2006 is more a testimony to the effectiveness of the other councils than a sign of negative feelings between British and Irish authorities.

THE ASSEMBLY OF NORTHERN IRELAND: POWERS, FUNCTIONS, AND STRUCTURES

The powers and competences of Northern Ireland's Legislative Assembly are, according to the Northern Ireland Act 1998, "transferred matters" that are not enumerated in the act but that exclude the specifically mentioned "excepted" and "reserved" matters.[17] Matters reserved to the Parliament at Westminster could eventually be devolved. They include: financial services and markets, national lottery, national minimum wage, navigation and merchant shipping, consumer safety (in relation to goods), civil aviation, and postal services. Policing services and justice belonged to this category before being devolved in 2010. Excepted matters are matters that are indefinitely reserved to the Parliament and Government of the United Kingdom. They include: the Crown, international relations, Parliament, defence, immigration and nationality, taxation, elections, and nuclear energy. Thus, transferred matters include education, health, agriculture, culture, and justice. A complete list will be provided in the discussion of the system of committees in the Assembly.

As a complex institution in a much-divided society, the Assembly is not limited to the traditional legislative and control parliamentary duties. It also plays a crucial role in the election of the Northern Ireland executive. Since 2006, as a further application of the power-sharing system between the communities, the first and deputy first ministers are elected to these positions by the Assembly in their capacity as leaders of the first and second largest Assembly groups. These groups come from the obligation for every member of the Assembly to designate herself or himself as "Unionist," "Nationalist," or "Other." These designations are crucial for securing effectiveness in power sharing. All the other ministers are chosen by the authorities of all major parties represented in the Assembly, applying the d'Hondt system of proportional representation to the share of seats obtained by these parties in the Assembly.[18] Chairpersons and deputy chairpersons of all statutory committees of the Assembly are also designated following the principles of this system. To the best of my understanding, the symbolically and substantively most important speeches or declarations in the Assembly are the solemn affirmations of the Pledge of Office that the prospective first minister, deputy minister, and all prospective ministers are required to make in order to assume their responsibilities. The most crucial elements of this pledge include: "to discharge in good faith all the duties of the office; commitment to non-violence and exclusively peaceful democratic means; to serve all the people of Northern Ireland equally, and to act in accordance with the general obligations on government to promote equality and prevent discrimination; to promote the interests of the whole community represented in the Northern Ireland Assembly towards the goal of a shared future; to participate fully in the

Executive Committee, the North South Ministerial Council and the British-Irish Council."[19]

In addition to the proportional appointing of ministers, the Assembly ensures effective power-sharing by requiring cross-community support for a variety of important topics: election of the Speaker, money bills, planned program for government, adoption and changes to the Standing Orders.[20] To secure cross-community support, the Assembly first uses the approach of parallel consent. This means that a proposition has the approval of an overall majority of participating members, but also of a majority within the members designated as "Unionist" and "Nationalist." If this fails, the Assembly uses the system called weighted majority. This means securing the support of 60 percent of all participating members, including at least 40 percent of all those who designate themselves as either "Unionist" or "Nationalist."[21] Effective power-sharing is further guaranteed by a procedure called the "petition of concern" through which the vote of at least 30 percent of the members in the Assembly can transform the consideration of any matter to require cross-community support, expressed through the system of weighted majority. The system is indeed complex, but recent empirical studies confirm that it works reasonably well.[22] Consociationalism encourages the elites of the respective communities to work together in a system devised to provide both power-sharing and communal autonomy. The idea is that, over time, trust between these elites will increase.[23] On the whole, it seems to me that this has worked reasonably well in the Assembly of Northern Ireland. Despite the current efforts of the Assembly in that direction, through a variety of typical pedagogical programs, it will still take much more time to bring the general public to engage more with the Assembly and to put greater trust in the system.[24]

The Speaker plays a crucial role in the Assembly of Northern Ireland. Lord Alderdice, from the Alliance Party, was the first Speaker from 1998 to 2004. The function is currently held by William Hay, from the DUP. The Speaker chairs the Business Committee, which schedules the work of the assembly, and the Assembly Commission, which oversees the administrative requirements of the Assembly in terms of property, staff, and services. Beyond the traditional but extended representational duties in light of the complex institutional and diplomatic environments of Northern Ireland, the Speaker has an essential responsibility to evaluate the competence of legislation before the first and final stages of a bill. This includes ensuring legal conformity with the European Convention on Human Rights.[25] It is also his or her duty to forward all bills to the Northern Ireland Human Rights Commission.[26] But the Speaker's primary function is as the Presiding Officer of the Assembly, with duties to act with authority and impartiality. Those duties and responsibilities stem from the Northern Ireland Act, 1998, and they are procedurally specified in the Standing Orders of the Assembly.[27]

The Assembly of Northern Ireland operates with an integrated, impressive, and in some ways original system of statutory and standing committees. There are twelve statutory committees. Eleven are directly linked to the work of the corresponding eleven line departments forming the bulk of the executive: culture, arts, and leisure; regional development; social development; education; finance and personnel; agriculture and rural development; justice; environment; employment and learning; enterprise, trade, and investment; and health, social security, and public safety. Each of these eleven committees has eleven members. Their chairpersons and deputy chairpersons are appointed, following the same logic as that prevailing for the selection of ministers, according to the d'Hondt system of proportionality. All five major parties in the assembly are represented in the committees. The chairperson, or at the very least the deputy chairperson, must come from a party other than the party of origin of the corresponding minister. In line with the Westminster system, statutory committees control the executive: scrutinizing the budget, amending laws, calling officials and ministers to their regular meetings, holding enquiries. What makes the Northern Irish system of statutory committees original is their co-responsibility, along with the executive, in the development of policy and of legislation. Each statutory committee works, at least in principle, hand in hand with its corresponding line department, at all stages of the conception and further development of policy and legislation. At times, statutory committees can also work concurrently.

In the opinion of parliamentary experts, this system, albeit original, tends to overburden the committees and their members.[28] In October 2013, the Assembly published a report on its own system of committees, generally supportive of the overall architecture. This judgment was accompanied by a caveat, since the number of committees could be reduced in 2015–16, possibly in coordination with the next elections expected in May 2016, if current talks about executive rationalization lead to a reduction in the number of line departments. The report of the Committee Review Group proposed changes that will sound familiar to experts of parliamentarianism: improve the day-to-day work of meetings, encourage more attendance, and stimulate the streamlining and transmission of information. There may, however, be an element of originality in the proposal to provide better ongoing or permanent training for members of the Legislative Assembly to perform their duties.[29]

The twelfth statutory committee is the Committee for the Office of the First Minister and the Deputy First Minister. Like other such committees, it has scrutiny, policy development, and consultation roles working closely with the office of the two most important actors in the executive. It is also intimately involved in the development of legislation. In the spirit of the whole institutional architecture, since the first minister comes from the DUP and the deputy first minister from Sinn Fein, the chairperson of this committee is Mike Nesbitt from the UUP, while the deputy chairperson is Chris Lyttle from the Alliance Party.

The Assembly of Northern Ireland operates as well with a system of six standing committees. Three deal with standard parliamentary issues of audit, procedures, and public accounts. The other three deserve special attention since they are related to the distinct political identity of Northern Ireland.

The Assembly and Executive Review Committee is of fundamental importance. As its name suggests, it can study and report to the Assembly, as well as to the British Secretary of State for Northern Ireland, about the whole executive and legislative architecture stemming from the Good Friday–Belfast Agreement of 1998. It is currently involved in an evaluation of the place of women in the Assembly and in the politics of Northern Ireland. In March 2014, it submitted an important report on the issue of Petitions of Concern in the Assembly. It concluded that there was no consensus between political parties to change the current system; nevertheless, the report remains instructive about the political culture of collaboration between parties in the assembly.[30] In previous years, the committee also studied in depth the devolution of policing and justice matters, prior to the devolution of these affairs in 2010.

The Business Committee operates in private meetings and is original in involving not only the whips or parliamentary leaders of political parties but also the Speaker in the organization and scheduling of activities in the Assembly.

Finally, the Standards and Privileges Committee reviews and reports on the conduct of members of the Assembly. It is currently reviewing the Code of Conduct for members adopted in 2009.[31] The Code of Conduct affirms and promotes the following principles: public duty, selflessness, integrity, objectivity, accountability, openness, honesty, leadership, equality, promoting good relations between members as well as between members and staff, and, finally, the principle of respect. In light of previous history in Northern Ireland, it is instructive to repeat here the code's formulation of the principle of respect: "It is acknowledged that the exchange of opinions, and ideas on policies may be robust but this should be kept in context and not extend to individuals being subjected to unreasonable and excessive personal attack. Members should keep in mind that rude and offensive behaviour may lower the public's regard for, and confidence in, Members and the Assembly itself. Members should therefore show respect and consideration for others at all times."[32]

CURRENT PROBLEMS AND CHALLENGES

The Assembly of Northern Ireland faces a number of internal difficulties. At the same time, many of its challenges deal with the evolution of politics in the civil society of both communities; in the relationships between Northern Ireland, the United Kingdom, and the Republic of Ireland; and in the relationship with the European Union. I start with the internal problems.

Personal relationships between members and overall political climate within the Assembly remain generally good, despite the current debate about flags and parades, discussed below. In recent years, one of the greatest accomplishments of the executive, as well as of the Assembly, remains the compromise that led to the transfer of policing and justice powers to Northern Ireland in 2010 following the Hillsborough Agreement.[33] Nevertheless, as can be deduced from previous analysis in this chapter, the Assembly has worked diligently to produce various reports on key institutional issues (relations between Assembly and executive, system of committees, petitions of concern) and concluded that no consensus existed to implement reforms, as desirable as they may be. Thus, it is not inappropriate to talk about a form of institutional stalemate.

As Rick Wilford noted more than a decade ago, a major structural problem for committees in the Assembly of Northern Ireland is that they suffer from overload. The reason is that, beyond their duties with regards to scrutiny, committees are also involved in "advising and assisting each of their associated departments in policy formulation, taking the committee stage of all primary legislation, scrutinising the policy, administration and expenditure of the departments, besides embarking on their own enquiries."[34] More generally, as Alan Trench remarked at our conference about the parliaments of autonomous nations in Quebec City in 2013, party discipline at Stormont is very strong, backbenchers have a strictly limited role, and the Assembly embarks on very little on its own. The parties that have been marginalized in each community in the last decade, UUP and SDLP, have at times considered sitting as opposition forces in the Assembly. It would be a very difficult decision to make, entailing major losses in influence and patronage. So far, both parties have been disinclined to cross this Rubicon.

The Assembly is of course facing problems and challenges that are linked to the overall political situation of Northern Ireland in its complex environment. Both the Republic of Ireland and Northern Ireland have been heavily hit by the economic and financial crisis of recent years in Europe. For the latter, this crisis has been combined with the economic rationalizations of the Cameron government in the UK. Economic prosperity between 1998 and 2008 had tended to assuage tensions in the North. The last few years have been much tougher. Moreover, the referendum that took place in Scotland on 18 September 2014 has implications for Northern Ireland, given its historically strong links with Scotland. The uncertainty around the political future of the latter has clouded the political climate. What would have happened if Scots had voted "Yes" in the referendum? I leave this question open. However, this issue is clearly linked to the possibility of yet one more referendum, or actually two referendums, more directly related to my topic here. The 1998 Good Friday–Belfast Agreement opened a door to the future reunification of Ireland as a whole. This would require a majority vote in a referendum in Northern Ireland, and a similar majority vote in the Republic. Gerry Adams and Sinn Fein politicians have regularly talked about such a referendum hypothesis in the past few years, with the first minister, Peter Robinson from the DUP, confidently stating that if it occurred, a clear majority would be in favour of staying with the United Kingdom. The ultimate decision on this issue belongs to the Secretary of State for Northern Ireland, currently Theresa Villiers, and of course she would not initiate anything of the sort without the move being supported by the British prime minister and cabinet. A referendum in Northern Ireland could not happen alone. It would have to take place concurrently with a referendum in the Republic with a majority supporting the integration of Northern Ireland. And there is one more referendum possibility that needs to be mentioned. Before and after the strong showing of the Euro-skeptic United Kingdom Independence Party in the European elections in 2014, David Cameron has stated that, if the Conservatives were to be re-elected in 2015, he would initiate a referendum about the withdrawal of the United Kingdom from the European Union. Now that the Conservatives have been re-elected with a majority government on 7 May 2015, it appears quite probable that Mr Cameron will make good on his promise, and this could happen in 2016 rather than in 2017. Beyond the positive contributions of the European Union economic support programs in Northern Ireland, experts have suggested that the "symbolism of Europe" (cooperation, talks, dialogue) has made an overall positive contribution to the transformation of the political culture of Northern Ireland.[35]

In the past two years, the single most important issue that has threatened, and still threatens, normalization and peace in Northern Ireland has to do with the politics of symbols and commemorations. Flags and parades have always been contested matters in Northern Ireland. In late December 2012, Belfast city council voted, despite the opposition of Unionists on that council, to reduce to about twenty per year the number of days the flag of the United Kingdom will be flown. This sparked major disturbances and gatherings by Loyalist protesters. Political elites on both sides, with outside help, worked hard in 2013 to come up with a proposed agreement that would have had to be signed by all five parties of the Northern Ireland Executive and Assembly to regulate parades, select commemorations, flags, and emblems, thus "contending with the past." The best effort document was completed in late December 2013 and in the end the talks between parties fell apart for lack of sufficient all-party consensus. Upon reading the ultimately failed proposed agreement, it appears clear that more progress was being made on the issue of parading than on the issue of flags and emblems. The two following excerpts are representative, first, of the goodwill involved in discussing the first matter and, second, the context of the ultimate failure of the talks:

> This requires that the tradition of parading, protesting and assembling be conducted in a way that contributes to the goal of building a shared and open society. Those who parade, commemorate and protest have just as strong an interest as those who do not in building a peaceful and prosperous Northern Ireland where reconciliation takes hold and all space is shared. Restraint and generosity in the exercise of freedom of expression, assembly, and association, as well as fulfilment of the associated responsibilities, can advance this goal … We reached no agreement on any of these proposals. Without a larger consensus on the place of Britishness and Irishness – for which there must be a special and protected place along-

side other identities, national or otherwise, represented within our
society – we could not reach a common position on the flying of
flags and the display of other emblems, which are in fact manifesta-
tions of these identities.[36]

Despite the difficulties, all parties involved persevered and, in late
December 2014, with the participation of the British and Irish governments, a new agreement was signed at Stormont House [home
of the British Secretariat of State in Northern Ireland] by the political parties in the troubled region.[37]

The accord first established a Commission on Flags, Identity, Culture
and Tradition, which should be operational in June 2015 to report within eighteen months. In order to deal with the weight of past history, the
agreement went forward with the idea of an Oral History Archive that
would allow many people, for their own sake and for the future, to provide their own narrative about the Troubles. This will be accompanied
by a Historical Investigation Unit, under the supervision of the Northern Ireland Policing Board, in charge of overlooking outstanding criminal cases. In light of the goodwill involved in the discussions, it was
further provided that the responsibility for parades would be devolved
by the British state to the Northern Irish Assembly.

The Stormont House agreement also increased substantially the financial commitments of the British state in Northern Ireland; details
about this matter should be part of the next throne and budget speeches to be delivered by the new British Conservative government led by
David Cameron at Westminster. And in time for the elections in Northern Ireland in 2016, it was also agreed that the number of members of
the Assembly would be reduced, from six to five members for each
Westminster constituency. There will also be a major reorganization of
the structures of government, reducing the number of departments
from twelve to nine. Finally, for my purposes in this chapter, an important obstacle to the emergence of an official opposition in the Assembly was lifted, as the Stormont House agreement promised public
funding and support for a political party that would choose to work in
the opposition rather than forming part of the political executive. It remains to be seen whether a political party will follow such a new path
in Northern Ireland in 2016.

As I finish revising this chapter in the spring of 2015, the political
and institutional climate in Northern Ireland is relatively quiet. The

parades held in July 2014 were among the most orderly in years. The 2015 summer parade season will be a good test for the spirit and letter of the recent Stormont House agreement. Despite all the goodwill of members of the executive and of the Assembly, Northern Ireland remains a profoundly divided society. The vast majority of students continue to go to segregated schools, isolated from the people, humanity, and narratives of the other community. In cities such as Belfast, Londonderry, and Craigavon, neighbourhoods of the two communities continue to be separated by "peace walls." There are currently fifty-nine such peace walls in place, about ten more than at the time of the Good Friday–Belfast Agreement. Leaders of both communities work in the hope of gradually reducing their number and eventually eliminating all of them by 2022.[38]

According to the figures of the 2011 census, there are around 1.8 million people living in Northern Ireland. Of these, 40 percent have a British only national identity, while 25 percent have an Irish only national identity and 21 percent define themselves as having a Northern Irish only national identity. To refine these figures, the census also allows us to understand that 48 percent of the population include British as a national identity, 28 percent include Irish as a national identity, and 29 percent state that Northern Irish is also part of their national identity. Forty-five percent of the population define themselves as Catholics or claim that they were brought up as Catholics. On the other hand, 48 percent state that they are Protestants or that they were brought up as Protestants. About one person out of six affirms no religious affiliation or identity.[39] The Assembly of Northern Ireland operates and exercises its functions in the context of these recent trends and figures, and in the larger context of the history of Northern Ireland, of Ireland, and of the British Isles.

A complex political identity is emerging in Northern Ireland. In the last fifteen years, political autonomy has been regained and enlarged. All parties and all communities, "Unionist," "Nationalist," and "Other," are to be commended for these results. As a legislative institution, the Assembly of Northern Ireland has continued some traditions of British-Westminster parliamentarianism while bringing forward innovations. It is thus a history of hope and of constraint. The last words should be left to the first minister and deputy first minister of the restored assembly in 2007, Ian Paisley, speaking at the time of the restoration of the Assembly, and Martin McGuinness of Sinn Fein, speaking in the Assembly in 2009, during the debates leading to the further devolution to Northern Ireland of justice and policing services.

Ian Paisley: "I can say to you today that I believe Northern Ireland has come to a time of peace, a time when hate will no longer rule. How good it will be to be part of the wonderful healing in this province today."[40]

Martin McGuinness: "We are at an important stage in the Administration's history. As someone who is absolutely committed to the success of the Assembly, the North/South institutions and the east-west institutions, I passionately want all of them to work. However, those institutions have to work on the basis of the agreements that we made – the Good Friday Agreement and the St Andrews Agreement – and in line with equality and partnership, which is how we show respect to one another."[41]

NOTES

1 President Obama made the speech in the context of the G8 Summit held in Northern Ireland in the summer of 2013. See http://www.theguardian .com/global/2013/jun/17/barack-obama-g8-belfast-blueprint-peace, accessed 26 December 2015.

2 At the conference on the Parliaments of Autonomous Nations held at the National Assembly of Quebec in early February 2013, Guy Laforest made the presentation on Northern Ireland with the help of MA student and conference organizer Rosalie Readman. I wish to thank Rick Wilford for kindly replying to my queries prior to the conference and I also wish to thank Alan Trench for his suggestions.

3 Rick Wilford, ed., *Aspects of the Belfast Agreement* (Oxford: Oxford University Press, 2001).

4 Paul Carmichael and Colin Knox, "Devolution, Governance and the Peace Process," *Terrorism and Political Violence* 16, no. 3 (2004): 593–4.

5 Garth Stevenson, *Parallel Paths: The Development of Nationalism in Ireland and Quebec* (Montreal & Kingston: McGill-Queen's University Press, 2006), 14.

6 John McGarry and Brendan O'Leary, "Consociational Theory, Northern Ireland's Conflict, and Its Agreement. Part I: What Consociationalists Can Learn from Northern Ireland," *Government and Opposition* 41, no. 1 (2006): 43–63.

7 Of course consociationalism can also fossilize the status quo between communities. For a discussion, see James Tilley, Geoffrey Evans, and Claire Michelle, "Consociationalism and the Evolution of Political Cleav-

ages in Northern Ireland, 1989–2004," *British Journal of Political Science* 38, no. 4 (2008): 699–717.

8 John McGarry and Brendan O'Leary, *The Northern Ireland Conflict: Consociational Engagements* (Toronto: Oxford University Press, 2004), 262.

9 Rick Wilford, "Designing the Northern Ireland Assembly," *Parliamentary Affairs* 53, no. 1 (2000): 57–90.

10 Stevenson, *Parallel Paths*, 330–1.

11 For an analysis of the most recent elections in 2011, see Neil Matthews, "The Northern Ireland Assembly Election 2011," *Irish Political Studies* 27, no. 2 (2012): 341–58.

12 Kristin Archick, "Northern Ireland: The Peace Process" (Washington, DC: Congressional Research Service, 2014), 6.

13 The fourth plenary session took place in early April 2014. See the communiqué at http://www.niassembly.gov.uk/News-and-Media/Press-Releases/Joint-Communique-from-the-Fourth-Plenary-of-the-North-South-Inter-Parliamentary-Association/, accessed 26 December 2015.

14 The latest version of the Memorandum of Understanding can be found at http://www.ofmdfmni.gov.uk/jmc-memorandum-of-understanding-2012.pdf, accessed 26 December 2015. After the 18 September 2014 Scottish referendum, all sides in and beyond Scotland agree that the machinery of intergovernmental relations, and the Memorandum of Understanding, will have to be upgraded.

15 The latest communiqué of the plenary meeting of the NSMC can be found at http://www.northsouthministerialcouncil.org/index/publications/joint-communiques/plenary-jc/plenary_jc_08_november_2013.htm, accessed 26 December 2015.

16 The latest summit communiqué of the BIC is available at http://www.britishirishcouncil.org/sites/default/files/22%20-%20Twenty%20Second%20Summit%20-%20Guernsey%20-%2013%20June%202014.pdf, accessed 26 December 2015.

17 For complete details, see the Northern Ireland Act 1998 at http://www.legislation.gov.uk/ukpga/1998/47/section/4, accessed 26 December 2015.

18 The Assembly of Northern Ireland provides the following summary explanation of this system at http://archive.niassembly.gov.uk/io/summary/d'hondt.htm, accessed 26 December 2015.

19 The full Pledge of Office can be consulted here: http://www.northernireland.gov.uk/index/your-executive/ministerial-code/ministerial-code-1.4-pledge-of-office. It includes a provision about promoting the rule of law and endorsing fully the Police Service of Northern Ireland and the criminal justice system, as stated in the 2006 St Andrews Agreement. Protestants and Unionists considered such a provision essential. Its acceptance

by Catholics and Nationalists was a key step toward the restoration of the Assembly in 2006–07, and eventually toward the devolution of justice and police services in 2010. On this matter, as on many others, Rick Wilford and Robin Wilson have written very insightfully. Rick Wilford and Robin Wilson, "Northern Ireland: Devolution Once Again," in Alain Trench, ed., *The State of Nations 2008* (Exeter: Imprint Academic Press, 2008), 98.

20 Rick Wilford, "Designing the Northern Ireland Assembly", 57–90.

21 McGarry and O'Leary, *The Northern Ireland Conflict: Consociational Engagements*, 290–1.

22 Richard S. Conley and Charles Dahan, "Legislative Behaviour in the Northern Ireland Assembly, 2007–2011: Conflict and Consensus in a Developing Consociational Democracy," *Political Studies* 61, no. 1 (2013): 179–97.

23 Nevertheless, as Rick Wilford argues, this is a form of the politics of constraint. Rick Wilford, "Northern Ireland: The Politics of Constraint, 1989–2004," *Parliamentary Affairs* 63 (2010): 134–5.

24 Alistar Clark and Rick Wilford, "Political Institutions, Engagement and Outreach," *Parliamentary Affairs* 65, no. 2 (2011): 386–7.

25 Niall Johnston, "The Northern Ireland Assembly: A New Beginning?" *The Journal of Legislative Studies* 8, no. 1 (2002): 5.

26 To find more about the commission, see http://www.nihrc.org/, accessed 26 December 2015. For many years, there has been a debate about the enshrinement of a distinctive Bill of Rights for Northern Ireland. Discussions so far have not been fruitful. It remains part of the unfinished business.

27 The Standing Orders were last amended on 17 June 2014. They can be consulted at http://www.niassembly.gov.uk/Assembly-Business/Standing-Orders/Standing-Orders/#1, accessed 26 December 2015.

28 Rick Wilford, "The Assembly and the Executive: A Discursive Appraisal," *Irish Political Studies* 16, no. 1 (2001): 233–43.

29 See the executive summary of the report at http://www.niassembly.gov.uk /Assembly-Business/Committees/Report-of-the-Committee-Review-Group-Review-of-the-Committee-System-of-the-Northern-Ireland-Assembly-October-2013/, accessed 26 December 2015.

30 A summary of the report can be consulted at http://www.niassembly.gov .uk/Assembly-Business/Committees/Assembly-and-Executive-Review /Reports/Review-of-Petitions-of-Concern/, accessed 26 December 2015.

31 The terms of reference for this review can be consulted at http://www .niassembly.gov.uk/Your-MLAs/Code-of-Conduct/Committee-on-Standards-and-Privileges—Review-of-the-Assemblys-Code-of-Conduct/, accessed 26 December 2015.

32　The Code of Conduct can be consulted at http://www.niassembly.gov.uk /Your-MLAs/Code-of-Conduct/The-Code-of-Conduct-together-with-the-Guide-to-the-Rules-Relating-to-the-Conduct-of-Members-amended-and-reissued-by-the-Committee-on-Standards-and-Privileges-for-2013-14/#5, accessed 26 December 2015.

33　Archick, "Northern Ireland: The Peace Process," 8–9.

34　Wilford, "The Assembly and the Executive: A Discursive Appraisal," 234.

35　Carmichael and Knox, "Devolution, Governance and the Peace Process," 615.

36　The proposed agreement can be consulted at http://www.northern ireland.gov.uk/haass.pdf, accessed 26 December 2015. See in particular pages 4 and 16.

37　The Stormont House agreement can be read at https://www.gov.uk /government/uploads/system/uploads/attachment_data/file/390672 /Stormont_House_Agreement.pdf, accessed 26 December 2015.

38　This information comes from the BBC's political blog on Northern Ireland by Mark Devenport, which can be consulted at http://www.bbc.com /news/uk-northern-ireland-21187673, accessed 26 December 2015.

39　The *Guardian* reported these figures in the following article: http://www.theguardian.com/news/datablog/2012/dec/11/2011-census-northern-ireland-religion-identity, accessed 26 December 2015.

40　These words were pronounced on the day Paisley and McGuinness affirmed their pledges of office. See the report at http://www.theguardian .com/uk/2007/may/08/northernireland.northernireland, accessed 26 December 2015.

41　Department of Justice, Northern Ireland, Hansard, Official Report, Debate on the Department of Justice Bill, Belfast, 1 December 2009, 205.

8

The Parliament of Canada

ANDRÉ LECOURS

The Parliament of Canada has been the formal arena for debate over national unity and the management of Quebec's claims for autonomy and recognition. Throughout the constitutional negotiations of the 1970s, 1980s, and 1990s, supporters of different visions of the country and of its federal structures put forth their ideas in the House of Commons and also in the Senate. Indeed, as an institution that embodies Canada's sovereignty and identity, Parliament has often had to take a stance on how Canadian nationhood could be reconciled with Quebec's national aspirations. In this context, parliamentary debates have featured different, sometimes antagonistic, positions, most often following partisan political lines. As a result, the Parliament of Canada has never spoken to the question of accommodating Quebec's nationalist claims with a unanimous voice.

This chapter discusses how the Parliament of Canada has expressed the Canadian identity vis-à-vis Quebec's assertions of national identity and their challenge of existing federal structures and policies. The chapter is divided into three sections. The first section provides some background to the Parliament of Canada and highlights important features of the Canadian political system that have strongly shaped its expression of Canadian nationhood, particularly when reacting to Quebec's demands for change. The second section analyses Parliament's position on four constitutional or political initiatives linked to the exposition of the Canadian national identity and its treatment of Quebec's identity: the 1982 Constitution Act; the failed Meech (1987) and Charlottetown (1992) accords; the Clarity Act (2000); and the motion recognizing that the Québécois form a nation within Canada (2006). The conclusion looks ahead to how recent changes in the partisan structure of Parliament may be ushering in new dynamics when it comes to the promotion of the Canadian identity.

THE PARLIAMENT OF CANADA: STRUCTURES AND
POLITICAL DYNAMICS

The Parliament of Canada is bicameral. Its lower house, the House of Commons, inherited the principle of responsible government from the Assembly of the Province of Canada and represents the only chamber of confidence in the federal parliamentary institutions. The members of the upper house, the Senate, are appointed by the prime minister. The Fathers of Confederation decided on the role of the upper house in the parliamentary system and sought to establish through it a form of territorial representation. In the end, the role of senators as unelected but, presumably, erudite persons was to give legislation a "sober second thought." The Senate was also intended to provide territorial representation since a specific number of senators (twenty-four) is assigned to every major "region" of the country (Ontario, Quebec, the Western provinces, and the Maritime provinces). However, the Senate's lack of democratic legitimacy stemming from the appointment procedure has prevented it from playing a forceful role in the federal legislative process and has resulted in the institution often being marginalized in the Canadian political system. For example, the legislation designed to frame any other referendum that could lead to the secession of a province (the Clarity Act) gave to the House of Commons only the responsibility to judge the clarity of the question and of a majority in favour of secession.

The crucial cleavages in the House of Commons are between members representing different political parties. This is helped by the fact that federal political parties have a high degree of discipline. When it comes to the place of Quebec in the Canadian federation, parties have had different, albeit changing, views, and this has conditioned the House of Commons' position. The Liberal Party of Canada (LPC), the historical party of French-Canadians, adopted fairly centralist preferences in the 1970s, 1980s, and 1990s, but veered toward a friendlier attitude toward the claims of Quebec governments in the early 2000s. The Conservative Party of Canada (CPC) (and its predecessor the Progressive Conservative Party of Canada) has been receptive to Quebec's claims for more autonomy and symbolic recognition since the early 1980s despite having been mostly associated with English-Canada and Protestantism for most of its history. The New Democratic Party (NDP) has attempted to reconcile its preference for centralized government as a social-democratic party concerned with equality with a position sympathetic to Quebec's claims. The Reform Party, which held seats in the

House of Commons from 1989 to 2000 and served as official opposition, opposed any formal recognition of Quebec's distinctiveness. Since its creation in 1990, the Bloc Québécois (BQ) has promoted the independence of Quebec. Because senators are appointed by the prime minister, only the two parties that have governed Canada (the LPC and the PC/CPC) are represented there. Party discipline applies, but a bit more loosely than in the House of Commons.

The presence of multiple parties within Parliament has meant that different visions of Canada and of the place of Quebec within the federation typically coexist at any one time. Yet, the ascendency of the executive over Parliament has meant that the vision of the party forming the Government of Canada, rather than a compromise between the various parties' positions, was translated into public policy.

MEGA-CONSTITUTIONAL POLITICS AND THE PARLIAMENT OF CANADA

The Quiet Revolution in Quebec during the 1960s involved a profound political change in the province that resulted in Quebec governments seeking constitutional changes that would either decentralize Canadian federalism while formally recognizing Quebec's distinctiveness (the position of the Quebec Liberal Party) or achieve independence albeit with some form of association with Canada (the position of the Parti Québécois, PQ). At the same time, Pierre Trudeau's LPC (from 1968 on) had different ideas on how to manage Quebec's growing nationalism. For Trudeau, integration through a foundational rights document rather than constitutional differentiation represented the best way to unite Canada. There were, therefore, two very different constitutional projects developing in the 1970s.

After 60 percent of Quebecers opted not to give the PQ government a mandate to negotiate independence with the Government of Canada in 1980, Pierre Trudeau decided to push for a package of constitutional change that would include, most importantly, a Charter of Rights and Freedoms. The Quebec government opposed the project. Interestingly, this opposition was not visible in the House of Commons where seventy-two out of the seventy-five members of Parliament representing Quebec ridings supported the so-called patriation of the Canadian Constitution. This speaks to the strong party discipline existing in the House, since out of the seventy-four Liberal members of Parliament from Quebec (out of a possible seventy-five), only two opposed the constitutional reform. Overall, the patriation, steered through the House by a majority Liberal government, was approved in the House of Commons by a vote of 246 to twenty-four. In the Senate, the result was closer (fifty-nine to twenty-three) and many Quebec Senators spoke against the reform. Senator Flynn, for example, echoed much of what was said in the Quebec National Assembly, arguing that Quebec "is the only province that is victimized in this process."[1]

After the constitutional reform of 1982, the fortunes of the LPC declined, especially in Quebec. Meanwhile, the Progressive Conservative Party, under its new leader Brian Mulroney, was denouncing the patriation without Quebec's consent and pledged, if it were to govern the country, to bring the province back into the constitutional fold with "honour and enthusiasm." The Progressive Conservatives won a huge majority in 1984 (211 out of 282) and its government proceeded to work on a constitutional reform designed to satisfy the Quebec government's "minimal conditions" if it were to sign the Canadian Constitution. The Meech Lake Accord involved a vision of Canadian federalism different from the 1982 Constitutional Act since it recognized Quebec as a "distinct society" and favoured decentralization through the right of a province to opt out of a shared-cost program with full compensation. It was initially agreed to by the governments of the ten provinces and the federal government. The Meech Lake Accord received overwhelming support in the House of Commons (242 to sixteen), with all Quebec members of Parliament voting in favour. The vote in the Senate was closer (forty-seven to twenty-eight).

Nothing coming out of Canada's Parliament gave a sense of what was to come. Indeed, the Meech Lake Accord proved unpopular outside Quebec as opinion leaders such as former prime minister Pierre Trudeau denounced it (more specifically its clause recognizing Quebec as a distinct society) as a betrayal of Canada. Opposition to the accord enabled the parliaments of Newfoundland and Manitoba to resist its ratification, which led to the demise of that constitutional agreement. The overwhelming support received by the Meech Lake Accord in Canada's Parliament did not reflect how it was perceived in Canadian society. The absence in Canadian political institutions of a house of provincial representation with strong democratic legitimacy is at the heart of this paradox. The vision of the country expressed by Canada's Parliament at that time was underpinned by the strong Conservative majority and party discipline and did not reflect the country's federal condition. The same is true for the subsequent Charlottetown Accord, which featured the Meech Lake Accord's content and a variety of other clauses. The Charlottetown Accord received overwhelming support in the House of Commons (233 to twelve) and in the Senate (fifty-eight to two), yet it was defeated in six of the ten provincial referendums held to seek out the opinion of Canadians. As a consequence of these results, the Charlottetown Accord was never implemented.

The failures of the Meech Lake and Charlottetown accords fed nationalism in Quebec, and the PQ, after winning the Quebec elections of 1994, organized a second referendum on sovereignty where the "yes"' camp fell just short of 50 percent. Afterward, the federal Liberal government sought the opinion of Canada's Supreme Court on the parameters of any future referendum on independence and followed up, in 2000, with legislation – the so-called Clarity Act. The Clarity Act was opposed by the Quebec National Assembly, which felt that the federal government was undermining the right of Quebecers to decide on the province's political future by imposing conditions related to both processes (the clarity of the question) and outcome (the clarity of the majority). The changes in the federal party system in the early 1990s, specifically the creation of the sovereignist BQ (which held a plurality of Quebec seats between 1993 and 2011), meant there was opposition to the Clarity Act in the House of Commons. Indeed, all BQ MPs, bringing their sovereignist perspective to the debate, voted against the legislation. Interestingly, the Clarity Act split both the NDP and the Progressive Conservatives and, despite the strong tradition of party discipline, some MPs from both of these opposition parties supported the legislation. Progressive Conservative MP André Bachand said in the House, "This has been a very difficult bill for us. I do not hide that fact. Our party's position has not changed. It is clear that some members will vote with the government. We have tried to explain our position. It was not easy and it has left scars within the party. We do not hide that either."[2]

In the end, the Clarity Act was adopted by a strong majority in the House of Commons (208 to fifty-five), but opposition to the bill reflected the fact that it was not well received among the Quebec political class. The majority in the Senate was smaller (fifty-two to thirty-four), due in part to the fact that the Clarity Act left to the House of Commons only ("elected representatives") the responsibility to determine what constitutes a clear question and a clear majority.

The period of mega-constitutional politics in Canada arguably ends with the Clarity Act. Yet, in 2006 the Conservative government introduced a motion in the House of Commons to "recognize that the Québécois form a nation within a united Canada." The debate on this motion in the House was surprisingly muted considering that the constitutional recognition of Quebec as a distinct society had triggered such opposition in many provinces during the 1980s and the early 1990s. Yet, support for this motion was very strong in the House of Commons (265 to sixteen) with only some Liberal MPs opposing it. Through this motion, the House expressed a vision of the Canadian identity coherent with the failed Meech Lake Accord, that is, accepting of multinationalism and asymmetry, but in opposition to the type of uniform identity promoted by the LPC beginning with Pierre Elliot Trudeau's leadership and by the Reform Party. This vision was supported by most in the Liberal Party and by the former Reformers who became Conservative MPs when the two parties merged. Of course, in the Conservative Party, discipline was no doubt strongly enforced, therefore silencing dissenting voices.

THE 2011 FEDERAL ELECTION AND ITS CONSEQUENCE FOR THE EXPRESSION OF THE CANADIAN IDENTITY IN PARLIAMENT

The 2011 federal election featured an important change in the federal party system, although it remains to be seen whether this change will be long term or temporary. The dominant federal party in Quebec since 1993, the sovereignist BQ, was reduced to four seats (down forty-three seats from the previous election). Most of the electoral support of Quebecers went to the NDP, which had previously never elected an NDP MP in Quebec during a general federal election. Indeed, the NDP took fifty-nine out of the seventy-five Quebec seats and formed, for the first time of its history, the official opposition. The diminished contingent of the BQ in the House of Commons means that the sovereignist view of Canada (that it is unwilling and incapable of accommodating Quebec's distinctiveness) will be much less present in the House of Commons, at least until the next election.

The new standing of the NDP as official opposition also changes identity dynamics in the House of Commons. As a social-democratic party concerned with equality, the NDP has always had centralist tendencies, but it was also most of the time open, at least in principle, to accommodating Quebec's distinctiveness. Now, with its parliamentary core hailing from Quebec (fifty-nine out of 103 seats), the NDP is clearly bringing a Quebec perspective into the House of Commons. For example, in 2013, the party expressed concerns about the 2000 Clarity Act, suggesting that 50 percent+1 could be a sufficient majority to trigger Quebec's independence.

As a forum for the expression of the Canadian identity and for debates on the place of Quebec in the Canadian federation, Canada's Parliament more often than not takes its lead from the executive. Indeed, strong party discipline helps executives with parliamentary majorities transform their visions of the country into public policy. In this context, transformations in the party system, more specifically when they correspond to change in the parties that can hope to form a government, are likely to affect the identity discourse in the House of Commons.

NOTES

1 Canada, *Debates of the Senate*, Ottawa, Tuesday, 8 December 1981, 3387.
2 Canada, *House of Commons Debates*, Ottawa, 15 March 2000, 4721.

9

The Westminster Parliament and Territorial Politics in the United Kingdom

ALAN TRENCH[1]

The United Kingdom is best understood as a parliamentary state. Parliament is its central political institution; while the Crown (embracing the monarchy and the executive branch of government) is the historic starting point, the key feature of the UK's constitution is the doctrine of parliamentary sovereignty. In the unwritten British constitution, the UK Parliament is supreme. There is no higher constitutional law and no legal limit to what Parliament can do, no Parliament can bind another, and Parliament has the power to legislate for all matters across the whole of the UK. While that doctrine has been under pressure in recent years, from the growing power of the executive and from membership of the European Union in particular,[2] it remains the underpinning of the UK. But the UK Parliament also governs a multi-national state. Symbolically, this is illustrated at the heart of the Palace of Westminster, where the ceiling of Central Lobby between the House of Commons and the House of Lords bears images of the patron saints and national emblems of each of its four component nations, England, Scotland, Wales, and Ireland. This often-overlooked territorial dimension of the UK's constitution confuses many observers. The UK is not a unitary state, and never was. Nor is it currently a federal system, or likely to become one, principally because of problems arising from England's relationship with the other parts of the UK. The UK should be regarded as a "state of unions,"[3] the outcome of a sequence of bilateral unions between England and its immediate neighbours.

This chapter will look at some key institutional issues arising from the relationship between the Westminster Parliament and "territorial politics" in Scotland and Wales (and to a lesser degree Northern Ireland).[4] It will focus on three areas that have been particularly problematic: how the Westminster Parliament fails to reflect territorial preferences accurately; the problems that arise from asymmetry and the role of Westminster as the sole legislature for England but one of two legislatures for Scotland, Wales, and Northern Ireland; and how the constitutional position of the Scottish, Welsh, and Northern Ireland devolved legislatures is safeguarded given the doctrine of parliamentary sovereignty. I will argue in this chapter that the UK has sought to come to pragmatic compromises in each of these areas, with varying degrees of success, but without any attempt to rethink in a fundamental way the nature of the United Kingdom after devolution.

WESTMINSTER
AND THE REPRESENTATION OF TERRITORY

Westminster has a rather schizophrenic approach toward territorial issues. Like parliaments in Canada (but in no other European country), the UK Parliament is elected using a single-member plurality system. Each member is elected by a single constituency or riding, and increasingly is expected actively to represent that constituency. This implies a close attachment to the interests of a particular locality, as well as historically promoting a two-party system in accordance with Duverger's law. During the twentieth century, the numbers of MPs became distorted, so that Scotland and Wales were over-represented compared to England on the basis of population.[5] In practice, however, the attachment of MPs to a particular constituency is shaped by a number of non-territorial factors, especially party identification (and the loyalty and discipline that come with it).

However, party-political competition has seen the UK party system become increasingly fragmented over the last fifteen or twenty years. A third party, the Liberal Democrats, emerged as a major factor in the 1980s; more recently, challenges from other parties such as the Scottish National Party (riding a surge of support after the Scottish independence referendum) and the anti-European Union UK Independence Party in England have further weakened Conservative-Labour dominance. The extent to which these lead to three- or four-party competition in individual constituencies is limited. There appears to be a complex pattern of two-party competition, with the Lib Dems often challenging Labour from the right in northern England and the Conservatives from the left in southern England. The entry of new parties (and collapse of the Lib Dem vote since 2010) clearly has a major impact on established parties, but it is unclear how this will affect voting in particular constituencies, or the number of MPs for each party.

Increasing variation in patterns of voting reinforce the problem. This became particularly evident from the 1980s onward, when the Conservative vote – below the UK average since the 1950s – declined heavily in Scotland and Wales (as well as parts of northern England). Consequently, those parts of the UK were subject to a Westminster government with limited local support. The use of a single-member plurality electoral system has led to further distortions in electoral outcomes, polarizing party choices, and so resulting in significantly disproportionate outcomes. These have benefited the Conservatives in England, and Labour in Scotland and Wales to date – with the Lib Dems losing out in England and Wales, the Conservatives in Scotland, and nationalist parties in both, given the shares of the vote they get in Westminster elections. This is illustrated for the 2010 election in tables 9.1, 9.2, and 9.3.

The result is that existing political differences across the UK have been magnified by the electoral system: England does not vote as strongly for the Conservatives as the number of English Conservative MPs suggests, nor have Scotland and Wales been the bastions of popular support for Labour that is suggested by the number of Labour MPs they elect. These distortions become particularly important when it comes to considering how the party balance from the various parts of the UK affects politics within Westminster, and the so-called "West Lothian question."

The prospect that Scotland will return a large number of Scottish National Party (SNP) MPs in the May 2015 general election, at the expense of Labour, intensifies these questions.[6] The mutual hostility of the Conservatives and SNP may help the SNP electorally, but complicate the operation of Westminster hugely, particularly if the election leads to minority or coalition government.

Electoral reform has been debated for many years. While the Liberal Democrats have been long-standing advocates of moving toward a proportional system, both Labour and the Conservatives have strongly resisted it and remained attached to the current majoritarian model, even as British politics has embraced multiple parties, not just two. If the major parties were serious about reducing territorial distortions in the electoral system, rather than using it as a political football, they would have embraced a proportional system long ago. However, the closest the UK has been to change was the referendum on whether the preferential (but not proportional) "alternative vote" system should be adopted, held in May 2011 and resoundingly rejected.[7]

Table 9.1
Shares of vote and parliamentary seats in England, 2010 UK general election

	Percentage of vote	Percentage of seats
Labour	28.1	35.8
Conservative	39.6	55.9
Lib Dem	24.2	8.1
UKIP	3.5	0
Green Party	1.0	0.2
BNP	2.1	0

Source: BBC News website, http://news.bbc.co.uk/1/shared/election2010/results/

Table 9.2
Share of votes and seats in Scotland, 2010 UK general election

	Percentage of vote	Percentage of seats
Labour	42.0	69.5
Conservative	16.7	1.7
Lib Dem	18.9	18.6
SNP	19.9	10.1

Source: BBC News website, http://news.bbc.co.uk/1/shared/election2010/results/

Table 9.3
Share of votes and seats in Wales, 2010 UK general election

	Percentage of vote	Percentage of seats
Labour	36.2	72.5
Conservative	26.1	20.0
Lib Dem	20.1	7.5
Plaid Cymru	11.3	7.5

Source: BBC News website, http://news.bbc.co.uk/1/shared/election2010/results/

CONSTITUTIONAL ANOMALIES OF DEVOLUTION:
THE WEST LOTHIAN QUESTION

Devolution has given rise to a major anomaly affecting the UK Parliament. This is the so-called "West Lothian question," which is not an anomaly of devolution as such, but of asymmetric devolution to Scotland, Wales, and Northern Ireland, while England remains governed by the UK Parliament alone. So Scottish, Welsh, and Northern Ireland

MPs continue to sit in Parliament and take part in debates and votes on matters that affect England but not the places that elected those MPs. This anomaly is named after the former MP for West Lothian in Scotland, Tam Dalyell, who pointed out that he would not be able to vote for matters like health or education that affected his constituents, as they would be devolved – but he would still be able to vote on health and education affecting England.

In practical terms, the impact of the West Lothian question has been limited. Westminster governments that have a UK-wide majority have normally had a majority in England as well. On only two occasions since 1945 has the UK Government's overall parliamentary majority depended on Scottish (or Scottish and Welsh) MPs – two Labour governments, one elected in October 1964 with a four-seat majority, and the minority government elected in February 1974. Both were replaced by majority Labour governments within a short while (in March 1966 and October 1974 respectively). There have been only three votes since 1999 where the government's majority has been smaller than the number of Scottish or devolved MPs voting – in other words, where MPs whose constituents were not directly affected by the issue at stake voted and their votes were decisive. All three votes occurred during the Blair Labour government, and related to controversial policies which had stirred up backbench revolts – to which Scottish MPs were less subject.[8]

The limited practical importance of the West Lothian issue does not stop it being a bone of political contention, particularly for the Conservative Party. Almost by definition, any Conservative UK government will have a majority of English MPs. Even if it does not rely on Scottish (or Scottish and Welsh) MPs for its majority, Labour governments have always had large numbers of MPs from Scotland and Wales as part of any majority, unlike the Conservatives. (The surge in support for the SNP suggests that Labour may lose many of its Scottish MPs but need SNP support to form a government instead.) The Conservatives' advocacy of this issue reflects the tension between their interests as a party whose electoral strength lies in England and their commitment to maintaining the union, while for Labour their interest in maintaining support across Britain has not been matched by their actions. The question raises public concern too; opinion polling evidence suggests that English voters are increasingly unhappy about the problem, even if they are not clear about what positive alternative they want.[9] Politically, the problem is likely to become worse after the 2015 election. The Conservatives have sought to stigmatize the SNP during the election campaign and question the legitimacy of any government relying on SNP support, while the SNP's new leader, Nicola Sturgeon, has indicated that her party's MPs in the new Parliament will take part in matters relating to England which also have an effect on Scotland, unlike in previous Parliaments.

There are four responses to the West Lothian question – other than doing nothing about it (which was the approach under the Blair and Brown Labour governments). One would be to develop a regional tier of government within England. Regionalization along these lines was tentatively tried by Labour in the early 2000s, but never developed very far and was rejected by the voters in a referendum in the first region outside London where it was tried, the North East, in 2004. The second solution would be to establish an English Parliament, with powers for England similar to those of the Scottish Parliament and the assemblies in Wales and Northern Ireland. But such a parliament would represent about 85 percent of the population of the UK as a whole, and would not be a stable solution (no federal system with such an imbalance between the size of constituent units has survived for long). The third solution is to reduce the number of Westminster MPs elected from Scotland, Wales, and Northern Ireland, in partial recognition of the more limited role Westminster plays in governing those parts of the UK. This happened during devolution to the Northern Irish Parliament in 1922–72, and so is sometimes called the "Stormont discount." But this approach would also reduce the voice of those territories when it comes to *non-devolved* matters – so one would be saying that Scottish or Welsh voters counted for less when it came to decisions about going to war, signing treaties, or the welfare system, because health and education were devolved. That is unlikely to be acceptable in the long term either.

The fourth solution is sometimes called the "in and out" solution, or "English votes for English laws." It would limit votes on at least some parliamentary stages of legislation affecting only England to MPs from England. There are serious practical problems with this: most Westminster legislation has provisions affecting England (or England and Wales), but also extending to the whole UK, or to Scotland, or to Northern Ireland. That would need to change to make "English votes for English laws" a reality. So would financing arrangements for devolved governments, since their funding under the Barnett formula is affected by changes in spending on "comparable functions" in England. That means that the devolved governments have an interest in spending on health or education in England, even if the substantive policy is devolved. (In reality, this makes little difference to how spending decisions are taken – and MPs have seldom sought to act as advocates for devolved governments in the way such a linkage assumes. However, the constitutional point stands.) There is also a "governability" problem. What would happen if the majority of English MPs were from a different party than Parliament as a whole – if a government which commanded the confidence of Parliament as a whole could not command support from English MPs for specific measures? These problems are potentially manageable, certainly more than those of other approaches to the West Lothian question, but they are not straightforward. It is therefore little surprise that they have been adopted as policy, first by the Conservative Party (following the report of a party Democracy Task Force in 2009), and then by the McKay Commission, set up by the Coalition UK Government in 2010.[10] The McKay recommendation was for the detailed consideration at committee and recommittal stages to be among English MPs only, a "legislative consent motion" for general approval of the bill limited to English MPs as well, but with all MPs able to vote on second reading (general consideration of the principles of a bill) and third reading (final approval of it) – an approach which seeks to balance English with UK-wide interests.[11] Making such an approach work in the longer term would require the Conservatives to be willing not to treat such a constitutional issue as a political football, which in turn means making some hard choices about the nature of the Conservatives' commitment to the union. Conservative behaviour since the Scottish referendum suggests that may be hard to achieve.

MANAGING RELATIONS BETWEEN WESTMINSTER AND THE DEVOLVED LEGISLATURES: THE SEWEL CONVENTION

Relations between the UK Parliament and the devolved legislatures are limited at best. On the day-to-day level, they are most cooperative and cordial with the National Assembly for Wales, which regularly facilitates sittings of Westminster committees in the Senedd in Cardiff. The Northern Ireland Assembly does likewise, though less often. The Scottish Parliament is protective of its position and prerogatives, and will not permit UK Parliament committees to meet on its premises. There are few other forums where elected members of the UK's various legislatures can meet and form social acquaintances or share experience – in contrast to intergovernmental liaison through the Joint Ministerial Committee and British Irish Council. Ironically, one of the few forums where members of all four legislatures do encounter each other is the British-Irish Inter-Parliamentary Body, formed to enable British MPs and members of the Dáil in the Republic of Ireland to meet, and in which the devolved legislatures now take part as well.

The most serious point of contact between devolved and UK parliaments arises from the working of the Sewel Convention. The convention provides that the "the UK Parliament would not normally legislate with regard to devolved matters except with the agreement of the devolved legislature."[12] This convention is key to safeguarding the prerogatives and position of the devolved legislatures, since it means Westminster gives up the power to legislate for matters for which the devolved parliament or assemblies are responsible. Given the difficulty of entrenching devolution, this provides a powerful safeguard, while also enabling a substantial measure of flexibility in how government works across the UK. However, very importantly, the convention does not apply just to "ordinary" policy matters but also to conferring or removing functions from the devolved executives and legislatures. It therefore has a fundamental constitutional importance, transforming devolution from being a delegation of power from a sovereign parliament (like local government) to a transfer to a constitutionally recognized and protected, if formally subordinate, tier of government. Moreover, it does so in a way that is both flexible in practice and recognizes the primarily political nature of the UK's constitution.

In reality, however, this convention regulates relations between executives more than legislatures. Its foundation remains the Memorandum of Understanding, an intergovernmental agreement, rather than any constitutional or statutory provision, or even a resolution of the UK Parliament. However, there are now suggestions that it will be put on a statutory basis for both Scotland and Wales, following the work of the Smith Commission.[13] Moreover, communication about the convention remains a matter between governments, not legislatures. In that sense, the convention subordinates devolved legislatures to their executives, not vice versa. That clearly runs contrary to a proper understanding of the principle of the separation of powers and legislative supremacy, however much practical sense it may make on the administrative level.

The key test of the standing of a constitutional convention in the British system is whether it is complied with when it is put under real pressure. This test produces a somewhat uncertain outcome. In one key case, when there were suggestions that the UK Parliament would pass legislation to which devolved consent had not been granted – the Scotland Act 2012, which conferred some tax-setting powers on the Scottish Parliament – it was complied with. The Scottish Parliament has never withheld legislative consent from Westminster legislation when it has been sought, although on some occasions (including the Scotland Act 2012 and the Welfare Reform Act 2012) it has been qualified. In Wales, however, legislative consent has been withheld on a number of occasions. In those cases, amendments have been laid before Westminster to remove the application in Wales of the provisions from which consent was withheld, so there was compliance in that sense – but the extent of compliance was in each case limited and minimal, so while there was compliance with the letter of the convention, the spirit was not fully respected.

CONCLUSION

Westminster has embraced the challenge of devolution to only a limited extent. It has made little attempt to make territorial representation more equitable or related to votes, although this might reduce some of the territorial tensions that have become serious since devolution. It has taken little action yet to address the anomaly of Scottish and Welsh MPs voting on matters relating only to England. It has acknowledged a principle that respects devolved autonomy and safeguards devolved functions, in an ingenious if possibly unintended way, but it has failed to give that principle any sort of formal recognition. Despite its profound importance, the Sewel Convention continues to rest on a weak constitutional foundation.

This mixed and tentative response to devolution is not a surprise, given the unwritten British constitution, which relies heavily on convention, custom, and practice, as understood and implemented principally by politicians. It reflects pragmatism and convenience more than principle or any syncretic understanding of the constitution as a whole. Yet these conventions and assumptions are under increasing strain, as they seek to accommodate an increasingly varied range of party actors and acrimonious conflict and can no longer rely on calculations of party advantage or tacit shared understandings to manage those.

The result of the 2015 general election will put these conventions and assumptions to a very severe test. The virtual elimination of the pro-UK parties in Scotland and election of a large number of SNP MPs dramatically changes the dynamics of Parliament. These MPs will not simply seek to advance the cause of further devolution for Scotland, or to advance policies (such as end to austerity economics or rejection of replacements for the Trident nuclear missile submarines). They will also seek to prove that the parliamentary system can no longer serve Scotland's interests, and that the incumbent UK Government (indeed, any incumbent UK government) is illegitimate in the eyes of Scottish voters. This creates particular difficulties for the pro-UK parties, since it is hard to see how *any* accommodation of such Scottish demands is possible, while ignoring or marginalizing the SNP at Westminster will only reinforce its arguments. This is not just a huge challenge to the nature of UK parliamentary democracy but also marks a dramatic advance for a party which owes its current political profile and significance to the establishment of a sub-state arena. It can now move its arguments to a statewide arena which has a questionable capacity to respond to such challenges, institutionally or politically. The UK's constitutional future will give much food for thought and analysis in coming years.

NOTES

1 This chapter was finalized in April 2015, before the result of the May general election was known.
2 Anthony King, *The British Constitution* (Oxford: Oxford University Press, 2007).
3 James Mitchell, "The United Kingdom as a State of Unions: Unity of Government, Equality of Political Rights and Diversity of Institutions," 24–47, in Alan Trench, ed., *Devolution and Power in the United Kingdom* (Manchester: Manchester University Press, 2007).
4 This discussion is chiefly concerned with England, Scotland, and Wales, and omits Northern Ireland. This is principally because Northern Ireland has a quite different party system; with the partial exception of the 2010 UK general election (when there was an alliance between the Conservatives and the Ulster Unionists), none of the British parties contest elections in Northern Ireland, and the Northern Ireland parties do not function in Great Britain.
5 Iain McLean, "Are Scotland and Wales Over-Represented in the House of Commons?" *Political Quarterly* 66, no. 4 (1995): 250–68.
6 The text of this chapter was finalized in April 2015, before the result of the May 2015 general election.
7 There is clear evidence of differential voting; the nationalist parties in Scotland and Wales perform more strongly in devolved than in Westminster elections. The Conservatives also tend to do better in devolved elections, where proportional systems mean votes for them are more likely to see representatives elected.
8 Guy Lodge, Meg Russell, and Oonagh Gay, "The Impact of Devolution on Westminster: If not Now, When?," 193–216, in Alan Trench, ed., *The*

Dynamics of Devolution: The State of the Nations 2004 (Exeter: Imprint Academic Press, 2004).

9 See, for example, C. Jeffery et al., *Taking England Seriously: The New English Politics. The Future of England Survey 2014* (Wales Governance Centre, Cardiff, 2014), http://sites.cardiff.ac.uk/wgc/files/2014/10/Taking-England-Seriously_The-New-English-Politics.pdf, accessed 30 December 2015.

10 United Kingdom, *Report of the Commission on the Consequences of Devolution for the House of Commons*, London, The McKay Commission, 2013. See also HM Government, *The Implications of Devolution for England* Cm 8969 (London, December 2014).

11 In Westminster practice, detailed line-by-line scrutiny takes place at committee stage, and that is when the bulk of amendments are tabled and considered. However, the quality of that scrutiny is distinctly variable.

12 United Kingdom, *Memorandum of Understanding and Supplementary Agreements between the United Kingdom Government, the Scottish Ministers, the Welsh Ministers, and the Northern Ireland, London*, London, The Stationery Office, 2013, paragraph 14.

13 The Smith Commission, *Report of the Smith Commission for further devolution of powers to the Scottish Parliament*, November 2014; HM Government, *Scotland in the United Kingdom: An Enduring Settlement* Cm 8990 (London, January 2015).

10

The Spanish Parliament: Its Role in the Definition of the National Community and the Politics of National Unity

CÉSAR COLINO

The Cortes Generales is the legislature of Spain, established by the 1978 Constitution. It is a bicameral parliament consisting of the Congress of Deputies (350 MPs), regarded as the lower chamber, and the Senate, considered the upper house. Although some of its history as a modern parliament can be traced back to the Restoration period (Restauración, 1876–1923) or the II Republic, 1931–39 (unicameral), it could be considered a young parliament, adopted anew during the post-Franco transition. Regarding the Senate, Art. 69 of the 1978 Spanish Constitution establishes a mixed composition, characterized by two types of senators – constituency elected senators (three-quarters), elected by direct universal suffrage through a majoritarian formula, and regionally appointed senators – a quarter. The latter are appointed by the Autonomous Communities (ACs), usually nominated by their regional parliaments through procedures regulated by their statutes of autonomy.

Given the transition's consensus-building requirements and the historic experience of instability and political violence during and after the Second Republic in the 1930s, the founding fathers agreed during the constituent legislature in 1977–78 on a sort of rationalized parliamentarism, a model that was less interested in controlling the government or empowering citizens than in guaranteeing the stability of the executives and strengthening the new emerging parties through the fusion of powers in the majority group in parliament. It chose to reinforce party groups vis-à-vis individual MPs. Also, it gave to the Congress of Deputies pre-eminence over the Senate in the legislative process. In practice, the most important powers of the Spanish Parliament are budgetary and the scrutiny of government policies but, as in other parliamentary or Westminster systems, the executive clearly dominates over the Parliament in the legislative agenda, regardless of the number of seats the majority party in Parliament achieves.

Several institutional arrangements and procedural rules, such as party regulations and the electoral system, have systematically favoured a two-party system with clear pluralities or majorities and highly disciplined parties. At the same time, the national Parliament has always featured some non-state-wide party groups (nationalists and regionalists) with members in both houses. Moreover, in its thirty-five years of operation and ten legislatures, the Spanish Parliament has not experienced a single case of coalition government. Single party executives, often supported by informal parliamentary coalitions with non-state-wide parties, have displayed very important degrees of authority to set and pursue their political and policy agendas.[1]

This predominance of the executive vis-à-vis the Congress of Deputies is due to several factors.[2] For example, Congress is organized procedurally (committees, initiatives, debates) in a way that promotes disciplined parliamentary groups to the detriment of individual MPs. Opposition groups in the lower house are fragmented and ideologically very different, making it difficult to achieve the coordination necessary to influence policy. Despite this, in some cases legislation in some policy areas has been passed through consensus and cooperation between the government and the opposition, including minority regionalist or nationalist groups.[3]

This preponderance of the government and Parliament's weak capacity of oversight, especially when there is a majority, does not mean that the Parliament is not a central political actor and setting in terms of representation, public visibility, the legitimation of democratic governance, and the recruitment of new politicians – ministers are almost always drawn from the Parliament, mainly the lower house. The Cortes Generales has been the main stage in decisive moments of recent Spanish political life and has been the main protagonist in Spanish constitutional debates. The media increasingly report on the annual parliamentary debates on national and constitutional issues and weekly question periods in both houses.

As regards the Senate, apart from its constitutional role as co-legislative power and its scrutiny and control prerogatives, its formal powers include some that are equal to those of the lower house in some regional-related issues, on which it may deliver its opinion before the other house does. These issues are the authorization of cooperation agreements among autonomous communities, the regulation of the Interterritorial Compensation Fund, the eventual implementation of measures to force regional governments to comply with their constitutional obligations, and the assessment of the need for issuing harmonizing laws. The Senate also intervenes in the reform of the regional statutes of autonomy and holds a debate (in theory annually) on the state of the "State of Autonomies" where all the regional presidents meet and symbolically use their co-official languages in the debates. In reality, these debates have only been held in 1994, 1997, and 2005. Lately, the Senate has also hosted the meetings of the Conference of Presidents.

In practice, the legislative influence of the Senate is minimal since it has only suspensive veto capacity. In most issues the Senate is subordinated to the Congress of Deputies and it is difficult for the second chamber to act as the channel for representation of regional interests in national policy-making or a forum for real intergovernmental cooperation. Recently, from 2004 to 2011, the upper house's party composition has differed from that of the Congress of Deputies, with the opposition parties (e.g., People's Party and Catalan nationalists) allied against the socialist government and repeatedly vetoing legislation passed by the lower chamber. In fact, the Senate vetoed and returned the national budget bill to the Congress in 2004, 2007, and 2008. Even in these cases, however, the Congress has been able to override the veto, negotiating a majority vote. This means that, in most cases, the role of representation of regional interests in national legislation and policies has been taken on by the parliamentary groups of nationalist or regionalist parties in the Congress, through their control and legislative initiatives, and their weight as necessary voting partners for the government group.[4] Most of the regional-related functions of the Senate are exercised by one of its specialized standing legislative committees, the General Committee of the Autonomous Communities, created in 1994 to give the Senate a more territorial orientation. It has a peculiar composition of fifty-two senators – twice as many senators as the other standing legislative committees, mostly regionally appointed – and representatives of central and regional governments, usually ministers, but also premiers, who are invited to join the senators in the hearings and debates of the committee. Regional ministers are also entitled to request the committee to convene.

Although the General Committee of the Autonomous Communities has no final decision-making power, it was becoming increasingly relevant as a forum for discussion and participation for regional governments in the late 1990s and 2000s. The number of its meetings increased from twenty-three in 1996 to 2000, to thirty-eight in 2000 to 2004, and forty-five in 2004 to 2008. By the mid-2000s, for example, during a two-year period, seventy-five regional ministers and three regional premiers participated in the sessions and debates of the committee alongside the senators and several ministers of the central government. However, this strange mix of legislators and members of the executive has not achieved the goal of serving as a forum for deliberation and intergovernmental cooperation. The committee has mainly been used by regional ministers and premiers of regions ruled by the national opposition parties as a new forum to attack the central government on party political grounds. In the present tenth legislature since 2011, with the People's Party dominating the Senate, the committee has been deactivated.

In sum, if we consider the main functions attributed to legislatures around the world, the predominant role and functions of both houses of the Spanish Parliament in the Spanish political system, a parliamentary system itself, have been those of representation and legitimation. Policy-making, political accountability, and recruitment have been visibly less important than in other countries' legislatures.

THE ROLE OF THE SPANISH PARLIAMENT IN DEFINING THE POLITICAL COMMUNITY AND INTEGRATING TERRITORIAL DIVERSITY: POLITICAL AUTONOMY, IDENTITY, AND RECOGNITION

The Spanish Parliament has several unique features related to its nature as a forum of territorial politics and as the arena for both debating national unity and constitutional issues and representing and integrating a diversity of state-wide and regional parties and interests. It has also been active, since the beginning of the current democratic institutions, in matters relative to the definition and promotion of a new Spanish national identity, based on the 1978 Constitutional Pact. At the same time, the Spanish Parliament has helped to recognize and reflect the diversity of nation-building projects and political communities constituting the Spanish state. Citizens of communities such as Catalonia and the Basque Country, with dual identities and minority nationalist movements representing citizens with exclusive regional identities, have been well represented according to their population in the Cortes Generales. In both cases, however, Catalan and Basque deputies and senators belonging to state-wide parties have usually outnumbered those representing nationalist parties from those ACs. Currently, for instance, of the forty-seven Catalan MPs, twenty-eight belong to state-wide parties (PP and PSOE) and nineteen to the ruling Catalan nationalist parties. In the case of the eighteen Basque deputies in Congress, for the first time there is a majority of nationalist deputies, with eleven seats.[5]

The Cortes Generales as Arena of Territorial Politics and Constitutional Policies

Although intergovernmental relations in Spain are dominated by the executives, with only a limited role for parliaments, and the Senate has failed to represent the ACs' interests in national policy-making, parliamentary groups of nationalist or regionalist parties have traditionally used the Parliament, through their scrutiny and legislative initiatives, to promote the interests of their (or all) ACs in national legislation. ACs have no veto power in national legislation, but in practice an AC ruled by a regionalist or nationalist party may exercise a near de facto veto position if the government party group needs this party's MPs support. This dynamic may affect all policy fields but is most relevant in constitutional and territorial policies regarding devolution of powers, regional funding, and the accommodation of minority nations.

ACs may also participate indirectly, through their regionally appointed senators, in national legislation, or scrutinize the central government through the Senate or by means of the MPs representing their governing regional parties in the Congress of Deputies. In addition, ACs can intervene in central legislation at the Spanish Parliament through the right of legislative initiative by regional parliaments, which may propose bills in the Spanish lower house. This right of legislative initiative has been exercised forty-two times during the seventh legislature (2000–04), thirty-four times in the eighth (2004–08), twenty-eight times in the ninth (2008–11), and fourteen times in the current tenth legislature since 2011. The procedure includes the public presentation and defence of the bill by representatives of the regional parliament at the plenary of the Congress of Deputies, which in some cases will have considerable media or public impact.

Last but not least, the Spanish Parliament becomes the centre of constitutional territorial politics – and the centre of national media attention from time to time – in its constitutional role in approving the regional statutes of autonomy and their amendments, in concert with the regional parliaments. Regional statutes of autonomy are quasi-constitutional laws in several respects, but they have the status of a national organic law, subject to the same approval requirements as organic laws at the Spanish Parliament. Both the ACs and the Spanish Parliament may initiate amendments to the regional statutes of autonomy and must jointly intervene and agree in the approval of the amendments. Thus, amendments may not be unilateral, but have to respond to both regional and national interests. The arbitration between the interests of the AC and the general interests represented by the central government and other ACs is theoretically assured through including a delegation of deputies from the proposing regional parliament that defends the regional amendment proposals in the discussions of the Committee for Constitutional Affairs in both the lower and upper houses. This implies that the Parliament becomes the arena of public bilateral negotiations and deliberation. In terms of public visibility, this procedure may include a first reading of the draft amendments in the plenary of the Congress of Deputies, where a representative of the regional parliament, who may be the regional premier, will defend the proposed amendments to the Statute of Autonomy. This occasion usually involves considerable solemnity, media attention, and the presence in the lower chamber of most regional higher authorities and politicians as guests.

There are other procedures and mechanisms through which the national Parliament may have a role in territorial and national unity issues – for example, through debates and prime ministers' speeches upon the occasion of the State of the Nation debate every year, through the debates on the State of the Autonomies held in the Senate, and through the use of written and oral questions and interpellations by deputies from different ACs and non-state-wide party groups.

Moreover, there can be inquiry committees and study subcommittees in the Senate (*ponencias*) for studying constitutional issues and proposing reforms. In 1994 a subcommittee was formed "for the study of the constitutional reform of the Senate" out of the joint meeting of the General Committee of the ACs and the Senate Constitutional Committee. It held its sessions throughout 1995 until the dissolution of Parliament in early 1996 and conducted important preparatory work, mainly based on hearings that summoned all the "fathers of the Constitution," the regional premiers, and a large group of prestigious academics. The study subcommittee final reports, although not leading to a political agreement, represented a good starting point for any future Senate reform. Currently, a subcommittee to study the "reinforcement of the Senate functions" has been created in 2012.

Finally, like other parliaments, the Cortes Generales plays a symbolic or "dignified" function in representing the Spanish nation and its unity, but also its diversity. The former is epitomized, for instance, in solemn occasions such as the crowning of the king, or the Oath of Allegiance to the Constitution by the Crown Prince of Asturias, or the opening of Parliament by the king, all of these usually done in a joint session of the Congress and the Senate.

Regarding diversity, the Parliament has also reflected and displayed symbolically the different nationalities and regions constituting the state. This has been done mainly by the upper house, the Senate, where all seventeen regional flags are flown at the entrance, and which usually serves as the seat of the meetings of the Conference of Presidents, received by the king in all solemnity. A very important issue regarding the symbolic recognition of diversity has been the use of all co-official languages in the Parliament. While the Congress of Deputies has been reluctant to renounce the exclusive use of the common Castilian-Spanish as *lingua franca* in its deliberations and records, the Senate has recognized and allowed the use of co-official languages – Catalan/Valencian, Galician, and Basque – providing simultaneous interpretation, since 2005 at meetings of the General Committee of the ACs, and since 2011 for the debates of motions in the plenary sessions. This was done at the request of thirty-four nationalist senators, through an amendment of its standing orders.

Some Landmark Parliamentary Debates on the National Community and Spain's Territorial Organization

A good way to understand the Spanish Parliament's contribution to the debates and political struggles surrounding the definition and renovation of the country's national identity and its internal diversity is to identify some relevant debates, documents, or texts that illustrate the importance of the Parliament for Spanish public life.[6]

First are the constitutional debates of the constituent Parliament during 1978.[7] After receiving a first constitutional draft elaborated by the seven "Fathers of the Constitution," the members of the Constitutional Committee of the Congress of Deputies deliberated for two months, with very sophisticated argumentations, and spent a great deal of time discussing, among other things, the nature of Spain as a nation. With the goal of asserting Spanish identity as a nation and simultaneously fully restructuring its territorial organization, they discussed at length provisions such as articles 1 and 2, which ascribed sovereignty to the whole Spanish people and introduced the term "nationalities" into the constitution. This controversial proposal required a great effort in consensus-building, since it sought to accommodate those who postulated the existence of a Spanish nation as the social basis for the Spanish state, and those so-called "peripheral" nationalist proposals that recognized the existence of differentiated substate national identities, especially in Catalonia and the Basque Country.

The debates among the constituent deputies and senators thus revolved around the concepts of nation, nationality, and region. Two main positions were observable: first, those interpreting "nation" and "nationality" as synonymous terms, giving them substantial political content associated with state formation and pointing to the contradiction posed by the simultaneous recognition of different "nationalities" in the constitution and second, those MPs who were willing to accept as a starting point the classical distinction between "political nation" and "cultural nation" or nationality, to justify the simultaneous constitutional recognition of a Spanish nation alongside nationalities and regions within it. Many MPs defended the character of Spain as a nation on the grounds of the classical objective and subjective criteria that usually define national entities, referring mainly to historical events and episodes of a political or military nature that made Spain an imagined community and constituted the national imagery of Spanish nationalism from the beginning of the nineteenth century, but also referring to linguistic and cultural factors, together with the notion that Spain was considered a nation by the vast majority of its inhabitants throughout history.[8] Only two minority groups defended the right of self-determination for the Spanish regions, but this position was defeated by the majority and not even defended by most of the regional nationalists.

Another example of debates on the nature of the Spanish national community can be seen during the 1980s when the Congress of Deputies debated the day of the national holiday. In 1981, on 26 and 31 March a harmonization bill intended to regulate the use of the terms "nation," "national," and "nationality" was discussed but was not passed. On 19 May of that year, a bill was discussed to declare 6 December, the day of approval of the 1978 Constitution, a national holiday. The debates revolved around two main dates, 6 December and 12 October, the traditional Hispanity day (*Día de la Hispanidad*) commemorating the Discovery of America.[9] The Basque and Catalan nationalist parliamentary groups and the socialists had proposed a bill in December 1980 to declare 6 December a national holiday. In support of the proposal they cited the preamble to the Spanish Constitution. They argued that 6 December 1978 was the date when "the Spanish people ratified overwhelmingly in peace and freedom, the Constitution of 1978." They also argued that the constitution marked the opening of a new phase in the life of the Spanish people, governed by the principles of justice, freedom, and democratic coexistence, which "all peoples and nationalities of Spain should celebrate." Most of the interventions in the debate argued in favour of this date, even the Catalan nationalists, represented by MP Miquel Roca, who argued that "the constitutional political system requires its own symbols and there is no better symbol in a democratic regime than its constitution, which is the representation of democracy and freedom." This bill was not passed because the legislature ended. The government subsequently declared through an executive decree in 1983 that 6 December was the National Holiday of Spain. Later, in November 1983, 6 December was also declared the National Holiday in a decree establishing it as solemn institutional celebration. Then, a bill declaring 6 December as the National Holiday was finally debated on 17 September 1987 in the Congress and 6 October in the Senate. In all these debates the civic versus more cultural or ethnic conceptions of the Spanish nation can be traced.

Other landmark debates that could be mentioned are the debates in the Senate about "the state of the State of Autonomies," held in 1994, 1997, and 2005. Some of these debates, in which for the first time the regional premiers used their co-official languages, dealt with the loyalty of Catalan nationalism to the constitutional state (see speech by Jordi Pujol on 26 September 1994), the tensions between symmetry and asymmetry (March 1997), and the need for intergovernmental cooperation (September 2005).

Finally, the debates about the reform of the Catalan Statute of Autonomy in 2006 can be referred to as landmark debates on the constitutional issues of national unity. A joint drafting subcommittee comprising eleven central state MPs (mostly Catalan deputies themselves) and eleven MPs from the regional Catalan Parliament produced a draft that was subsequently discussed at the Standing Legislative Committee for Constitutional Affairs, also with a joint composition of parliamentarians of both central and regional parliaments (fifty and fifty MPs). This is a typical example of the Spanish Parliament serving as an arena for negotiations and detailed deliberations to reach an agreement accommodating Catalonia's aspirations for recognition and additional power and resources. The long discussions over several sessions in March 2006 of all the proposed amendments reflected very accurately the range of arguments and positions in the debate on the unity and the plurinationality of Spain.

THE RECENT PARLIAMENTARY POLITICS
OF NATIONAL UNITY:
DEALING WITH SELF-DETERMINATION DEMANDS
AND THE RECENT SECESSIONIST CHALLENGE (2004–14)

One of the most significant challenges that the Spanish Parliament has confronted in recent years has been the attempt by Basque and Catalan regional governments and nationalist parties to see a right of self-determination recognized by the Spanish Parliament. On several occasions since 2004, with the Ibarretxe Plan coming from the Basque Parliament as a proposed amendment to the Basque Statute of Autonomy, and recently, since 2012, after the secessionist turn of mainstream Catalan nationalism and its ruling party, the Cortes Generales has rejected the idea of a unilateral possibility of sovereignty-association (as proposed in the Ibarretxe Plan) or self-determination for the Spanish autonomous communities in public debates and votes on several motions and legislative proposals. We can pinpoint the reaction of the majority of both houses in response to these secessionist demands referring to a number of recent parliamentary initiatives and debates.

On 1 February 2005 the Ibarretxe Plan was submitted to the Cortes as an amendment to the Statute of Autonomy of the Basque Country. The Basque premier Ibarretxe defended the proposal at a first plenary session of Congress and it was rejected by 90 percent of the house. Still, in 2008 Ibarretxe tried to hold a consultation on the "right to decide"; the Constitutional Court prevented this, arguing, as most parties had done in Parliament, that the single owner of the "right to decide" was the Spanish people as a whole and the Basque government lacked jurisdiction to call a referendum on Spanish-wide constitutional issues.

Since the fall of 2012, Catalan MPs have also presented several initiatives in the Congress or the Senate. For example, on 9 October there was a motion, initiated by the nationalists of ERC, requesting that the central government transfer to the Catalan Parliament its exclusive competence to call for a referendum on the independence of Catalonia. This motion was rejected with the votes of PP, PSOE, and UPyD and was supported by ERC, CiU, Plural Left, and PNV. In the preamble to the initiative, ERC noted that the referendum is one of the main instruments of popular participation, which "should be" a standard expression of government policy mechanism.[10] Several days later, in a Senate question period on 23 October, there was an intense debate between Prime Minister Rajoy and the Catalan nationalist senators when they questioned the prime minister about his opinion on the recent Edinburgh Agreement to hold a referendum in Scotland.

One year later, on 29 October 2013, Rosa Díez, the leader of UPyD, submitted a motion in order for the Congress of Deputies to solemnly reject the right to decide and the sovereignist plan of Catalonia's premier Artur Mas, emphasizing that only the Spanish people as a whole can exercise the right to decide and be consulted since national sovereignty is indivisible. This motion was in part a reaction to the declaration of the Catalan Parliament in January describing the Catalan people as a "sovereign political and legal subject." The motion was supported by PP, PSOE – after some hesitation and this time divided with its Catalan backbenchers abstaining – UPyD, UPN, and Foro Asturias (265 MPs) and was opposed by nine left or nationalist parties in the lower house (CiU, PNV, IU, ICV, CHA (Chunta Aragonesista), ERC, Amaiur, BNG, and Compromís), totaling forty-eight MPs. This motion represented the first time that the Spanish Parliament has taken a position since the Catalan premier had declared his intention of organizing a consultation on the independence of Catalonia.

A similar debate took place on 17 February 2014, when the same party, UPyD, submitted a motion that the Congress of Deputies should reject the secessionist plan of the Catalan government. Around 85 percent of the house voted in favour of this motion, with votes from UPyD, PP, and PSOE, plus two votes of the non-party group, with 272 votes in favour, forty-three against, and one abstention. On the one hand, the motion requested that "the Congress expressly and emphatically reject the secessionist plan of the Government of Catalonia approved by the Catalan Parliament on 27 September" and urged the Government of Spain to use *"all legal instruments* to remedy the open breach of the law and of judicial decisions that have systematically been committed by the Catalan Government." In this case, there was no debate on the first point among the supporters of the motion, but the second point, the intervention of the central government, was more controversial, and was finally qualified in its formulation, since the socialist group argued that the Parliament cannot do the job of the judiciary, including the Constitutional Court; should the Catalan government act illegally there would be other powers or actors who have the responsibility for judging and sanctioning it.

On 27 February 2014, during the annual State of the Nation debate at the Congress of Deputies, several positions on the issue of Catalan demands were evident. As usual, MPs of the lower house tabled and voted on motions addressed to the government at the end of the debate. The positions on the issue of Catalonia expressed in these debates can be divided into three main categories. First, there were the motions by the PP defending the values contained in the constitution and rejecting those that overstep the limits of the constitution and the principles of sovereignty and legality. This motion was supported by the PP majority group, Navarrese and Asturian regionalists. The Socialist Party abstained while the other groups voted against. Second, there is a "sovereignist" block that presented several motions, all very similar, that called for a dialogue between the central government and the Catalan government in order to make the consultation announced by the Catalan government possible (these proposals by CiU, Plural Left, Republican Left of Catalonia, and Amaiur were defeated by the votes of the popular group and UPyD). The socialists again abstained. The third main position, the so-called "third way" advocated by the socialist group (PSOE), proposed the creation of a parliamentary subcommittee in which a process of debate and dialogue takes place in order to make constitutional amendments enabling the accommodation of the Catalan question in a new constitutional framework. This motion was not supported by any other parliamentary group and was defeated.

Finally, we should refer to a very solemn debate that took place in the Congress on 8 April 2014, namely, the debate on the Catalan Parliament's proposed bill on an organic law of delegation requesting the transfer of powers to authorize, convene, and hold a referendum on the political future of Catalonia on 9 November. Three representatives of the Catalan Parliament from three different parties presented their arguments (the Catalan premier refused to do it himself as the Basque premier had done in 2005). As expected, after a seven-hour debate, an overwhelming majority (86 percent, 299 MPs) of the Congress voted down the proposal. The bill was supported by forty-seven MPs with one abstention. The no vote was cast by the ruling PP, the Socialist Party, UPyD, the Navarrese People's Union (UPN), and Foro Asturias. The yes votes were cast by nationalist parties from Catalonia and the Basque Country and leftist-green-nationalist ICV. During the debate, Prime Minister Mariano Rajoy argued that although sovereignty lies with the Spanish people, making a regional referendum constitutionally impossible, Catalan nationalists are free to lobby for, and propose, an amendment to the constitution. The socialist opposition leader Pérez Rubalcaba also rejected the notion of a regional referendum and offered instead a new "federal state model" that would give greater powers to the ACs. Catalan nationalist parties dismissed these two options and vowed to carry on with their plans through other channels. "We will not desist, we will promote other ways." These options were the passing of its own legislation at the Catalan Parliament enabling regional referendums or an outright unilateral declaration of independence.[11]

CONCLUDING REMARKS

After the debate in the Spanish Parliament in April 2014, constitutional reform proposals and the issue of Catalonian self-determination seem to have returned temporarily to the media discussion and the public arena outside Parliament. Given that the legislature of the Congress of Deputies expires at the end of the this year and early elections have also been called for the Catalan Parliament for the next fall, and given that regional elections in most ACs are approaching in May 2015, several issues of national unity and constitutional amendment will be publicly discussed and included in electoral manifestos and electoral pledges in the next months. All these factors indicate that the next legislative term of the Spanish Parliament, with no clear majorities, will represent both a challenge and an opportunity for negotiation and consensus-seeking on proposals for constitutional renewal and accommodation of Catalonia. This will certainly give back to the Cortes Generales the protagonist role it has enjoyed several times since the founding moments of the current Spanish democratic system.

NOTES

1 Eva Sáenz Royo, "El papel del parlamento español en la democracia de partidos," *Revista de Derecho Político UNED*, no. 73 (2008): 149–76; Lynn M. Maurer, "Parliamentary Influence in a New Democracy: The Spanish Congress," *The Journal of Legislative Studies* 5, no. 2 (1999): 24–45.

2 Natalia Ajenjo and Ignacio Molina, "Spain: Majoritarian Choices, Disciplined Party Government and Compliant Legislature," in Bjørn Erik Rasch and Georg Tsebelis, eds, *The Role of Governments in Legislative Agenda Setting* (London: Routldedge, 2011), 164–83.

3 Alejandro Mújica and Ignacio Sánchez-Cuenca, "Consensus and Parliamentary Opposition: The Case of Spain," *Government and Opposition* 41, no. 1 (2006): 86–108; Bonnie N. Field, "Minority Government and Legislative Politics in a Multilevel State: Spain under Zapatero," *South European Society and Politics* 14, no. 4 (2009): 417–34; Bonnie N. Field, "Minority Parliamentary Government and Multilevel Politics: Spain's

System of Mutual Back Scratching," *Comparative Politics* 46, no. 3 (2014): 293–312.

4 Mireia Grau, "The Spanish Lower Chamber of Parliament: An Intergovernmental Arena? The Representation and Integration of Territorial Interests within the Congreso de los Diputados," in Rudolf Hrbek, ed., *Legislatures in Federal Systems and Multi-level Governance* (Baden-Baden: Nomos, 2010), 11–33.

5 See Josu Erkoreka, "Vascos, nacionalistas y nacionalistas vascos en las Cortes Generales," Blog de Josu Erkoreka, 2011/09/08, http://josuerkoreka .com/2011/09/page/3/, accessed 29 December 2015.

6 See, for instance, Hector Grad and Luisa Martín Rojo, "'Civic' and 'Ethnic' Nationalist Discourses in Spanish Parliamentary Debates," *Journal of Language and Politics* 1, no. 2 (2002): 225–67.

7 See Fernando Domínguez García, *Más allá de la nación. La idea de España como "Nación de naciones"* (Barcelona: Fundación Rafael Campalans, 2006); David Sánchez Cornejo, "Los senadores reales y el debate sobre la organización territorial del Estado en los trabajos parlamentarios de la constitución de 1978," in *La transición a la democracia en España: actas de las VI Jornadas de Castilla-La Mancha sobre Investigación en Archivos* (Guadalajara: Anabad Castilla-La Mancha, 2004), 1–19.

8 Fernando Domínguez García, "Nación de naciones."; David Sánchez Cornejo, "Los senadores reales y el debate sobre la organización territorial del Estado en los trabajos parlamentarios de la constitución de 1978."

9 See Jaume Vernet i Llabet, "El debate parlamentario sobre el 12 de octubre: Fiesta Nacional de España," *Ayer*, no. 51 (2003), 135–52.

10 Spain, *Diario de Sesiones del congreso de los diputados*, X legislatura, no. 63, 9 October 2012, 21.

11 For some parliamentary exchanges relating to regional referenda see *Diario de Sesiones del congreso de los diputados*, X legislatura, no. 192, 8 April 2014.

Conclusion

GUY LAFOREST AND ANDRÉ LECOURS

Minority nations have proven resilient over the years but, as the histories of their parliaments show, they have also had to manage important change. In all likelihood, more change is coming. After all, our world is not static; it never has been. As we conclude this book on the parliaments of autonomous nations, Russia's assertiveness in the East Ukraine, the collapse of oil prices, the terrorist attacks in Paris, and the atrocities committed on behalf of the Islamic State (ISIS) in the Middle East have all increased the relevance of the expression coined by our colleague Alain-G. Gagnon. Indeed, we live in an age of change and uncertainty.[1]

In this global atmosphere of vulnerability, all political communities are affected by a constellation of environmental problems, security issues, often-unjust economic development, and all kinds of social disintegrations, without forgetting a wide array of institutional pathologies of democracy (corruption, voter apathy, and mistrust of elites, among others). However, in addition to these perils or trouble areas, Gagnon argues that minority nations face other challenges. At the heart of these challenges lies the task of empowerment, not only vis-à-vis the central state but also as a political project reinforcing groups and communities in their midst. As we argued in the introduction, the parliaments of autonomous nations, joined in this endeavour by their governments and civil societies, must face these challenges with limited state powers and often in competition with the nation-building projects of central state authorities. In most if not all of the cases covered here, the parliaments of autonomous and minority nations have been able in the last couple of decades, with varying degrees of success and exhaustiveness, to realize some of the central goals attributed to them by Gagnon. They have "made history" by contributing to the enrichment and diversification of liberal constitutionalism, for instance through referendum processes in Scotland and Quebec, as well through the peace agreements and institutional reconstructions in Northern Ireland.[2] They have "made a society" by working to profoundly transform their civil societies, perhaps no more so than in Catalonia and Flanders. In Gagnon's terms, they have deepened democracy through nationalism and not in opposition to it, with a range of assertiveness that may seem lower in Galicia and Wales, and a level of complexity that reaches unparalleled heights in the Basque Country and in Northern Ireland.

This concluding section offers some thoughts on the short- and mid-term future of the parliaments of autonomous nations.

Considering the events of the last few years, it makes sense to recapitulate the circumstances in which the parliaments of autonomous nations will have to meet their challenges in the unfolding chapter of the age of change and uncertainty, starting with the case of Scotland. Following the report of the Smith Commission in late November 2014,[3] and in the aftermath of the publication by the United Kingdom government of the first draft of a refurbished Scotland Act,[4] it appears very likely that the next British speech from the throne, to be delivered in Parliament by the Queen following the formation of a government after the next 7 May 2015 general election, will include the proposal of a substantial array of new powers for the Scottish Parliament and for the Scottish government. This proposal will be made by a government once again led by David Cameron, but with the Conservatives sufficiently strong to govern alone. The presence at Westminster of a huge contingent of fifty-six elected deputies from the SNP will heighten the stakes. So will Cameron's promise to hold a referendum on UK membership in the European Union before the end of 2017. In Scotland, public opinion is strongly opposed to any idea of British exit from the European Union. Meanwhile, institutional logic follows its course. For instance, legal measures have already been adopted to authorize all citizens in the sixteen to eighteen year age bracket to vote in the next Scottish general election in May 2016. Moreover, the Scottish Parliament will soon be granted first constitutional enshrinement of its permanence in British law, plus greater authority to control its own affairs, including more autonomy in the conduct of elections in Scotland. The Scottish Parliament will also enjoy wider fiscal autonomy accompanied by forms of accountability in that context that remain to be specified, and also more powers and freedoms in many fields of public policy related to welfare, along with the recognition that the entire machinery of intergovernmental relations in the United Kingdom will have to be rethought. The concretization of such an ambitious agenda in all its aspects could take years, but there seems to be an all-party consensus in Britain to deliver significant parts of it as rapidly as possible. The Scottish agenda will, of course, have consequences for the other nations of the United Kingdom and for their parliaments. The leader of the Welsh government, Carwyn Jones, suggested in the aftermath of the publication of the Smith Commission report that Wales should have the same new devolved powers as Scotland. Peter Robinson, leader of the Democratic Ulster Party and first minister of Northern Ireland did not go as far, but he also believes that all institutional levels in the United Kingdom will need to be profoundly refashioned. In the meantime, as Guy Laforest argued in a preceding chapter, Northern Ireland will continue to address the politics of symbols and of internal reconciliation, while its legislative assembly will need to give more voice to an effective opposition.

In his post-referendum speech, Prime Minister David Cameron said the new "settlement" would have to be fair to not only the people of Scotland but also "to everyone in England, Wales and Northern Ireland as well."[5] Thus, the future of the United Kingdom will be shaped by its minority nations and by England. As the Scottish Parliament gains more powers, the "West Lothian question," discussed by Alan Trench in his chapter, only grows in importance and, in all likelihood, has to find an answer. More broadly, the referendum gave Scotland exposure in England like rarely before. The English population becoming more "'aware" of Scotland could very well complicate negotiations over the next settlement, especially since some of the guarantees contained in the "vow" of the three unionist leaders a week prior to the referendum (for example, keeping the Barnett formula) are interpreted, in the context of more autonomy for Scotland, as unfair to England by many of its MPs.

The dire conditions of the global economy will impose tough decisions on all parliaments surveyed in this book, but nowhere more so than in Spain, where levels of unemployment, particularly among youth, remain extraordinarily high. These constraints certainly apply to the Parliament of Galicia, and to a lesser extent to the Parliament of the Basque Country because of the immense fiscal autonomy bestowed on this jurisdiction (and Navarra, as well, we might add). In the context of the total absence of meaningful dialogue between the Spanish government and Catalan authorities about the organization of a self-determination referendum, the government of Artur Mas allowed for the setting up of a citizen participation process on the future of Catalonia, which took place on 9 November 2014. In the absence of real dialogue, the whole issue has been marred by a barrage of judiciary recourses. In addition to the current economic, constitutional, and political complexities that accompany the absence of a stable majority in Parliament, Artur Mas has also felt the relentless pressures of a militantly sovereignist civil society given a very coherent voice in Parliament through the leader of the Left Republican Party (ERC), Oriol Junqueras. These realities have prompted Mas to clear the way for an early election, to be held on 27 September 2015. The governing party (the nationalist federation formed by Democratic Convergence (CDC), and Democratic Union (UDC) seems poised to go into the electoral campaign with a common sovereignist platform with ERC, but with two independent lists of candidates. As we finish writing in the early months of 2015, current polls in no way guarantee the kind of distribution of forces that would allow the next government to act with a clear, convincing majority in Parliament. With the sudden irruption of Podemos (Podem, in Catalan) as a major political party at the Spanish level but also in all autonomous communities including Catalonia, it is likely that at least seven and possibly eight political parties will be represented in the next Catalan Parliament.[6] The Catalan elections will be followed, in all likelihood in the second half of November 2015, by a general Spanish election whose results are also currently quite unpredictable, with Podemos, led by Pablo Iglesias Turrion, and Ciudadanos, led by Albert Rivera, threatening to break open a system characterized by the hegemony of the Popular Party (PP, led by Mariano Rajoy and presently forming a majority government) and the Spanish Socialist Workers Party (PSOE, led by Pedro Sanchez). With elections looming as well in Galicia and in the Basque Country no later than October 2016, all parliaments of the autonomous nations in Spain will soon operate with transformed distributions of political forces to face their respective challenges.

In most of Spain outside the three historical nationalities, there is little patience for self-determination claims. The rising secessionist support in Catalonia, in particular, is further straining the relationship between Catalonia and the rest of the country. The uncompromising position of Spanish parties on a Catalan referendum finds strong anchoring in most of Spanish civil society outside Catalonia and reflects a historical conception of Spain as a mononational country. This conception greatly complicates the way forward for Catalonia as it looks to reconfigure its relationship with the Spanish state.

In Flanders, as well as in Quebec, general elections took place in the spring of 2014 (7 April in Quebec, 25 May in Flanders), leading to the formation of new governments bringing to their respective autonomous parliaments a mostly economic rhetoric aimed at streamlining, evaluating, rationalizing, and ultimately reducing state bureaucracies and the functioning apparatuses of government. In Flanders, Geert Bourgeois, at the helm of the nationalist and independentist New Flemish Alliance (N-VA), leads the new coalition government. The other groups in the coalition are the Christian Democrats Party (CD&V) and the Liberals and Open VLD. These three parties are also members of a new Belgian coalition government presided over by Charles Michel, leader of the francophone party Mouvement réformateur (MR). The most important politician in Belgium, however, remains Bart de Wever, the mayor of Antwerp and president of the N-VA. He has been instrumental in helping to secure the sixth major constitutional reform of the Belgian state, which was implemented between 2012 and 2014, transforming the Senate into a chamber of the federated entities and transferring more than 20 billion euros in spending revenues to the regional and community parliaments, along with a vast array of new powers. The new Flemish Parliament, officially at work since late September 2014, combines the powers of the Flemish region and of the Flemish community in the enormously asymmetrical Belgian brand of federalism. It will be hard pressed to find the right balance between the new government's rhetoric of austerity, its own heightened obligations of legislating and scrutiny that come with its augmented powers, and potential future reforms of the state.

The peculiarity of Flemings being a numerical majority within Belgium has meant that the Belgian state has adapted gradually but fundamentally to the preferences of their parties. The strength of the N-VA, now a partner in the federal coalition government, will in all likelihood keep state reform on the political agenda for many years. This is much to the despair of francophone parties, whose preference is always the constitutional status quo. With the Parti socialiste outside the federal executive, new political configurations are developing in Belgium, in large part as a response to the government formation crises of recent years. This newfound fluidity might give new hope to a political system that seemed to have come dangerously close to paralysis.

In Quebec, where we end our journey, the new federalist and moderately nationalist government led by Philippe Couillard delivered the broad lines of its program in front of the members of the Assemblée Nationale (Legislative Assembly) on 21 May 2014. At the helm of the Liberal Party (PLQ), Philippe Couillard should normally lead his majority government (with seventy seats held by the Liberals out of a total of 125) until the next election, to be held on 1 October 2018. At the beginning, the work of the governing party in Parliament will be helped by the resignation of Pauline Marois, who had led the Parti Québécois (PQ) to victory in 2012, a victory rendered modest by her ability to form only a minority government. The PQ, a sovereignist and traditionally moderately social-democratic party, stands now as the first party of the opposition in parliament (with thirty seats). It elected media mogul Pierre-Karl Péladeau as its new leader in mid-May 2015. Two other parties are represented in the Legislative Assembly: the Coalition for the Future of Quebec (CAQ, led by François Legault, with twenty-two seats), a moderately nationalist party from the centre-right; and Québec solidaire (QS, co-led by Françoise David and Andres Fonticella, with three seats), a more radically social-democratic and independentist party of the left. In the face of an estimated annual budget deficit of CAD$4 billion, the government led by Philippe Couillard has embarked on an ambitious project to re-evaluate all forms of government programs and public spending. In this context, the Assemblée Nationale du Québec and its members have already started to debate substantial reforms to the vast network of administrative structures in the two most important areas of Quebec's autonomous legislative authority, education and health. Furthermore, since the establishment in 2007 of a commission of inquiry led by Gérard Bouchard and Charles Taylor into the relationships between majority and minorities over issues of cultural and religious differences and accommodations, Quebec society and its political elites have been hard-pressed to better define a just and stable approach in the management of diversity that would favour intercultural reciprocal interactions and a form of secularism that would conform to overarching societal values such as freedom of conscience and religion, equality without discrimination for all – and particularly in the relationships between men and women – and enduring social cohesion and integration.[7] One of the standing committees of the Assembly, the Committee on the Relations between Citizens (Commission des Relations avec les Citoyens), has embarked on a major consultation which will lead to a new policy on immigration, diversity, and inclusion.[8] As the importance of these issues continues to rise on the agendas of almost all countries in Europe and in the Americas, the policy options chosen by the governing and legislative authorities of Quebec will be studied very seriously by all the other parliaments of autonomous nations, and particularly in Catalonia and Flanders where similar cultural and religious dilemmas have arisen with the acceleration of immigration fluxes in the past couple of decades.

In the rest of Canada, the victory of the PLQ in the 2014 Quebec elections was received with much satisfaction. As the PQ seemed to be poised for a win early in the election campaign, many outside the province were dreading a third referendum on independence. Another referendum might still take place, but in the short to medium term the most likely scenario is that both a formal attempt at secession and efforts to constitutionally address the "Quebec question" will be put on indefinite hold. Overall, Canada is in the peculiar situation where Quebec's independence is less likely than at any time in the last twenty-five years but Quebecers' attachment to the country appears weaker than ever before.

In a variety of writings, German political philosopher and sociologist Claus Offe has argued that all liberal democracies must, in addition to the requirement for leaders to exercise political judgment and for citizens to show civil courage, combine certain levels of state capacity, a system of governance in accordance with the rule of law, effective accountability, and substantial contestations.[9] We see no reason to believe that these requirements and duties do not apply to the governments, civil societies, and parliaments of autonomous nations. In his book on the age of uncertainty, Alain-G. Gagnon suggests that minority nations in multinational polities ought to recalibrate their politics of emancipation by following a number of ethical beacons. They should seek the kind of cleverness that translates into moderation, demanding the same from others and applying this principle in the management of their own internal diversity.[10] The politics of minority and autonomous nations, and markedly so in their legislative debates – as frequently illustrated in our book – is characterized by the rhetoric of dignity. This goes far beyond national pride and empty symbolism. Meaningful spheres of autonomy reinforce individual as well as collective senses of dignity. In multinational polities, the various partners ought to take much greater account of the sense of dignity of the significant others with whom they share, at least in part, the frontiers of political community. Undergirding these first two principles is the recognition that the humanistic politics that is relevant in the age of uncertainty requires an ethic that emphasizes hospitality. Others with whom we live ought to be accepted with their differences, with their opacity. This requires a disposition toward generosity. However, the more complex a multinational and pluricultural polity is or becomes, the more urgent the need to clarify the common moral, legal, and political rules that will be shared and accepted by all. Moderation, dignity, hospitality. If these three words were written at the entrance of all the parliaments of autonomous nations surveyed in our book, if the ethical principles they inform were the shared basis of debates taking place and of laws being adopted in these perennially important spaces of political life, our world would be all the better for it. Reflecting on the past and current practices of the parliaments surveyed in our book, we have reasons to be optimistic. At least moderately.

Multinational states have an inherent level a complexity that is far greater than that of mononational states. The territorial dimension of their governance is permeated by the issue of self-determination, and the question of (where and who is) the *demos* is constantly in play. As a result, the question of the relationship between minority nations (including their parliaments) and the state (and its own parliament) can never be completely solved or settled, including in the unlikely event of a secession. Rather, this relationship requires constant management and special preparedness for surprising outcomes. Indeed, minority nations are both bearers and actors of change and uncertainty.

NOTES

1 Alain-G. Gagnon, *Minority Nations in the Age of Uncertainty: New Paths to National Emancipation and Empowerment* (Toronto: University of Toronto Press, 2014).
2 Ibid., 5–6.
3 The Smith Commission, https://www.smith-commission.scot/smith-commission-report/, accessed 5 February 2015.
4 Statement by the Prime Minister, https://www.gov.uk/government /publications/scotland-in-the-united-kingdom-an-enduring-settlement, accessed 5 February 2015.
5 Statement by the Prime Minister, https://www.gov.uk/government/news /scottish-independence-referendum-statement-by-the-prime-minister, accessed 10 February 2015.
6 Podemos-Podem has developed a rhetoric that combines an anti-globalization and anti-corruption logic, populist approaches, and a desire to substantially transform the Spanish political system including the 1978 constitution. Beyond ERC, CIU (the combination of CDC and UDC), and Podemos-Podem, the other parties already present in Parliament who could have members after September 2015 are the Socialist Party (PSC), the Popular Party (PP), the Party of the Citizenry (C's), Initiative for Catalunya Greens (ICV), and finally the small, radical, left-wing party of Catalan independence Popular Unity Candidates (CUP).

7 For a recent analysis of the report submitted by Bouchard and Taylor, see Guy Laforest, *Interpreting Quebec's Exile within the Federation: Selected Political Essays* (Brussels: Peter Lang, 2015), 111–22.

8 http://www.assnat.qc.ca/en/travaux-parlementaires/commissions/crc /mandats/Mandat-26361/index.html.

9 See Claus Offe, *Europe Entrapped* (Cambridge: Polity Press, 2015); see also by the same author *Les démocraties modernes à l'épreuve* (Paris: l'Harmattan, 1997).

10 Gagnon, *Minority Nations in the Age of Uncertainty*, 97.

Contributors

CÉSAR COLINO is associate professor in the Department of Political Science and Public Administration at the Spanish National Distance-Learning University (UNED) in Madrid. His recent research has focused on comparative federalism, in particular diversity management, intergovernmental relations, fiscal federalism, and constitutional reform in federations.

MIREIA GRAU CREUS holds a PhD in social and political sciences from the European University Institute in Florence, Italy, and is senior researcher at the Institut d'Estudis Autonòmics of the Government of Catalonia.

MICHIEL ELST, PhD, is legal advisor at the Flemish Parliament and guest professor at the University of Antwerp. His major areas of research are constitutional and parliamentary law, information law, and Russian law.

JOSÉ JULIO FERNANDEZ is Valedor do Pobo (Ombudsman in the Autonomous Community of Galicia, Spain) and professor of constitutional law at Santiago de Compostela University where he is the director for the Security Studies Centre. He has been a consultant for many international law programs designed to promote cooperation and institutional development.

MARIE-CHRISTINE GILBERT received her PhD from the University of Ottawa. Her work focuses on Canadian federalism, specifically antifederalist thought in a historical perspective. She has coauthored several book chapters, including "A Comparative Look at Federalism and Intergovernmental Relations: Germany, Australia, Belgium, the United States, and Canada" in *Quebec-Ontario Relations: A Shared Destiny?* (2013).

MARTINE GOOSSENS holds a PhD in history and MA in public management. She has been secretary-general of the Flemish Parliament since 2005, and has published on the history of the Flemish Parliament.

MICHAEL KEATING is professor of politics at the University of Aberdeen and director of the Economic and Social Research Council (ESRC) Centre on Constitutional Change. He is Fellow of the British Academy, Royal Society of Edinburgh, Academy of Social Sciences, and European Academy. He has worked extensively on nationalism, regionalism, and European politics.

GUY LAFOREST is professor in the Department of Political Science at Université Laval in Quebec City. His major areas for research are political theory, intellectual history in Canada and Quebec, theories of federalism and of nationalism, and constitutional politics in Canada.

ANDRÉ LECOURS is professor in the School of Political Studies at the University of Ottawa. His main research interests are Canadian politics, European politics, nationalism (with a focus on Quebec, Scotland, Flanders, Catalonia, and the Basque country), and federalism.

ALBERTO LÓPEZ BASAGUREN is professor of constitutional law at University of the Basque Country (UPV/EHU) in Bilbao, Spain. His major areas for research are the law on national and linguistic minorities, federal constitutions, claims for secession in democratic systems, territorial autonomy in Spain, and constitutional law of European integration.

FRANÇOIS ROCHER is professor in the School of Political Studies at the University of Ottawa. His main research interests are constitutional politics, citizenship, pluriethnic and plurinational diversity, Canadian federalism, and nationalism in Quebec.

ALAN TRENCH is a lawyer and political scientist who has worked at the Constitution Unit at University College London, the University of Edinburgh, and the University of Ulster. He is also currently specialist adviser to the House of Commons Welsh Affairs Committee.

CARLES VIVER is professor of constitutional law at the Pompeu Fabra University (Barcelona), director of the Institut d'Estudis Autonòmics, and president of the Advisory Council of National Transition of the Government of Catalonia. His research focuses on the territorial organization of the state. He is former justice (1992–2001) and deputy president (1998–2001) of the Spanish Constitutional Court.

Index

Page references followed by *t* indicate a table; page references followed by *fig* indicate a figure.